Enterprise Application Development with Ext JS and Spring

Develop and deploy a high-performance Java web application using Ext JS and Spring

Gerald Gierer

PUBLISHING

BIRMINGHAM - MUMBAI

Enterprise Application Development with Ext JS and Spring

First published: December 2013

Production Reference: 1131213

Published by Packt Publishing Ltd.
Livery Place
35 Livery Street
Birmingham B3 2PB, UK.

ISBN 978-1-78328-545-7

www.packtpub.com

Cover Image by Kerry Thomson (kezthommo@activ8.net.au)

Credits

Author
Gerald Gierer

Reviewers
Eric Mansfield
Justin Rodenbostel
Ernst Schmidt
Alexandre Arcanjo de Queiroz

Acquisition Editor
Joanne Fitzpatrick

Lead Technical Editor
Susmita Panda

Copy Editors
Alisha Aranha
Roshni Banerjee
Sarang Chari
Janbal Dharmaraj
Tanvi Gaitonde
Mradula Hegde
Dipti Kapadia
Gladson Monteiro
Deepa Nambiar
Karuna Narayanan
Kirti Pai
Laxmi Subramanian

Technical Editors
Ritika Singh
Pratish Soman
Harshad Vairat

Project Coordinator
Anugya Khurana

Proofreader
Jonathan Todd

Indexer
Priya Subramani

Graphics
Yuvraj Mannari

Production Coordinator
Shantanu Zagade

Cover Work
Shantanu Zagade

About the Author

Gerald Gierer has been involved in enterprise web application projects for more than 15 years and continues to find his work challenging and rewarding. He started his software development career working with C, PowerBuilder, and Unix, until the rise of the Internet and Java caught his attention. In 2000, he made a conscious decision to focus on Internet application development using the Java language.

The frustration of working with the first **Enterprise JavaBeans (EJB)** implementations was the predominant reason he investigated the alternatives that could make enterprise development more productive. In 2004, he first heard of the Spring framework and quickly realized how comprehensive and well-designed an alternative this was to EJB. Since then he has architected and developed many Spring projects using a range of view technologies including JSP, JSF, Struts, Tiles, Freemarker, DWR, and YUI.

In 2009, he became aware of Ext JS and was immediately struck by the power of this JavaScript framework. Having spent countless hours building complex web pages from scratch, Ext JS was a breath of fresh air for the client realm. He has been working with Ext JS ever since.

He lives in Geelong, Australia, but often spends time in Europe, having lived and worked for five years in Munich. In his spare time, he enjoys keeping fit, brewing beer, being outdoors, and rock climbing—a passion that has kept him sane for more than 25 years.

Acknowledgments

Most of all I would like to thank my loving wife Katja for her boundless love and support for everything I do. Without her understanding, patience, and positive encouragement this book would simply not have been possible. Thank you meine Suesse!

To my loving parents, who have given me the gift of seeing the world with a positive outlook that can make such a difference when the going gets tough; you are, and continue to be, an inspiration.

To my friend Gabriel Bezas, thank you for showing me the path so many years ago. Your friendship and advice has been invaluable.

To my colleagues over the years I would like to thank (in no particular order) Alfred Merk, Steve Terry, Hans Hochreiter, Karin Langner, Steffen Haigis, Arthur Marschall, Ralf Haeussler, Zoltan Levardy, and Ernst Schmidt. Each of you has contributed to the evolution of this book.

Finally, thanks to the team at Gieman IT Solutions; Adam, Ben, Di (3T logos and design), Jane (book illustrations), Tracy, and Reece. You gave me a reason to write this book.

About the Reviewers

Eric Mansfield has 20 years of development experience at some of the world's largest media and entertainment conglomerates—including Sony Music, Universal, Scripps, Sony Pictures, and MTV—that brings a detailed, practical approach to building high-quality applications. He has been an early adopter of the Spring framework and has a passion for clean, user-friendly design and doing things right the first time. He lives in Austin, Texas with his wife and enjoys golfing and playing the piano.

Justin Rodenbostel is a senior software architect with Redpoint Technologies, based in Chicago, Illinois. He has more than 12 years' experience in full-stack application development using a variety of technologies, including Spring, Grails, Rails, .NET, and various JavaScript frameworks. On the Web, he can be found blogging at http://justinrodenbostel.com. Apart from his work, he stays busy as a husband and father of three, and when he's lucky, can be found brewing beer in his garage.

Ernst Schmidt is a designer and frontend engineer with a focus on rich web applications. He has worked with Sencha frameworks from the very beginning and has an in-depth understanding of Ext JS internals and architecture.

Recently, he is working with Sony Music and Universal Music Group leading the design and implementation of user interface frameworks for digital supply chain applications.

He lives in the Bay Area with his wife and two sons.

Alexandre Arcanjo de Queiroz, a Brazilian software developer, graduated from the Faculty of Technology of São Paulo, a renowned institution of his country. He has experience in developing backend and frontend applications using the Java EE platform in the Unix environment. He is also a GNU/Linux user.

Currently, he is working in Indra Company, a Spanish multinational company present in more than 128 countries, developing applications for the telecommunications segment.

I would like to thank my family who supports me at every moment of my life and my friends who believe in my potential.

www.PacktPub.com

Support files, eBooks, discount offers and more

You might want to visit www.PacktPub.com for support files and downloads related to your book.

Did you know that Packt offers eBook versions of every book published, with PDF and ePub files available? You can upgrade to the eBook version at www.PacktPub.com and as a print book customer, you are entitled to a discount on the eBook copy. Get in touch with us at service@packtpub.com for more details.

At www.PacktPub.com, you can also read a collection of free technical articles, sign up for a range of free newsletters and receive exclusive discounts and offers on Packt books and eBooks.

http://PacktLib.PacktPub.com

Do you need instant solutions to your IT questions? PacktLib is Packt's online digital book library. Here, you can access, read and search across Packt's entire library of books.

Why Subscribe?

- Fully searchable across every book published by Packt
- Copy and paste, print and bookmark content
- On demand and accessible via web browser

Free Access for Packt account holders

If you have an account with Packt at www.PacktPub.com, you can use this to access PacktLib today and view nine entirely free books. Simply use your login credentials for immediate access.

Table of Contents

Preface

Enterprise application development is an art form rarely acknowledged in this fast-paced technical world. This book describes the patterns and strategies that will simplify large-scale development projects using two of the most popular technologies available: the Spring Framework and Sencha Ext JS. Each chapter defines and builds a concise layer in the enterprise application stack, condensing an approach to web development that was gained from many years of developing real-world projects. We cover quite an extensive conceptual ground, so be prepared for an interesting journey!

This book is not an introduction to Java, JavaScript, or any web development concepts. There are significant amounts of practical code in both Java and JavaScript languages, so an understanding of these technologies is required. If you are not familiar with Java and associated concepts such as object-oriented programming, you may be challenged when following the examples and explanations. The same can be said for Ext JS development; you need to have some experience with the fundamental concepts, including the framework APIs, to follow most examples.

You do not need to be an expert, but beginners may wish to start their journey elsewhere.

Regardless of your experience and background, the practical examples provided in this book are written in a way to thoroughly cover each concept before moving on to the next chapter.

What the book covers

Chapter 1, Preparing Your Development Environment, discusses the installation and configuration for the development environment, including the Java Development Kit, NetBeans, and MySQL. We will also introduce Maven, create a new NetBeans project, and deploy the project to the GlassFish 4 application server.

Chapter 2, The Task Time Tracker Database, defines the Task Time Tracker (3T) database design and helps configure NetBeans as a client of the MySQL server. We create and populate all the tables and identify the possible enhancements that could be appropriate for enterprise use.

Chapter 3, Reverse Engineering the Domain Layer with JPA, helps us reverse engineer the 3T database using the NetBeans IDE to create a domain layer of JPA entities. These entities are explored and refactored as we examine and define core JPA concepts.

Chapter 4, Data Access Made Easy, introduces the Data Access Object (DAO) design pattern and helps implement a robust data access layer using the domain classes we defined in the previous chapter. Java generics and interfaces, the Simple Logging Facade for Java (SLF4J), the JPA EntityManager, and transactional semantics are also introduced.

Chapter 5, Testing the DAO Layer with Spring and JUnit, introduces the configuration of a JUnit testing environment and the development of test cases for several of our DAO implementations. We introduce the Spring Inversion of Control (IoC) container and explore the Spring configuration to integrate Spring-managed JUnit testing with Maven.

Chapter 6, Back to Business – The Service Layer, examines the role of the service layer in enterprise application development. Our 3T business logic is then implemented by the Data Transfer Objects (DTO) design pattern using Value Objects (VO). We also examine writing test cases prior to coding the implementation—a core principle of test-driven development and extreme programming.

Chapter 7, The Web Request Handling Layer, defines a request handling layer for web clients that generates JSON data using the Java API for JSON processing, which is a new API introduced in Java EE 7. We implement the lightweight Spring controllers, introduce Spring handler interceptors, and configure Spring MVC using Java classes.

Chapter 8, Running 3T on GlassFish, completes our Spring configuration and allows us to deploy the 3T application to the GlassFish 4 server. We also configure the GlassFish 4 server to run independently of the NetBeans IDE, as would be the case in enterprise environments.

Chapter 9, Getting Started with Ext JS 4, introduces the powerful Ext JS 4 framework and discusses the core Ext JS 4 MVC concepts and practical design conventions. We install and configure our Ext JS development environment using Sencha Cmd and the Ext JS 4 SDK to generate our 3T application skeleton.

Chapter 10, Logging On and Maintaining Users, helps us develop the Ext JS 4 components that are required for logging on to the 3T application and maintaining users. We will discuss the Ext JS 4 model persistence, build a variety of views, examine application concepts, and develop two Ext JS controllers.

Chapter 11, Building the Task Log User Interface, continues to enhance our understanding of the Ext JS 4 components as we implement the task log user interface.

Chapter 12, 3T Administration Made Easy, enables us to develop the 3T Administration interface and introduces the Ext JS 4 tree component. We examine dynamic tree loading and implement drag-and-drop tree actions.

Chapter 13, Moving Your Application to Production, will help us prepare, build, and deploy our 3T project to the GlassFish server. We introduce Ext JS theming, integrate Sencha Cmd compiling with Maven to automate the Ext JS 4 app-all.js file generation process, and learn how to deploy our production build on the GlassFish server.

Appendix, Introducing Spring Data JPA, provides a very brief introduction to Spring Data JPA as an alternative to the implementation discussed in *Chapter 4, Data Access Made Easy*.

What you need for this book

The examples in this book can be run on any Windows, Mac, or Linux platform that supports the following software:

- Java Development Kit (JDK) 1.7
- NetBeans 7.4+
- MySQL 5+
- Sencha Cmd

All of the software are available for free download at the websites listed in the appropriate chapters.

Who this book is for

This book is particularly relevant to those working in large-scale web application development projects, including application architects, Java developers, and Ext JS developers.

Application architects

Architects understand the big picture from a technical perspective and are responsible for laying out a blueprint for development standards. This book will introduce you to the power of the Spring Framework and Sencha Ext JS and how you can best leverage these technologies when designing your next project.

Java developers

Regardless of your level of understanding, you will learn how the Spring Framework encourages good programming practices. This includes a clean, layered structure that is easy to enhance and maintain. Those new to Spring will be surprised at how little effort is required to achieve significant results. For both new and experienced Spring developers, the focus will be best practices for enterprise web development to allow seamless integration with Sencha Ext JS clients. If you have never worked with Sencha Ext JS, you will be surprised at how quickly powerful UIs can bring backend data to life.

Ext JS developers

Sencha Ext JS is a powerful framework that is used to build enterprise applications that are cross-browser compliant. This book will solve real-world problems right from analysis to providing fully functional solutions. You will see the many stages of development that are usually hidden from Ext JS developers; you will also get introduced to the steps required to produce JSON data for client consumption. The chapters focusing on the Ext JS components will introduce simple strategies for maintainable development based on the latest MVC design patterns.

Conventions

In this book, you will find a number of styles of text that distinguish between different kinds of information. Here are some examples of these styles, and an explanation of their meaning.

Code words in text, folder names, filenames, file extensions, pathnames, dummy URLs, and user input are shown as follows: "The ManageTaskLogs definition is as follows:"

A block of code is set as follows:

```
Ext.define('TTT.store.Task', {
    extend: 'Ext.data.Store',
    requires: ['TTT.model.Task'],
    model: 'TTT.model.Task',
    proxy: {
        type: 'ajax',
        url:'task/findAll.json',
        reader: {
            type: 'json',
            root: 'data'
        }
    }
});
```

When we wish to draw your attention to a particular part of a code block, the relevant lines or items are set in bold:

```
controllers: [
  'MainController',
  'UserController',
  'TaskLogController'
],
models: [
  'User',
  'Project',
  'Task',
  'TaskLog'
],
stores: [
  'User',
  'Project',
  'Task',
  'TaskLog'
]
```

Any command-line input or output is written as follows:

```
sencha -sdk ext compile -classpath=app page -yui -in index.html -out build/index.html
```

New terms and **important words** are shown in bold. Words that you see on the screen, in menus or dialog boxes for example, appear in the text like this: "Adding a new task log will preserve the currently selected **Date** and **Project**, if present:".

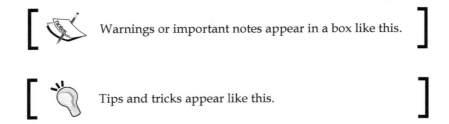

Warnings or important notes appear in a box like this.

Tips and tricks appear like this.

Reader feedback

Feedback from our readers is always welcome. Let us know what you think about this book—what you liked or may have disliked. Reader feedback is important for us to develop titles that you really get the most out of.

To send us general feedback, simply send an e-mail to feedback@packtpub.com, and mention the book title via the subject of your message.

If there is a topic that you have expertise in and you are interested in either writing or contributing to a book, see our author guide on www.packtpub.com/authors.

Customer support

Now that you are the proud owner of a Packt book, we have a number of things to help you to get the most from your purchase.

Downloading the example code

You can download the example code files for all Packt books you have purchased from your account at http://www.packtpub.com. If you purchased this book elsewhere, you can visit http://www.packtpub.com/support and register to have the files e-mailed directly to you.

Errata

Although we have taken every care to ensure the accuracy of our content, mistakes do happen. If you find a mistake in one of our books—maybe a mistake in the text or the code—we would be grateful if you would report this to us. By doing so, you can save other readers from frustration and help us improve subsequent versions of this book. If you find any errata, please report them by visiting http://www.packtpub. com/submit-errata, selecting your book, clicking on the **errata submission form** link, and entering the details of your errata. Once your errata are verified, your submission will be accepted and the errata will be uploaded on our website, or added to any list of existing errata, under the Errata section of that title. Any existing errata can be viewed by selecting your title from http://www.packtpub.com/support.

Piracy

Piracy of copyright material on the Internet is an ongoing problem across all media. At Packt, we take the protection of our copyright and licenses very seriously. If you come across any illegal copies of our works, in any form, on the Internet, please provide us with the location address or website name immediately so that we can pursue a remedy.

Please contact us at copyright@packtpub.com with a link to the suspected pirated material.

We appreciate your help in protecting our authors, and our ability to bring you valuable content.

Questions

You can contact us at questions@packtpub.com if you are having a problem with any aspect of the book, and we will do our best to address it.

Preparing Your Development Environment

1

This chapter will install and configure your development environment. The **Rapid Application Development (RAD)** tool is **NetBeans**, an open source, cross-platform **Integrated Development Environment (IDE)** that can be used for creating visual desktop, mobile, web, and **Service-Oriented Architecture (SOA)** applications. NetBeans officially supports Java, PHP, JavaScript, and C/C++ programming languages, but it is best known for providing a complete toolset for all the latest **Java Enterprise Edition (Java EE)** standards (currently Java EE 7).

The database of choice for this book is MySQL, the world's most widely used open source **Relational Database Management System (RDBMS)**. MySQL is the most popular choice of database for web applications hosted on Linux platforms and continues to deliver outstanding performance in a multitude of applications. Its small footprint and ease of use makes it perfect for development use on a single computer.

The application server used in this book is **GlassFish 4**, which comes bundled with the NetBeans download. GlassFish is installed as part of the NetBeans installation, and the tight integration between the two makes configuring GlassFish a simple process. GlassFish is an open source, production-quality application server that implements all the Java EE 7 features. It has enterprise-grade reliability and is considered by many to be the best open source application server available. GlassFish 4 is the **Reference Implementation (RI)** for the Java EE 7 specification, a full description of which can be found at `https://glassfish.java.net/downloads/ri/`.

All of these development tools are freely available for PC, Mac, and Linux. Each tool has extensive examples, comprehensive tutorials, and online support forums available.

It should be noted that although this chapter focuses on NetBeans, MySQL, and GlassFish, it is possible for you to configure any appropriate combination of tools that they are familiar with. The development tasks outlined in this book can just as easily be followed using Eclipse, Oracle, and JBoss—although some described configuration details may require minor modifications.

In this chapter, we will perform the following tasks:

- Install the MySQL Database server
- Install the Java SDK
- Install and configure the NetBeans IDE
- Create the application project and explore Maven
- Run the project in GlassFish

Installing MySQL

MySQL can be downloaded from `http://www.mysql.com/downloads/mysql`. Select the appropriate MySQL Community server for your operating system and architecture. It is important to follow the instructions, making note of installation directories and paths for future reference. After downloading and running the setup file, you should select the **Developer Default** installation for this book.

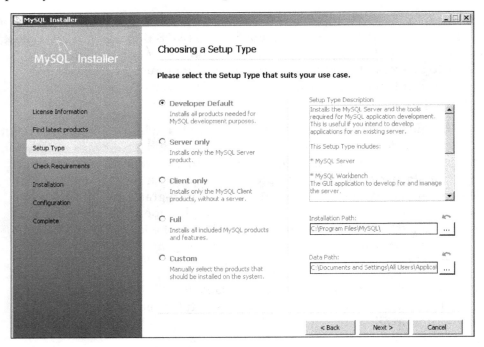

Choosing the default settings is best unless you are familiar with MySQL. This will include setting the default port to 3306, enabling TCP/IP networking, and opening the required firewall port for network access (not strictly required for a developer machine where all apps are running on the same environment, but required if you are configuring a dedicated MySQL server).

Regardless of the environment, it is important to set a root user password during the installation process. We will use the root user to connect to the running MySQL server to execute commands.

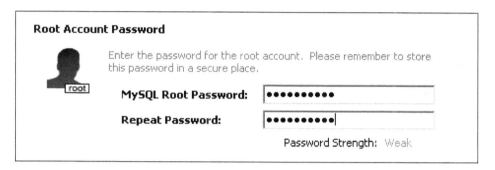

The rest of this book will assume the root user has the password `adminadmin`. This is not a very secure password but should be easy to remember!

We recommend that the MySQL server is configured to start when the operating system starts. How this is done will depend on your environment, but it is usually performed at the end of the **Initial Configuration** action. Windows users will have the option to start the MySQL server at system startup. Mac users will need to install the **MySQL Startup Item** after the server has been installed.

Should you decide not to start MySQL when the operating system starts, you will need to start the MySQL server manually whenever required. How this is done will once again depend on your environment, but you should start your server now to confirm that the installation was successful.

Unix and Linux users will need to install MySQL as appropriate for their operating system. This may include the use of **Advanced Packaging Tool (APT)** or **Yet another Setup Tool (YaST)**, or even the installation of MySQL from source. There are detailed instructions for various operating systems found at http://dev.mysql.com/doc/refman/5.7/en/installing.html.

At the end of the configuration process, you will have a running MySQL server ready to be used in *Chapter 2, The Task Time Tracker Database*.

Installing the Java SE Development Kit (JDK)

The **Java SE Development Kit (JDK)** can be downloaded from `http://www.oracle.com/technetwork/java/javase/downloads/index.html`. You may choose to skip this step if you already have the JDK 7 Update 45 (or later) installed on your system.

 Do not select the NetBeans bundle as it does not contain the GlassFish server.

You will need to accept the JDK 7 License Agreement before selecting the appropriate distribution. After downloading the JDK, run the setup program and follow the instructions and prompts.

Installing the NetBeans IDE

NetBeans can be downloaded from `https://netbeans.org/downloads/`. The
distribution requires a valid JDK to be already installed on your platform. At the
time of this writing, I used JDK 7 Update 45, but any JDK 7 (or higher) version
would be fine. There are several distribution bundles; you will need to select the
Java EE bundle.

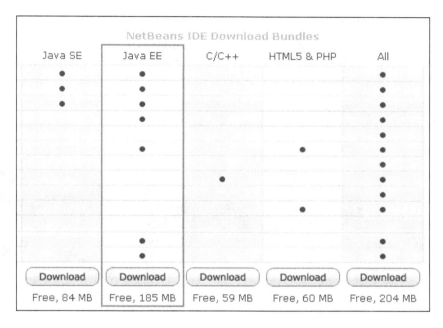

The latest version at the time of this writing was NetBeans 7.4, which introduced
significant new features, including extended HTML5 and JavaScript support.
For the first time, NetBeans also included editing and code completion support
for the Ext JS framework.

To install the software, simply download and follow the detailed instructions
available from the NetBeans website. This will take you through a sequence
of setup screens as follows:

1. The GlassFish 4 server is automatically selected. You do not need to
    install Tomcat.

2. Accept the terms in the license agreement.

3. Accept the terms of the JUnit license agreement. JUnit is used for testing in
    Chapter 5, Testing the DAO Layer with Spring and JUnit.

4. Note the installation path of the NetBeans IDE for future reference. Select the appropriate JDK that was installed previously (if there is more than one JDK on your system).

5. Note the installation path for the GlassFish 4 server for future reference.

6. The final screen summarizes the installation. Ensure to **Check for Updates** before clicking on **Install** to start the process.

The process may take several minutes depending on your platform and hardware.

When the installation is complete, you can run NetBeans for the first time. If you had a previous version of NetBeans installed, you may be prompted to **Import Settings**. The default opening screen will then be displayed as follows:

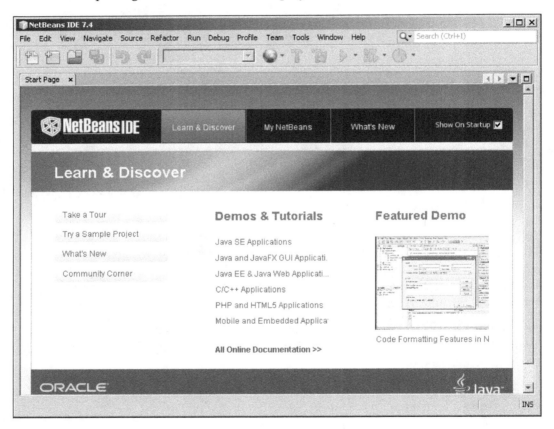

The most useful panels can now be opened from the menu:

- **Projects**: This panel is the main entry point to your project sources. It shows a logical view of important project content, grouped into appropriate contexts.

- **Files**: This panel shows the actual file structure of the project node as it exists on your filesystem.

- **Services**: This panel displays your runtime resources. It shows a logical view of important runtime resources such as the servers and databases that are registered with the IDE.

At this stage, the first two panels will be empty but the **Services** panel will have several entries. Opening the **Servers** panel will display the installed GlassFish 4 Server as seen in the following screenshot:

Introducing Maven

Apache Maven is a tool that is used for building and managing Java-based projects. It is an open source project hosted at `http://maven.apache.org` and comes bundled with the NetBeans IDE. Maven simplifies many steps common to all Java development projects and provides numerous features, including the following:

- The provision of convention over configuration. Maven comes with a series of predefined targets for performing certain well-defined tasks including compilation, testing, and packaging of projects. All tasks are managed through a single configuration file: `pom.xml`.

- A consistent coding structure and project framework. Each Maven project has the same directory structure and location for source files, test files, build files, and project resources. This common structure brings us easily up to speed with projects.
- A consistent build system with numerous plugins to make common tasks easy.
- The ability to execute tests as part of the build process.
- A highly flexible and powerful dependency management system. This allows software developers to publish information and share Java libraries through (external or remote) Maven repositories hosted on the Internet. Libraries are then downloaded and cached locally by Maven for use in the project.

We encourage you to visit the Maven website to explore the many features available. NetBeans will use Maven to create and manage the web application project.

Creating the Maven Web Application project

A NetBeans project encapsulates all the source code and related components required to maintain and develop an application. Navigate to **File | New Project** from the menu to start the process:

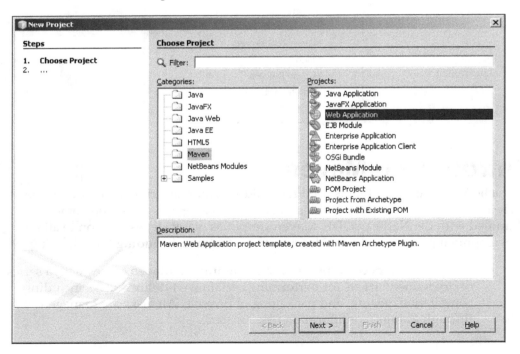

Select **Maven** in the **Categories** listing and **Web Application** from the **Projects** listing, as shown in the preceding screenshot, before selecting the **Next** button. This will present you with the project configuration screen with the following fields:

- **Project Name**: This specifies the display name of the project in the project window. This name is also used to create the project folder and must not contain spaces.

> Our project is called Task Time Tracker. This tool will allow users to manage the time spent on different tasks for different projects. The project name field is the lowercase, nonspaced translation of the name of the project: `task-time-tracker`.

- **Project Location**: This specifies the filesystem root folder where you want to store the project metadata and source code. We normally create a project-specific folder at the root level of a drive, rather than burying it deep within a folder structure under NetBeans. This makes it easier to find and copy files into the project.

> Windows users should create a project folder under `c:\projects`. Mac users may wish to replace this with `/Users/{username}/projects` and Unix users with `/home/{username}/projects`. The rest of the book will refer to this location in all examples as *the project folder*.

- **Project Folder**: The project folder is read-only and generated based on the name of the project and the project location.

- **Artifact Id**: This is a read-only Maven-specific property to identify the project and is based on the project name.

- **Group Id**: This is another Maven property that represents a top-level container for multiple artifacts. It usually represents the **Top-Level Domain (TLD)** of the organization owning the project.

> The **Group Id** for the project is `com.gieman`, the company of the author.

- **Version**: This is another Maven property that represents the version of the artifact. The default version is **1.0-SNAPSHOT**, which we will change to `1.0`. As projects evolve and new versions are released, Maven will keep track of the different builds based on their versions.

- **Package**: The IDE will automatically create a Java source package structure based on this field. We will use the package `com.gieman.tttracker`.

You should now have entered the following project details:

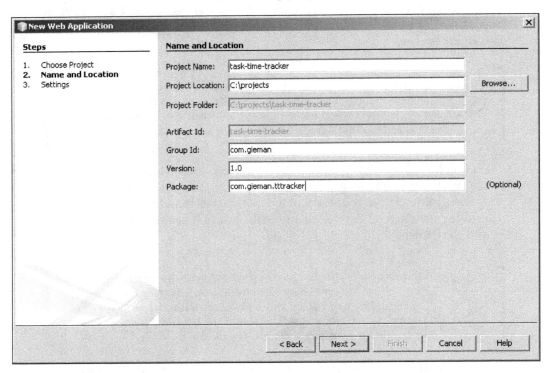

Click on the **Next** button to view the final screen. Do not change the default GlassFish Server 4.0 and Java EE 7 settings before clicking on the **Finish** button. You will now see activity in the **Project Creation** output tab as the project is created and configured. Opening the **Project** and **Files** panels will allow you to see the project structure:

Downloading the example code

You can download the example code files for all Packt books you have purchased from your account at http://www.packtpub.com. If you purchased this book elsewhere, you can visit http://www.packtpub.com/support and register to have the files e-mailed directly to you.

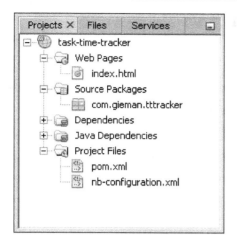 

Right-clicking on the project name in either tab will allow you to select the **Properties** for the project. This will display all properties and paths relevant to the project under different categories:

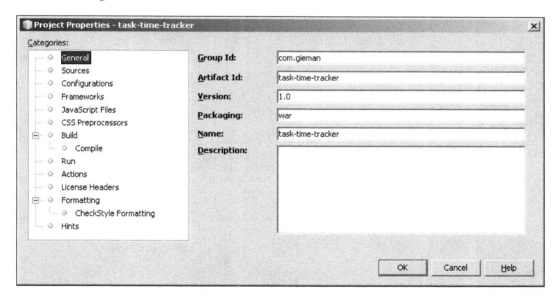

You should not need to change these properties for the remainder of the book.

Understanding the POM and dependency management

Each Maven project has a `pom.xml` configuration file at the root level of the NetBeans project. Click on the **Files** view and double-click on the `pom.xml` file to open it in the editor:

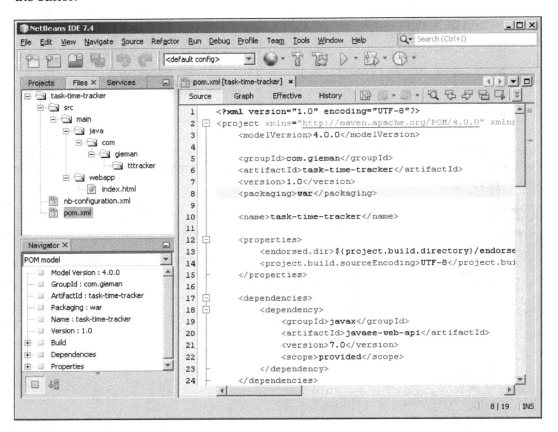

You should see the **Navigator** window open in the bottom-left panel. This displays an outline of the file being edited and is very helpful when navigating through large files. Double-clicking on a node in the **Navigator** will position the cursor at the appropriate line in the editor.

If the **Navigator** window does not open (or has been closed), you can open it manually by navigating to **Window | Navigating | Navigator** from the menu.

The **Project Object Model (POM)** fully defines the project and all required Maven properties and build behaviors. There is only one dependency shown in `pom.xml`:

```
<dependencies>
  <dependency>
    <groupId>javax</groupId>
    <artifactId>javaee-web-api</artifactId>
    <version>7.0</version>
    <scope>provided</scope>
  </dependency>
</dependencies>
```

This dependency identifies that the project requires Java EE 7 for building. This entry ensures the full Java EE 7 APIs are available for Java coding in the Task Time Tracker project. Our project also requires the Spring Framework, which must now be added as additional dependencies. Typing in the editor will result in autocompletion help to determine the correct dependencies. After adding the Spring Framework `groupId` and `artifactId` entries, as shown in the following screenshot, the *Ctrl + Space* bar keyboard shortcut will open the available matching entries for the `artifactId` starting with the text `spring`:

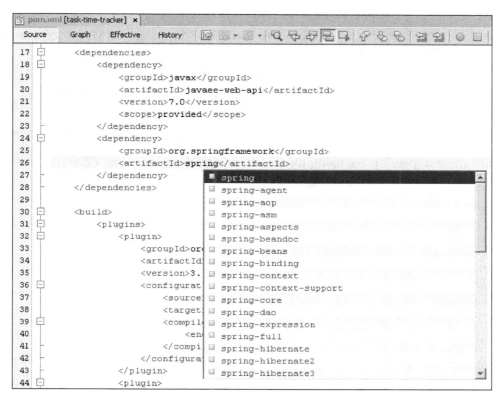

If this autocomplete list is not available, it may be due to the Maven repository being indexed for the first time. In this situation you will then see the following screenshot at the bottom of the editor:

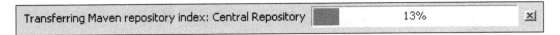

Be patient and in a few minutes the indexing will be finished and the autocomplete will become available. Indexing is required to download available entries from the Maven repository.

The required Spring Framework components are as follows:

- `spring-context`: This is the central artifact required for Spring's dependency injection container
- `spring-tx`: This is the transaction management abstraction required for implementing transactional behavior
- `spring-context-support`: These are various application context utilities, including Ehcache, JavaMail, Quartz, and FreeMarker integration
- `spring-jdbc`: This is the JDBC data access library
- `spring-orm`: This is the **Object-to-Relation-Mapping (ORM)** integration for JPA development
- `spring-instrument`: This is for the weaving of classes
- `spring-webmvc`: This is the **Spring Model-View-Controller (MVC)** for Servlet environments
- `spring-test`: This is the support for testing Spring applications with JUnit

To add these dependencies using the latest Spring release version (3.2.4) requires the following additions to the `pom.xml` file:

```
<dependency>
  <groupId>org.springframework</groupId>
  <artifactId>spring-context</artifactId>
  <version>3.2.4.RELEASE</version>
</dependency>
<dependency>
  <groupId>org.springframework</groupId>
  <artifactId>spring-context-support</artifactId>
  <version>3.2.4.RELEASE</version>
</dependency>
<dependency>
```

```
      <groupId>org.springframework</groupId>
      <artifactId>spring-tx</artifactId>
      <version>3.2.4.RELEASE</version>
   </dependency>
   <dependency>
      <groupId>org.springframework</groupId>
      <artifactId>spring-jdbc</artifactId>
      <version>3.2.4.RELEASE</version>
   </dependency>
   <dependency>
      <groupId>org.springframework</groupId>
      <artifactId>spring-orm</artifactId>
      <version>3.2.4.RELEASE</version>
   </dependency>
   <dependency>
      <groupId>org.springframework</groupId>
      <artifactId>spring-instrument</artifactId>
      <version>3.2.4.RELEASE</version>
   </dependency>
   <dependency>
      <groupId>org.springframework</groupId>
      <artifactId>spring-webmvc</artifactId>
      <version>3.2.4.RELEASE</version>
   </dependency>
   <dependency>
      <groupId>org.springframework</groupId>
      <artifactId>spring-test</artifactId>
      <version>3.2.4.RELEASE</version>
   </dependency>
```

Understanding dependency scope

The final Spring Framework dependency is only required for testing. We can define this by adding a scope attribute with value test. This tells Maven that the dependency is only required when running the testing phase of the build and is not required for deployment.

```
   <dependency>
      <groupId>org.springframework</groupId>
      <artifactId>spring-test</artifactId>
      <version>3.2.4.RELEASE</version>
      <scope>test</scope>
   </dependency>
```

The `javaee-web-api` dependency that was automatically created by NetBeans has a scope of `provided`. This means the dependency is not required for deployment and is provided by the target server. The GlassFish 4 server itself is the provider of this dependency.

If the `scope` attribute has not been included, the dependency JAR will be included in the final build. This is the equivalent of providing a scope entry of `compile`. As a result, all the Spring Framework dependency JARs will be included in the final build file.

A full explanation of the Maven dependency mechanism and scoping can be found at `http://maven.apache.org/guides/introduction/introduction-to-dependency-mechanism.html`.

Defining Maven properties

The Spring Framework dependencies defined in `pom.xml` all have the same version (3.2.4.RELEASE). This duplication is not ideal, especially when we wish to upgrade to a newer version at a later time. Changes would be required in multiple places, one for each Spring dependency. A simple solution is to add a property to hold the release version value as shown in the following code:

```
<properties>
<endorsed.dir>${project.build.directory}/endorsed</endorsed.dir>
<project.build.sourceEncoding>UTF-8</project.build.sourceEncoding>
<spring.version>3.2.4.RELEASE</spring.version>
</properties>
```

This custom property, which we have named `spring.version`, can now be used to replace the multiple duplicates as follows:

```
<dependency>
<groupId>org.springframework</groupId>
  <artifactId>spring-context-support</artifactId>
  <version>${spring.version}</version>
</dependency>
```

The `${spring.version}` placeholder will then be substituted with the `properties` value during the build process.

Understanding Maven-build plugins

The Maven build process executes each defined build plugin during the appropriate build phase. A full list of build plugins can be found at http://maven.apache.org/plugins/index.html. We will introduce plugins as needed in subsequent chapters, but the default plugins created by the NetBeans IDE are of interest now.

The maven-compiler-plugin controls and executes the compilation of Java source files. This plugin allows you to specify both the source and target Java versions for compilation as shown in the following code:

```
<plugin>
  <groupId>org.apache.maven.plugins</groupId>
  <artifactId>maven-compiler-plugin</artifactId>
  <version>3.1</version>
  <configuration>
    <source>1.7</source>
    <target>1.7</target>
    <compilerArguments>
      <endorseddirs>${endorsed.dir}</endorseddirs>
    </compilerArguments>
  </configuration>
</plugin>
```

Changing these values to 1.6 may be required when compiling projects for older Java servers running on the earlier versions of Java.

The maven-war-plugin builds a WAR file for the project as follows:

```
<plugin>
  <groupId>org.apache.maven.plugins</groupId>
  <artifactId>maven-war-plugin</artifactId>
  <version>2.3</version>
  <configuration>
    <failOnMissingWebXml>false</failOnMissingWebXml>
  </configuration>
</plugin>
```

The default generated WAR filename is {artifactId}-{version}.war, which can be changed by including the warName configuration property. We will be adding properties to this plugin when building the project for production release in the final chapter. A full list of maven-war-plugin options may be found at http://maven.apache.org/plugins/maven-war-plugin/war-mojo.html.

The `maven-dependency-plugin` copies dependency JAR files to the defined output directory as shown in the following code:

```
<plugin>
  <groupId>org.apache.maven.plugins</groupId>
  <artifactId>maven-dependency-plugin</artifactId>
  <version>2.6</version>
  <executions>
    <execution>
      <phase>validate</phase>
      <goals>
        <goal>copy</goal>
      </goals>
      <configuration>
        <outputDirectory>${endorsed.dir}</outputDirectory>
        <silent>true</silent>
        <artifactItems>
          <artifactItem>
            <groupId>javax</groupId>
            <artifactId>javaee-endorsed-api</artifactId>
            <version>7.0</version>
            <type>jar</type>
          </artifactItem>
        </artifactItems>
      </configuration>
    </execution>
  </executions>
</plugin>
```

This is useful to see which JARs are used by the project and to identify what transitive dependencies are required (dependencies of dependencies).

We will modify this plugin to copy all compile-time dependencies of the project to a directory in `${project.build.directory}`. This special build directory is under the root folder of the project and is named `target`, the target destination of the build process. The updated entry will now look as follows:

```
<plugin>
  <groupId>org.apache.maven.plugins</groupId>
  <artifactId>maven-dependency-plugin</artifactId>
  <version>2.1</version>
  <executions>
    <execution>
```

```
      <id>copy-endorsed</id>
      <phase>validate</phase>
      <goals>
        <goal>copy</goal>
      </goals>
      <configuration>
        <outputDirectory>${endorsed.dir}</outputDirectory>
        <silent>true</silent>
        <artifactItems>
          <artifactItem>
            <groupId>javax</groupId>
            <artifactId>javaee-endorsed-api</artifactId>
            <version>7.0</version>
            <type>jar</type>
          </artifactItem>
        </artifactItems>
      </configuration>
    </execution>
    <execution>
      <id>copy-all-dependencies</id>
      <phase>compile</phase>
      <goals>
        <goal>copy-dependencies</goal>
      </goals>
      <configuration>
        <outputDirectory>
          ${project.build.directory}/lib
        </outputDirectory>
        <includeScope>compile</includeScope>
      </configuration>
    </execution>
  </executions>
</plugin>
```

As we are now performing two executions in the single plugin, each execution needs its own `<id>`. The second execution, with ID `copy-all-dependencies`, will copy all dependent JARs with the scope `compile` to the `target/lib` directory.

Executing the Maven build

The simplest way to execute a build is to click on the **Clean and Build Project** button in the toolbar. You can also right-click on the project node in the **Projects** tab and select **Clean and Build** from the menu. The build process will then execute each defined phase in the POM, resulting in Java code compilation, dependency resolution (and copying), and finally, WAR file generation. Opening the target directory structure will display the build result as follows:

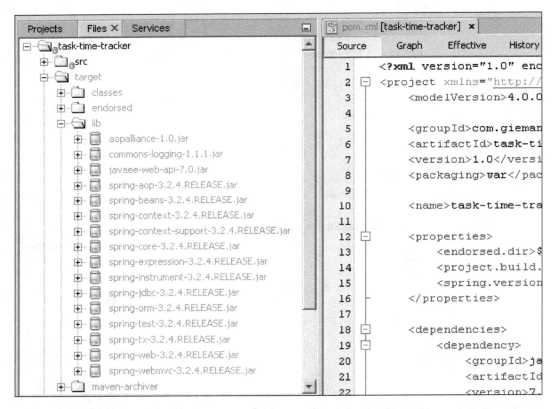

Even though we have not written a single line of code, the generated WAR file `task-time-tracker-1.0.war` can now be deployed to the GlassFish server.

Starting the GlassFish 4 server

Opening the **Services** tab and expanding the **Servers** node will list the GlassFish server that was installed during the NetBeans installation process. You can now right-click on the **GlassFish Server 4.0** node and select **Start** as shown in the following screenshot:

The **Output** panel should now open at the bottom of your NetBeans IDE and display the startup results. Select the **GlassFish Server 4.0** tab to view the details.

The fifth-last line identifies that the server has started and is listening to port 8080, written as 8,080 in the log:

INFO: Grizzly Framework 2.3.1 started in: 16ms - bound to [/0.0.0.0:8,080]

You can now open your preferred browser and view the page
`http://localhost:8080`.

 Note that depending on your environment, you may have other applications listening to port 8080. In these circumstances, you will need to substitute the correct port, as defined in the GlassFish server output, in place of 8080.

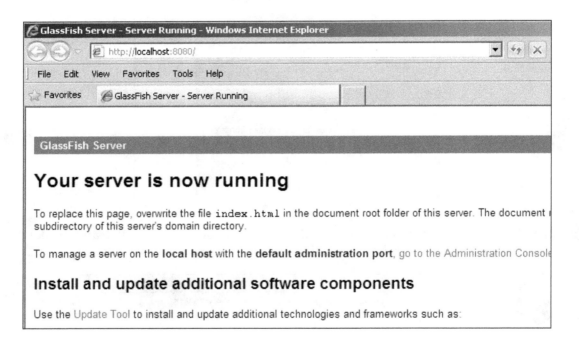

You can now stop the server by right-clicking on the **GlassFish Server 4.0** node and clicking on **Stop**.

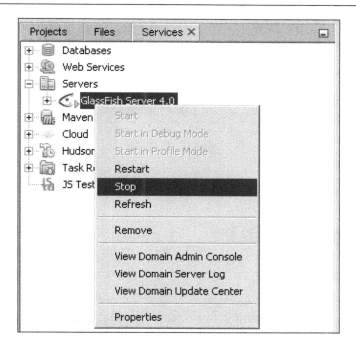

Running the Task Time Tracker project

We have already built the project successfully; it is now time to run the project in GlassFish. Click on the **Run** toolbar item to start the process as follows:

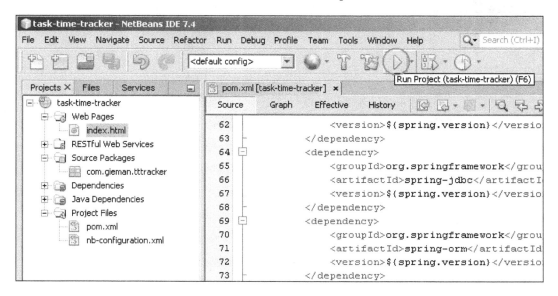

The output should display the process, first building the project followed by starting and deploying to the GlassFish server. The final step will open your default browser and display the world-renowned message that is loved by all developers, as shown in the following screenshot:

Congratulations! You have now configured the core components for developing, building, and deploying a Spring Java project. The final step is to change the text on the default page. Open the index.html file as shown in the following screenshot:

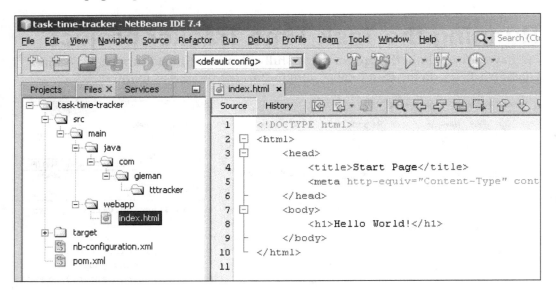

Change `<title>` to `Task Time Tracker Home Page` and the `<h1>` text to `Welcome to Task Time Tracker!`. Save the page and refresh your browser to see the change.

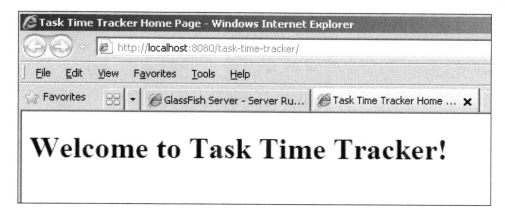

Didn't see the updated text change on browser refresh? Under some circumstances, after deploying to GlassFish for the first time, the changes made in the `index.html` file may not be seen in the browser when you refresh the page. Restarting your NetBeans IDE should fix the issue and ensure subsequent changes are immediately deployed to GlassFish when any project resource is saved.

Summary

In this chapter, you have been introduced to some of the key technologies we will be using in this book. You have downloaded and installed the MySQL database server, the JDK, and the NetBeans IDE. We then introduced Maven and how it is used to simplify the building and management of Java projects. We finally deployed our skeleton Task Time Tracker project to GlassFish without writing a single line of code.

Although we have added the Spring Framework to our project, we are yet to delve into how it is used. Likewise, we are yet to mention Sencha Ext JS. Be patient, there is plenty more to come! The next chapter will introduce our Task Time Tracker database tables and start our development journey.

2
The Task Time Tracker Database

This chapter defines the **Task Time Tracker** (**3T**) database design and configures NetBeans as a client of MySQL server.

The 3T application will be used to keep track of the time spent on different tasks for different company projects. The main entities are:

- **Company**: This is the entity that owns zero or more projects. A company is independent and can exist in its own right (it has no foreign keys).

- **Project**: This represents a grouping of tasks. Each project belongs to exactly one company and may contain zero or more tasks.

- **Tasks**: These represent activities that may be undertaken for a project. A task belongs to exactly one project.

- **Users**: They are participants who undertake tasks. Users can assign time spent to different tasks.

- **Task log**: This is a record of the time spent by a user on a task. The time spent is stored in minutes.

These entity definitions result in a very simple database design:

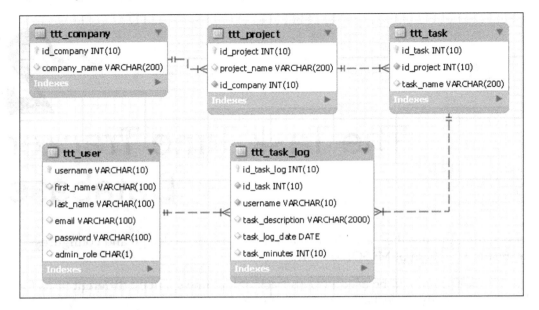

We will prefix all of our 3T tables with `ttt_`. Large enterprise databases may contain hundreds of tables, and you will soon appreciate the prefixing of table names to group related tables.

Connecting NetBeans with MySQL

Click on the **Services** tab in the NetBeans IDE, and navigate to **Databases | Drivers**. You will see that NetBeans comes with several different database drivers:

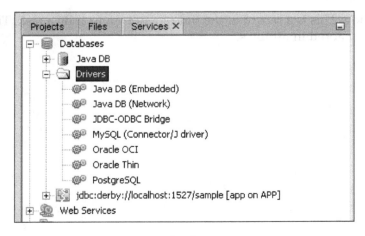

Right-click on the **Databases** node, and click on **Register MySQL Server...**as shown in the following screenshot:

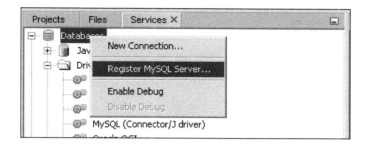

For Windows users, this will open a dialog box with default settings. Enter the admin password used when installing MySQL server in the previous chapter, and check the **Remember Password** option:

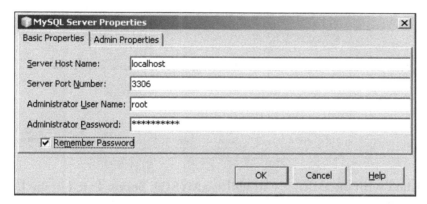

Mac users will see a different window prior to setting the connection properties. Select the MySQL driver before clicking on the **Next** button:

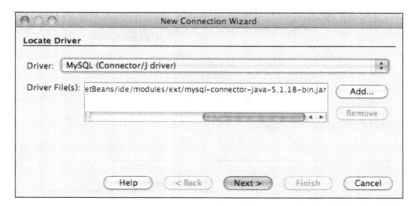

This will then allow you to specify the required database connection details:

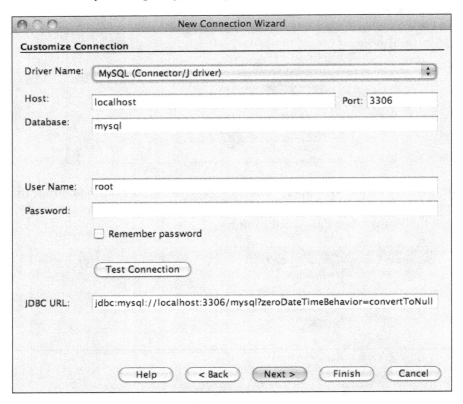

When finished with these tasks, you will see **MySQL Server** listed in the **Databases** node. Right-click on the server, and select **Connect** to connect to the server (if not already connected):

This will connect NetBeans to MySQL server and list the available databases. Right-click on the server, and select **Create Database** as shown in the following screenshot:

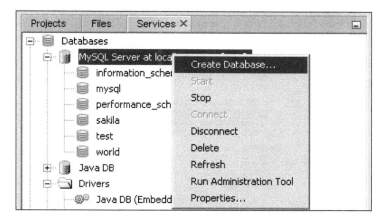

Enter the database name as shown in the following screenshot, and click on **OK** to create the database:

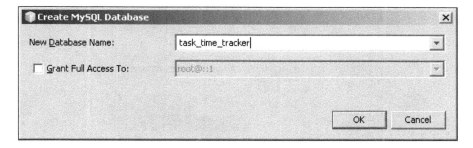

The final step is to connect to the newly created **task_time_tracker** database. Right-click on **task_time_tracker** and select **Connect...** as shown in the following screenshot:

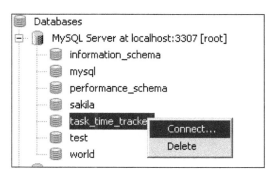

This will add a MySQL database connection entry for the **task_time_tracker** database, which can be opened by right-clicking on it whenever required:

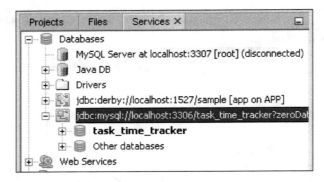

Now you can right-click on the database connection and select the **Execute Command...** option to open the **SQL Command** editor in the workspace:

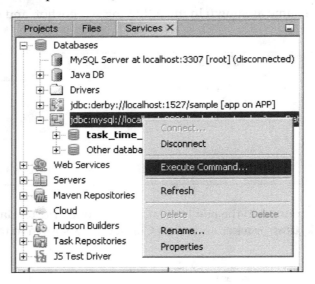

The **SQL Command** editor is where you will type and execute commands against
the database:

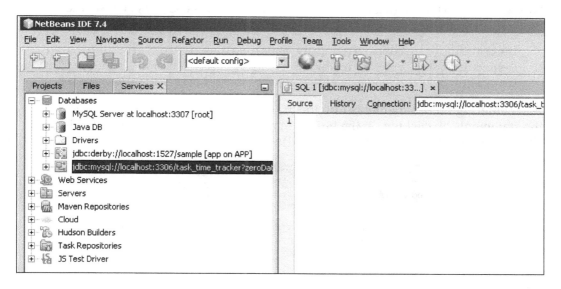

The 3T database

The following SQL statements define the MySQL tables used in 3T. It is possible to
use any database, and MySQL-specific code is highlighted to identify differences
with ANSI SQL.

The company table

A company has projects for which we need to keep track of the time spent on
different tasks. The company is, hence, the first table that needs to be defined.
It is a very simple structure:

```
create table ttt_company(
  id_company  int unsigned not null auto_increment,
  company_name varchar(200) not null,
  primary key(id_company)
);
```

The `auto_increment` keyword is used by MySQL to identify a number column that should automatically be incremental (the default rate of increment is by one number) based on the current highest value in the column. This is used to generate the `id_company` primary key values. Let's add some company data:

```sql
insert into ttt_company(company_name) values ('PACKT Publishing');
insert into ttt_company(company_name) values ('Gieman It Solutions');
insert into ttt_company(company_name) values ('Serious WebDev');
```

After entering these statements into the **SQL Command** editor, you can execute the statements by clicking on the button in the top-right corner of the following screenshot (the Run SQL button is circled):

```
  SQL Command 1   ×

  Source    History   Connection: jdbc:mysql://localhost:3306/task_time_tracker?zeroDateTimeBehavior=conve...   ▼    

1     create table ttt_company(
2         id_company        int unsigned not null auto_increment,
3         company_name      varchar(200) not null,
4         primary key(id_company)
5     );
6     insert into ttt_company(company_name) values ('PACKT Publishing');
7     insert into ttt_company(company_name) values ('Gieman It Solutions');
8     insert into ttt_company(company_name) values ('Serious WebDev');
9
```

The output of these statements will be shown at the bottom of the IDE:

```
  Output - SQL Command 1 execution

Executed successfully in 0 s, 1 rows affected.
Line 6, column 1

Executed successfully in 0.031 s, 1 rows affected.
Line 7, column 1

Executed successfully in 0.031 s, 1 rows affected.
Line 8, column 1

Execution finished after 0.266 s, 0 error(s) occurred.
```

You can now view the inserted data by executing the following statement in the **SQL Command** editor:

```
select * from ttt_company;
```

Alternatively, you can also right-click on the table node in the databases and select **View Data...**:

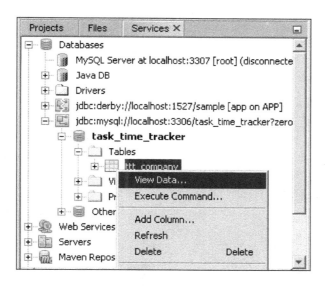

This will result in the following screenshot:

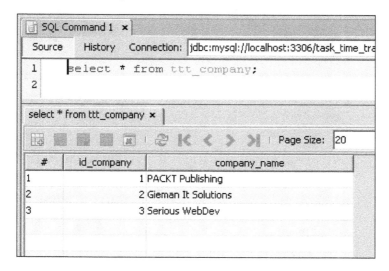

The projects table

A company may have any number of projects with each project belonging to exactly one company. The table definition is as follows:

```
create table ttt_project(
  id_project  int unsigned not null auto_increment,
  project_name varchar(200) not null,
  id_company  int unsigned not null,
  primary key(id_project),
  foreign key(id_company) references ttt_company(id_company)
);
```

Once again, we can add some data:

```
insert into ttt_project(project_name, id_company) values
  ('Enterprise Application Development with Spring and ExtJS', 1);
insert into ttt_project(project_name, id_company) values ('The
  Spring Framework for Beginners', 1);
insert into ttt_project(project_name, id_company) values
  ('Advanced Sencha ExtJS4 ', 1);
insert into ttt_project(project_name, id_company) values ('The 3T
  Project', 2);
insert into ttt_project(project_name, id_company) values
  ('Breezing', 2);
insert into ttt_project(project_name, id_company) values ('Gieman
  Website', 2);
insert into ttt_project(project_name, id_company) values
  ('Internal Office Projects', 3);
insert into ttt_project(project_name, id_company) values
  ('External Consulting Tasks', 3);
```

In these `insert` statements, we have provided the foreign key to the company table and once again allowed MySQL to generate the primary keys. Executing these commands and browsing the `ttt_project` table data should be displayed as shown in the following screenshot:

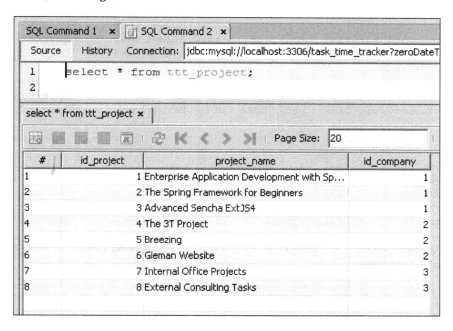

The tasks table

A project may have any number of tasks with each task belonging to exactly one project. The table and test data can now be added as follows:

```
create table ttt_task(
   id_task    int unsigned not null auto_increment,
   id_project  int unsigned not null,
   task_name  varchar(200) not null,
   primary key(id_task),
   foreign key(id_project) references ttt_project(id_project)
);
```

We will now add a range of tasks for some of our projects:

```
insert into ttt_task(id_project, task_name)values (1, 'Chapter 1');
insert into ttt_task(id_project, task_name)values (1, 'Chapter 2');
insert into ttt_task(id_project, task_name)values (1, 'Chapter 3');

insert into ttt_task(id_project, task_name)values (2, 'Chapter 1');
insert into ttt_task(id_project, task_name)values (2, 'Chapter 2');
insert into ttt_task(id_project, task_name)values (2, 'Chapter 3');

insert into ttt_task(id_project, task_name)values (3, 'Preface');
insert into ttt_task(id_project, task_name)values (3, 'Appendix');
insert into ttt_task(id_project, task_name)values (3, 'Illustrations');

insert into ttt_task(id_project, task_name)values (4, 'Database
    Development');
insert into ttt_task(id_project, task_name)values (4, 'Java
    development');
insert into ttt_task(id_project, task_name)values (4, 'Sencha
    Devcelopment');
insert into ttt_task(id_project, task_name)values (4, 'Testing');
```

Executing these commands and browsing the `ttt_task` table data will display the following screenshot:

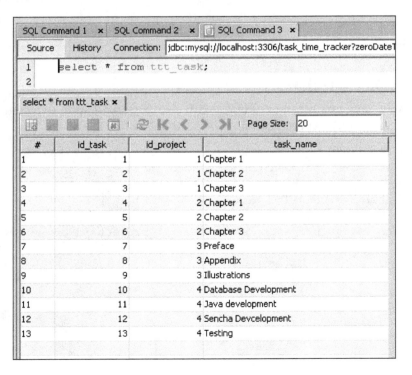

The user table

The next table in our design holds user information:

```
create table ttt_user(
   username          varchar(10) not null,
   first_name        varchar(100) not null,
   last_name         varchar(100) not null,
   email             varchar(100) not null unique,
   password          varchar(100) not null,
   admin_role        char(1) not null,
   primary key(username)
);
```

Note that the `admin_role` column will be used to identify if a user has administrative permissions in the 3T application. We will now add two users:

```
insert into ttt_user(username, first_name, last_name, email,
   password, admin_role)
   values ('jsmith', 'John', 'Smith', 'js@tttracker.com', 'admin',
   'N');
insert into ttt_user(username, first_name, last_name, email,
   password, admin_role)
   values ('bjones', 'Betty', 'Jones', 'bj@tttracker.com',
   'admin','Y');
```

Running this set of commands will create the user table and then insert our two test users as displayed in the following screenshot:

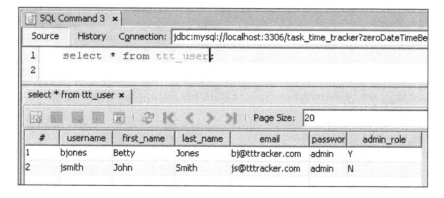

The task log table

The final table will be used to enter the time spent on different tasks.

```
create table ttt_task_log(
   id_task_log    int unsigned not null auto_increment,
   id_task    int unsigned not null,
   username    varchar(10) not null,
   task_description varchar(2000) not null,
   task_log_date  date not null,
   task_minutes   int unsigned not null,
   primary key(id_task_log),
   foreign key(id_task) references ttt_task(id_task),
   foreign key(username) references ttt_user(username)
);
```

We will now add some data to this table for our user John Smith (jsmith). Note that the time spent on each task is in minutes and that the MySQL function now() is used to return the current timestamp:

```
insert into ttt_task_log (id_task, username, task_description,
   task_log_date,task_minutes)
   values(1,'jsmith','Completed Chapter 1 proof reading',now(),
   120);
insert into ttt_task_log (id_task, username, task_description,
   task_log_date,task_minutes)
   values(2,'jsmith','Completed Chapter 2 draft',now(), 240);
insert into ttt_task_log (id_task, username, task_description,
   task_log_date,task_minutes)
   values(3,'jsmith','Completed preparation work for initial
   draft',now(), 90);
insert into ttt_task_log (id_task, username, task_description,
   task_log_date,task_minutes)
   values(3,'jsmith','Prepared database for Ch3 task',now(), 180);
```

In a similar way, we will insert some test data for Betty Jones (bjones):

```
insert into ttt_task_log (id_task, username, task_description,
   task_log_date,task_minutes)
   values(1,'bjones','Started Chapter 1 ',now(), 340);
insert into ttt_task_log (id_task, username, task_description,
   task_log_date,task_minutes)
   values(2,'bjones','Finished Chapter 2 draft',now(), 140);
insert into ttt_task_log (id_task, username, task_description,
   task_log_date,task_minutes)
   values(3,'bjones','Initial draft work completed',now(), 450);
insert into ttt_task_log (id_task, username, task_description,
   task_log_date,task_minutes)
   values(3,'bjones','Database design started',now(), 600);
```

The result of these `insert` statements can now be viewed as shown in the following screenshot:

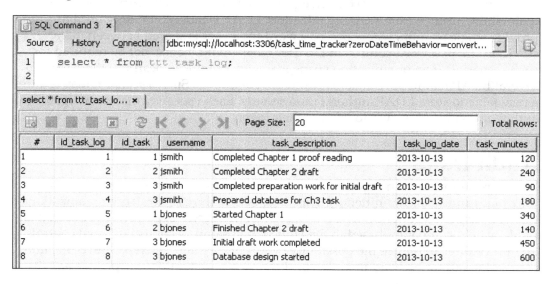

Enterprise options for the 3T database

The table and column definitions provided previously are the simplest required for our 3T project. There are, however, several potential options that could be added to enhance the structure for enterprise use.

Password encryption

Enterprise applications would require that the password field be encrypted for security purposes using a unidirectional algorithm. Passwords should never be stored in plain text, and it should never be possible to view the password in the database (as we can currently do). It is beyond the scope of this book to cover password security strategies, but a very good explanation of the core principles can be found at `http://www.jasypt.org/howtoencryptuserpasswords.html`.

MySQL provides a number of password encryption functions that could be used for this purpose. We suggest you browse the documentation at `https://dev.mysql.com/doc/refman/5.7/en/encryption-functions.html` to understand the different options available.

LDAP integration

Many enterprises use **LDAP** (**Lightweight Directory Access Protocol**) for maintaining users within their organization. LDAP is most commonly used to provide single sign-on, where one password for a user is shared between many services. The password column in the user table would, hence, not be required for such scenarios. If an organization spans many geographical locations, there may be several LDAP realms spread across different continents. Such a scenario may require a new table to store LDAP authorization servers. Each user may then be assigned an authorization LDAP server to process their logon.

Audit trails

Enterprise systems often require extensive audit trails (when and why an action took place and who committed it). This is especially the case for large organizations that are publicly held. The **Sarbanes-Oxley Act** (**SOX**), for example, requires that all publicly held companies based in the United States must establish internal controls and procedures to reduce the possibility of corporate fraud. Such processes include identifying authorized and unauthorized changes or potentially suspicious activity over any period of time.

The questions "Who, When, and Why" are the basis of audit trails that need to be considered when designing an enterprise database. Simply adding a few additional columns to all tables is a very good start:

```
who_created varchar(10) not null
who_updated varchar(10) not null
when_created datetime default current_timestamp
when_updated datetime on update current_timestamp
```

Note that this syntax is for MySQL, but similar functionality will be available for most databases. The `who_created` and `who_updated` columns will need to be updated programmatically. The developer will need to ensure that these fields are set correctly during processing of the relevant action. The `when_created` and `when_updated` columns do not need to be considered by the developer. They are automatically maintained by MySQL. The `when_created` field will be automatically set to the `current_timestamp` MySQL function that represents the query start time to establish the exact moment in time that the record is inserted into the database. The `when_updated` field will auto update each time the record itself is updated. Adding these four additional columns will ensure that a basic level of audit tracking is available. We now have the ability to view who created the record and when in addition to who performed the last update and when. The `ttt_company` table, for example, could be redesigned as follows:

```
create table ttt_company(
   id_company        int unsigned not null auto_increment,
   company_name      varchar(200) not null,
   who_created varchar(10) not null,
   who_updated varchar(10) not null,
   when_created datetime default current_timestamp,
   when_updated datetime on update current_timestamp,
   primary key(id_company)
);
```

Logon activity audits

This provides the ability to track basic user activity including who logged on, when they logged on, and from where they logged on. It is another crucial piece of the enterprise audit trail and should also include tracking of invalid logon attempts. This information will need to be maintained programmatically and requires a table with a structure similar to the following code:

```
create table ttt_user_log(
   id_user_log int unsigned not null auto_increment,
   username varchar(10) not null,
   ip_address varchar(20) not null,
   status char not null,
   log_date datetime default current_timestamp,
   primary key(id_user_log)
);
```

The status field could be used to identify the logon attempt (for example, **S** could represent successful and **F** could represent failed while **M** could represent a successful mobile device logon). The information required would need to be defined in the context of the compliance requirements of the enterprise.

Custom audit tables

There is often the need to audit every action and data change for a particular table. In situations such as this, the "when" and "who" updated fields are not enough. This situation requires an audit (or snapshot) table that contains all fields in the original table. Each time a record is updated, the current snapshot is written to the audit table so that each change is available for auditing purposes. Such tables may also be called archive tables as the evolution of data is archived on every change. Custom audit tables such as these are usually not maintained programmatically and are managed by the RDBMS, either by triggers or by built-in logging/archiving functionality.

Summary

This chapter has defined a database structure that will be used to build the 3T application. We have connected to the MySQL server and executed a series of SQL statements to create and populate a set of tables. Each table uses `autoincrement` columns to allow MySQL to automatically manage and generate primary keys. Although the table structures are not complex, we have also identified possible enhancements that could be appropriate for enterprise use.

In *Chapter 3, Reverse Engineering the Domain Layer with JPA*, we will start our Java journey by reverse engineering our database to create a set of **Java Persistence API (JPA)** entities. Our JPA domain layer will become the data heart of our 3T application.

3
Reverse Engineering the Domain Layer with JPA

The domain layer represents the real-world entities that model the heart of your application. At the highest level, the domain layer represents the application's business domain and fully describes the entities, their attributes, and their relationships with one another. At its most basic level, the domain layer is a set of **Plain Old Java Objects** (**POJOs**) that define the Java representation of the database tables being mapped onto your application. This mapping is achieved through JPA.

The **Java Persistence API** (**JPA**) is one of the most significant advances in the Java EE 5 platform, replacing the complex and cumbersome entity beans with the far simpler POJO-based programming model. JPA provides a standard set of rules for **Object Relational Mapping** (**ORM**), which are simple, intuitive, and easy to learn. Database relationships, attributes, and constraints are mapped onto POJOs using JPA annotations.

In this chapter we will do the following:

- Reverse engineer the 3T database using the NetBeans IDE
- Explore and define JPA annotations for our domain layer
- Introduce the **Java Persistence Query Language** (**JPQL**)

Understanding the reasons for using JPA

JPA is a productivity tool that allows developers to focus on business rather than write low-level SQL and JDBC codes. It completely eliminates the need to map a Java `ResultSet` to Java domain objects and greatly reduces the amount of effort required to produce a usable and functional application. A JPA-based application will be easier to maintain, test, and enhance. More importantly, the quality of your application code will significantly increase and the domain entities will become self-documenting.

From personal experience, I estimate the time taken to write a traditional SQL application (without JPA, coding the CRUD SQL statements directly) to be in the order of 10-15 times longer than with the JPA approach. This translates into an enormous saving of time and effort for enterprise applications where cost saving can amount to many man-months of work. During the lifecycle of an application, when maintenance, bug fixes, and enhancements are taken into account, cost savings alone may be the difference between success and failure.

Understanding JPA implementations

The JPA specification initially evolved from the combined experiences of key ORM implementations including TopLink (from Oracle), Hibernate, and Kodo to name a few. These products revolutionized Java database interactions by abstracting the underlying SQL from the domain layer and simplifying the development effort required to implement the core CRUD operations (Create, Read, Update, and Delete). Each implementation supports the JPA standards in addition to their own proprietary APIs. TopLink, for example, provides caching enhancements that are outside of the JPA specification as well as sophisticated query optimizations for Oracle databases. The implementation that you select may depend on the requirements of your application (for example, distributed caching) and also on the underlying database itself.

The GlassFish 4 server comes bundled with the open source **EclipseLink** JPA implementation, and this is what we will be using in our book. More information about the EclipseLink project can be found at `http://www.eclipse.org/eclipselink/`. You don't need to download any files as the EclipseLink dependencies will be automatically added to your `pom.xml` file during the reverse engineering process.

Reverse engineering with NetBeans

The **New Entity Classes from Database** wizard is one of the most helpful and time-saving wizards in NetBeans. It generates a set of entity classes from an existing database connection, extracting and annotating all the fields and defining relationships between the classes. To access the wizard, navigate to **File | New File**. This will open the **New File** window, where you can then select the **Persistence** category followed by the **Entity Classes From Database** file type:

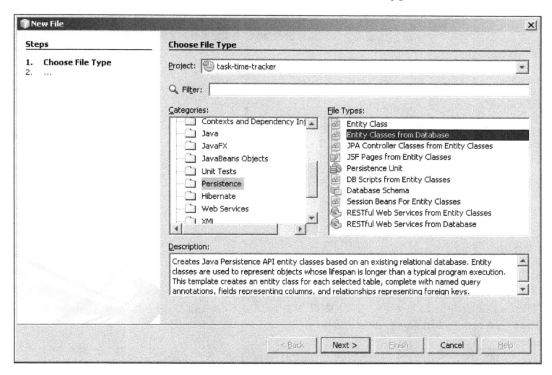

Click on **Next** to display the **Database Tables** screen where you can create a **New Data Source**:

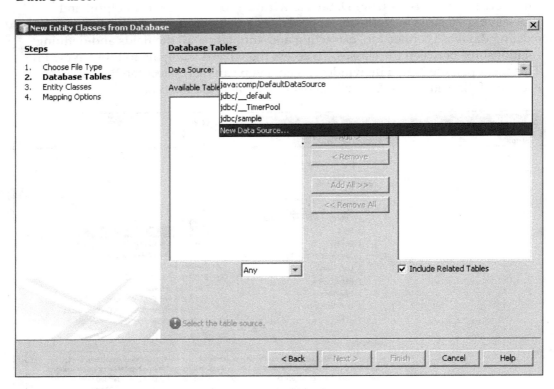

This will allow you to enter the **JNDI Name** and to select the **Database Connection** that was created in the previous chapter:

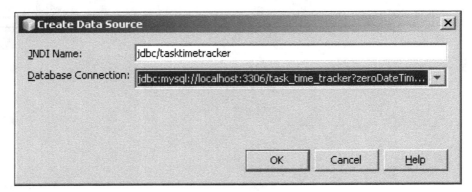

The wizard will now read all the tables and display them in the **Available Tables** list. Select all the tables and add them to the **Selected Tables** list as shown:

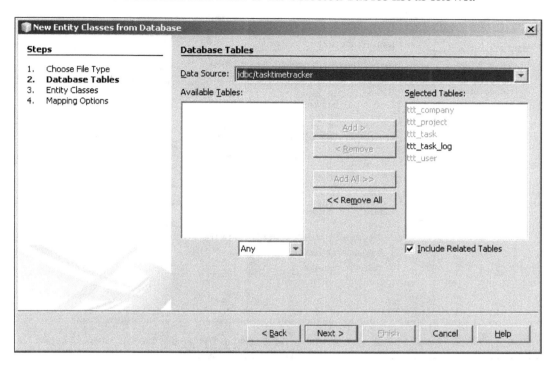

Click on the **Next** button. This will display the following screen with entity class generation properties. Change the **Class Name** for each entity to remove the **Ttt** prefix by double-clicking on each **Class Name** row to edit this property as shown (the screenshot shows the User entity prior to editing). Why do we remove this **Ttt**? Simply because the reverse engineering process automatically creates a class name based on the table name and the **Ttt** prefix does not add anything to our design. The next change has to be done in the package name. Add **domain** to the package name as shown. This will generate new entity classes in the **com.gieman.tttracker.domain** package that will represent our business domain objects and the associated helper classes. Keeping our classes in well-defined, separate packages according to usage or purpose enhances our ability to maintain the application easily. For large enterprise applications, a well-defined Java package structure is crucial.

The final step is to uncheck the **Generate JAXB Annotations** checkbox. We don't need to generate XML via JAXB, so we will not need the additional annotations.

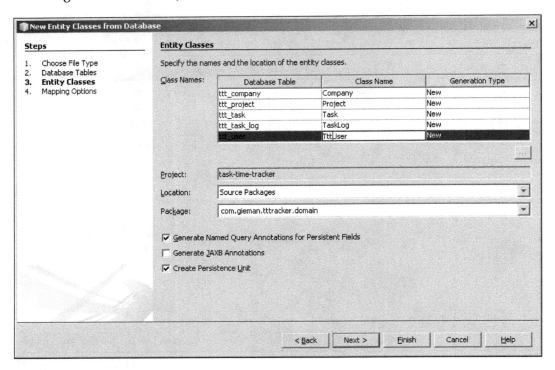

Now click on the **Next** button, which will show the following screen. The final step involves selecting the appropriate **Collection Type**. There are three different types of collections that can be used and all can be used with equal success. We will change the default **Collection Type** to **java.util.List** as the sort order is often important in an application's business logic and the other types do not allow sorting. On a more personal level, we prefer using the `java.util.List` API over the `java.util.Set` and `java.util.Collection` APIs.

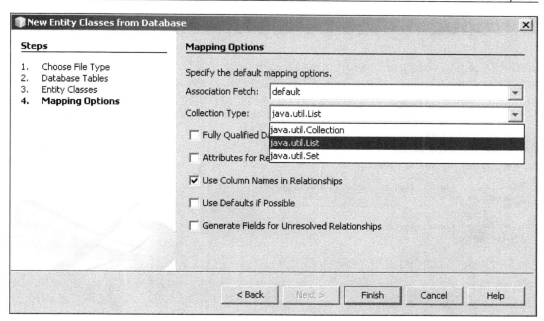

Click on the **Finish** button to start the reverse engineering process. When the process is complete, you can open the src/java nodes to view the generated files, as shown in the following screenshot:

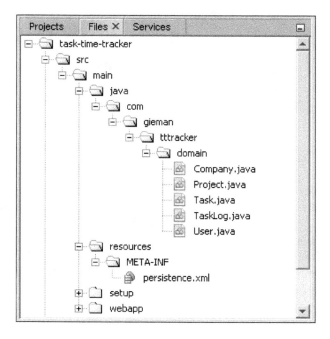

Introducing the persistence.xml file

The persistence.xml file is generated during the reverse engineering process and defines the JPA configuration for a set of entity classes. This file is always located in the META-INF directory at the root of the classpath. Maven projects have a special directory named resources located in the src/main directory, which contains additional resources applicable for building the Java project. The resources directory is automatically copied by Maven to the root of the classpath when building the project. Open the file by double-clicking on it to display the **Design** view of the file in the editor:

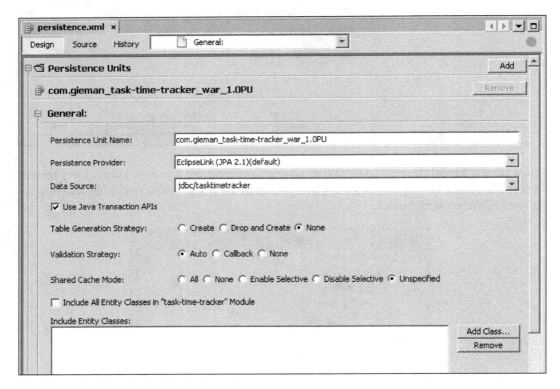

The **Design** view contains several properties that are used to configure the persistence unit behavior. We will stick to the simplest settings, but we encourage you to explore the different strategies that may be useful for your own application's needs. For example, projects that require tables to be automatically created will appreciate the **Table Generation Strategy** of **Create** or **Drop and Create**. Selecting the different options and switching to the **Source** view will help us to quickly identify the appropriate properties in the persistence.xml file.

Click on the **Source** button at the top to view the default file contents in the text format:

```
persistence.xml ×
Design   Source   History

 1   <?xml version="1.0" encoding="UTF-8"?>
 2   <persistence version="2.1" xmlns="http://xmlns.jcp.org/xml/ns/persistence" xmln
 3     <persistence-unit name="com.gieman_task-time-tracker_war_1.0PU" transaction-t
 4       <provider>org.eclipse.persistence.jpa.PersistenceProvider</provider>
 5       <jta-data-source>jdbc/tasktimetracker</jta-data-source>
 6       <exclude-unlisted-classes>true</exclude-unlisted-classes>
 7       <properties/>
 8     </persistence-unit>
 9   </persistence>
10
```

Change the default `persistence-unit` node `name` attribute value to `tttPU` instead of the long autogenerated name. This value will be used in your Java code to refer to this persistence unit and is easy to remember. The `provider` node value is automatically set to the appropriate EclipseLink class, and the `jta-data-source` node value is automatically set to the data source used during the reverse engineering wizard. The `exclude-unlisted-classes` setting will define whether the classpath is scanned for annotated entity classes. Change this to `false`. For large projects, this is the safest way of ensuring that classes are not omitted accidentally. It is also possible to specify each class explicitly in the following way:

```
persistence.xml ×
Design   Source   History

 1   <?xml version="1.0" encoding="UTF-8"?>
 2   <persistence version="2.1" xmlns="http://xmlns.jcp.org/xml/ns/persistence
 3     <persistence-unit name="tttPU" transaction-type="JTA">
 4       <provider>org.eclipse.persistence.jpa.PersistenceProvider</provider>
 5       <jta-data-source>jdbc/tasktimetracker</jta-data-source>
 6       <class>com.gieman.tttracker.domain.Company</class>
 7       <class>com.gieman.tttracker.domain.Project</class>
 8       <class>com.gieman.tttracker.domain.Task</class>
 9       <class>com.gieman.tttracker.domain.TaskLog</class>
10       <class>com.gieman.tttracker.domain.User</class>
11       <exclude-unlisted-classes>true</exclude-unlisted-classes>
12       <properties/>
13     </persistence-unit>
14   </persistence>
```

This is fine for small projects but not very practical if you have hundreds of entity classes. In the previous example, the exclude-unlisted-classes property is set to true, meaning that only the specified classes will be loaded without the need for classpath scanning. We prefer the first method for defining our JPA classes, where the classpath is scanned for all the annotated entity classes by setting exclude-unlisted-classes to false.

The final configuration item of interest is the transaction-type attribute. There are two different types of transactions supported by this item, of which we have JTA set by default. **JTA (Java Transaction API)** denotes that transactions will be managed by a Java EE transaction manager provided by the GlassFish server in our application. We will explore the RESOURCE_LOCAL alternative to JTA when we build our test cases in *Chapter 5, Testing the DAO Layer with Spring and JUnit*. In this situation, the transactions will be managed locally without a Java EE container.

Refactoring the Java classes

The classes generated by the reverse engineering process can be improved upon with a little refactoring to make the code more readable and easier to understand. Some of the autogenerated properties and fields have id in their name when we are actually referring to classes, while the collection of java.util.List objects have list in their name. Let's start with the Company.java file.

The Company.java file

This file represents the Company entity. Double-click on the file to open it in the editor and browse through the contents. This class is a simple POJO with set and get methods for each property in addition to the standard hashCode, equals, and toString methods. The class has a no-arg constructor (required by the JPA specification as domain objects must be created dynamically without any properties), a second constructor that takes only the primary key, and a full (all arguments) constructor. We will make the code more readable by making a few minor changes to the Company.java file.

The first change is to rename the field projectList to projects everywhere in the file. This can be easily achieved by selecting the projectList field, and then selecting **Refactor | Rename** from the menu:

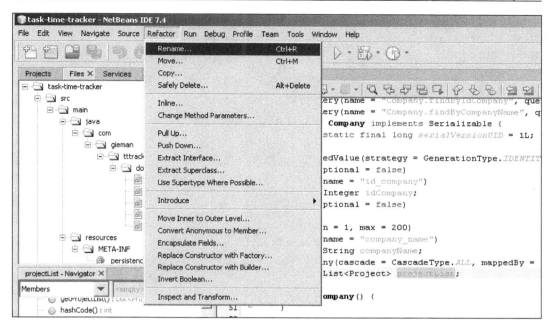

You can now change the field name to **projects**. Make sure that you also select the **Rename Getters and Setters** option before clicking on the **Refactor** button.

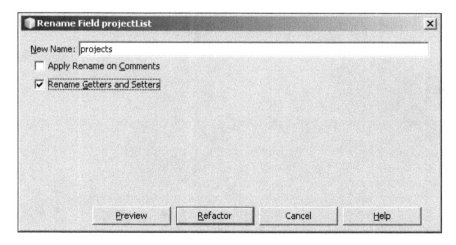

Making these changes will change the field name and generate new get and set methods for the `projects` field.

The final change for the `Company.java` file is renaming the `mappedBy` property from `idCompany` to `company`. The appropriate lines should now look like the following code:

```
@OneToMany(cascade = CascadeType.ALL, mappedBy = "company")
private List<Project> projects;
```

The final refactored `Company.java` file should now look like the following code snippet:

```
package com.gieman.tttracker.domain;

import java.io.Serializable;
import java.util.List;
import javax.persistence.Basic;
import javax.persistence.CascadeType;
import javax.persistence.Column;
import javax.persistence.Entity;
import javax.persistence.GeneratedValue;
import javax.persistence.GenerationType;
import javax.persistence.Id;
import javax.persistence.NamedQueries;
import javax.persistence.NamedQuery;
import javax.persistence.OneToMany;
import javax.persistence.Table;
import javax.validation.constraints.NotNull;
import javax.validation.constraints.Size;

@Entity
@Table(name = "ttt_company")
@NamedQueries({
    @NamedQuery(name = "Company.findAll", query = "SELECT c FROM
Company c"),
    @NamedQuery(name = "Company.findByIdCompany", query = "SELECT c
FROM Company c WHERE c.idCompany = :idCompany"),
    @NamedQuery(name = "Company.findByCompanyName", query = "SELECT c
FROM Company c WHERE c.companyName = :companyName")})
public class Company implements Serializable {
    private static final long serialVersionUID = 1L;
    @Id
    @GeneratedValue(strategy = GenerationType.IDENTITY)
    @Basic(optional = false)
    @Column(name = "id_company")
    private Integer idCompany;
    @Basic(optional = false)
```

```
@NotNull
@Size(min = 1, max = 200)
@Column(name = "company_name")
private String companyName;
@OneToMany(cascade = CascadeType.ALL, mappedBy = "company")
private List<Project> projects;

public Company() {
}

public Company(Integer idCompany) {
    this.idCompany = idCompany;
}

public Company(Integer idCompany, String companyName) {
    this.idCompany = idCompany;
    this.companyName = companyName;
}

public Integer getIdCompany() {
    return idCompany;
}

public void setIdCompany(Integer idCompany) {
    this.idCompany = idCompany;
}

public String getCompanyName() {
    return companyName;
}

public void setCompanyName(String companyName) {
    this.companyName = companyName;
}

public List<Project> getProjects() {
    return projects;
}

public void setProjects(List<Project> projects) {
    this.projects = projects;
}

@Override
```

```
        public int hashCode() {
            int hash = 0;
            hash += (idCompany != null ? idCompany.hashCode() : 0);
            return hash;
        }

        @Override
        public boolean equals(Object object) {
            if (!(object instanceof Company)) {
                return false;
            }
            Company other = (Company) object;
            if ((this.idCompany == null && other.idCompany != null) ||
    (this.idCompany != null && !this.idCompany.equals(other.idCompany))) {
                return false;
            }
            return true;
        }

        @Override
        public String toString() {
            return "com.gieman.tttracker.domain.Company[ idCompany=" +
    idCompany + " ]";
        }

    }
```

JPA uses the convention-over-configuration concept to simplify the configuration of entities. This is achieved by using annotations with sensible defaults to keep the entity definitions lean. Now, let's look at the key JPA annotations in this file.

The @Entity annotation

This is a marker annotation that indicates to the JPA persistence provider that the Company class is an entity. JPA scans for the @Entity annotations when exclude-unlisted-classes is set to false in the persistence.xml file. Without the @Entity annotation, the persistence engine will ignore the class.

The @Table annotation

The @Table annotation defines the underlying database table that is represented by this entity class. The @Table(name = "ttt_company") line tells the persistence provider that the Company class represents the ttt_company table. Only one table annotation can be defined in any entity class.

The @Id annotation

The @Id annotation defines the primary key field in the class and is required for each entity. The persistence provider will throw an exception if the @Id annotation is not present. The Company class property representing the primary key in the ttt_company table is the Integer idCompany field. There are three additional annotations attached to this field, of which the following annotation is specific to primary keys.

The @GeneratedValue annotation

This annotation identifies how the persistence engine should generate new primary key values for the insertion of records into the table. The strategy=GenerationType.IDENTITY line will use the MySQL autoincrement strategy in the background to insert records into the ttt_company table. Different databases may require different strategies. For example, an Oracle database table could use a sequence as the basis for primary key generation by defining the following generator annotations:

```
@GeneratedValue(generator="gen_seq_company")
@SequenceGenerator(name="gen_seq_company", sequenceName="seq_id_
company")
```

 The primary key generation is independent of the class itself. The persistence engine will handle the generation of the primary key for you as defined by the generation strategy.

The @Basic annotation

This is an optional annotation that is used to identify the nullability of the field. The @Basic(optional = false) line is used to specify that the field is not optional (may not be null). Likewise, the @Basic(optional = true) line could be used for other fields that may be nullable.

The @Column annotation

This annotation specifies the column to which the field is mapped. The @Column(name = "id_company") line will, hence, map the id_company column in the ttt_company table to the idCompany field in the class.

The @NotNull and @Size annotations

These annotations are part of the `javax.validation.constraints` package (the Bean Validation package was introduced in Java EE 6) and define that the field cannot be null as well as the minimum and maximum sizes for the field. The `company_name` column in the `ttt_company` table was defined as `varchar(200) not null`, which is the reason why these annotations were created during the reverse engineering process.

The @OneToMany annotation

A `Company` class may have zero or more `Projects` entities. This relationship is defined by the `@OneToMany` annotation. In words, we can describe this relationship as *One Company can have Many Projects*. In JPA, an entity is associated with a collection of other entities by defining this annotation with a `mappedBy` property. We have refactored the original `mappedBy` value to `company`. This will be the name of the field in the `Project.java` file after we have refactored the `Project` file in the next section.

The @NamedQueries annotation

The `@NamedQueries` annotations deserve an explanation in their own right. We will look at these in detail later.

The Projects.java file

As you may have guessed by now, this file represents the `Project` entity and maps to the `ttt_project` table. Double-click on the file to open it in the editor and browse the contents. We will once again do a bit of refactoring to clarify the autogenerated fields:

- Rename the autogenerated `idCompany` field to `company` using the refactoring process. Don't forget to rename the get and set methods.
- Rename the autogenerated `taskList` field to `tasks`. Don't forget the get and set methods again!
- Rename the `mappedBy` value from `idProject` to `project`.

The final refactored file should now look like the following code:

```
package com.gieman.tttracker.domain;

import java.io.Serializable;
import java.util.List;
import javax.persistence.Basic;
import javax.persistence.CascadeType;
```

```
import javax.persistence.Column;
import javax.persistence.Entity;
import javax.persistence.GeneratedValue;
import javax.persistence.GenerationType;
import javax.persistence.Id;
import javax.persistence.JoinColumn;
import javax.persistence.ManyToOne;
import javax.persistence.NamedQueries;
import javax.persistence.NamedQuery;
import javax.persistence.OneToMany;
import javax.persistence.Table;
import javax.validation.constraints.NotNull;
import javax.validation.constraints.Size;

@Entity
@Table(name = "ttt_project")
@NamedQueries({
    @NamedQuery(name = "Project.findAll", query = "SELECT p FROM
Project p"),
    @NamedQuery(name = "Project.findByIdProject", query = "SELECT p
FROM Project p WHERE p.idProject = :idProject"),
    @NamedQuery(name = "Project.findByProjectName", query = "SELECT p
FROM Project p WHERE p.projectName = :projectName")})
public class Project implements Serializable {
    private static final long serialVersionUID = 1L;
    @Id
    @GeneratedValue(strategy = GenerationType.IDENTITY)
    @Basic(optional = false)
    @Column(name = "id_project")
    private Integer idProject;
    @Basic(optional = false)
    @NotNull
    @Size(min = 1, max = 200)
    @Column(name = "project_name")
    private String projectName;
    @JoinColumn(name = "id_company", referencedColumnName = "id_
company")
    @ManyToOne(optional = false)
    private Company company;
    @OneToMany(cascade = CascadeType.ALL, mappedBy = "project")
    private List<Task> tasks;

    public Project() {
    }
```

```java
    public Project(Integer idProject) {
        this.idProject = idProject;
    }

    public Project(Integer idProject, String projectName) {
        this.idProject = idProject;
        this.projectName = projectName;
    }

    public Integer getIdProject() {
        return idProject;
    }

    public void setIdProject(Integer idProject) {
        this.idProject = idProject;
    }

    public String getProjectName() {
        return projectName;
    }

    public void setProjectName(String projectName) {
        this.projectName = projectName;
    }

    public Company getCompany() {
        return company;
    }

    public void setCompany(Company company) {
        this.company = company;
    }

    public List<Task> getTasks() {
        return tasks;
    }

    public void setTasks(List<Task> tasks) {
        this.tasks = tasks;
    }

    @Override
```

```
public int hashCode() {
    int hash = 0;
    hash += (idProject != null ? idProject.hashCode() : 0);
    return hash;
}

@Override
public boolean equals(Object object) {
    if (!(object instanceof Project)) {
        return false;
    }
    Project other = (Project) object;
    if ((this.idProject == null && other.idProject != null) ||
(this.idProject != null && !this.idProject.equals(other.idProject))) {
        return false;
    }
    return true;
}

@Override
public String toString() {
    return "com.gieman.tttracker.domain.Project[ idProject=" +
idProject + " ]";
}

}
```

The @ManyToOne annotation

This annotation represents a relationship between entities; it is the reverse of the `@OneToMany` annotation. For the `Project` entity, we can say that *Many Projects have One Company*. In other words, a `Project` entity belongs to a single `Company` class, and (inversely) a `Company` class can have any number of `Projects` entities. This relationship is defined at the database level (that is, the foreign key relationship in the underlying tables) and is achieved in the `@JoinColumn` annotation:

```
@JoinColumn(name = "id_company", referencedColumnName = "id_company")
```

The `name` property defines the name of the column in the `ttt_project` table that is the foreign key to the `referencedColumnName` column in the `ttt_company` table.

Bidirectional mapping and owning entities

It is essential to grasp the very important concept of how one entity is related to another through the @ManyToOne and @OneToMany annotations. The Company class has a list of mapped Projects entities defined as follows:

```
@OneToMany(cascade = CascadeType.ALL, mappedBy = "company")
private List<Project> projects;
```

Whereas, the Project class has exactly one mapped Company entity:

```
@JoinColumn(name="id_company", referencedColumnName="id_company")
@ManyToOne(optional=false)
private Company company;
```

This is known as bidirectional mapping, one mapping on each class for each direction. A many-to-one mapping back to the source, as in the Project entity back to the Company entity, implies a corresponding one-to-many mapping on the source (Company) back to the target (Project). The terms **source** and **target** can be defined as follows:

- **Source**: This is an entity that can exist in a relationship in its own right. The source entity does not require the target entity to exist and the @OneToMany collection can be empty. In our example, a Company entity can exist without a Project entity.

- **Target**: This is an entity that cannot exist on its own without a reference to a valid source. The @ManyToOne entity defined on the target cannot be null. A Project entity cannot exist in our design without a valid Company entity.

The **owning entity** is an entity that understands the other entity from a database perspective. In simple terms, the owning entity has the @JoinColumn definition describing the underlying columns that form the relationship. In the Company-Project relationship, Project is the owning entity. Note that an entity can be both a target as well as a source as shown in the following Project.java file snippet:

```
@OneToMany(cascade = CascadeType.ALL, mappedBy = "project")
private List<Task> tasks;
```

Here, Project is the source for the Task entity relationship and we would expect a reverse @ManyToOne annotation on the Task class. This is exactly what we will find.

The Task.java file

This file defines the `Task` entity that represents the `ttt_task` table. Open the file and perform the following refactoring:

- Delete the autogenerated `taskLogList` field and also delete the associated get and set methods. Why do we do this? There may be many millions of task logs in the system for each `Task` instance and it is not advisable to hold a reference to such a large set of `TaskLog` instances within the `Task` object.

- Rename the autogenerated `idProject` field to `project`. Don't forget to delete the get and set methods again.

After making the preceding changes, you will see that some of the imports are no longer required and are highlighted by the NetBeans IDE:

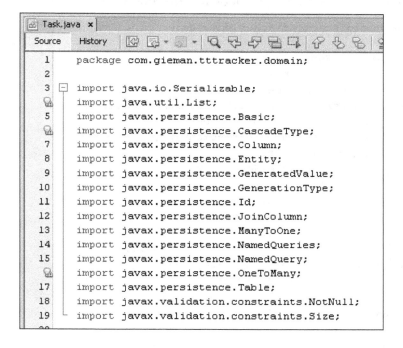

The keyboard combination of *Ctrl + Shift + I* will remove all the unused imports. Another alternative is to click on the icon, shown in the following screenshot, to open the menu and select a **Remove** option:

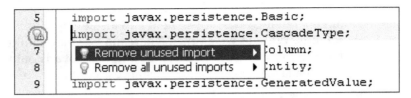

It is good practice to have clean code and removing the unused imports is a simple process.

The final refactored file should now look like the following code snippet:

```java
package com.gieman.tttracker.domain;

import java.io.Serializable;
import javax.persistence.Basic;
import javax.persistence.Column;
import javax.persistence.Entity;
import javax.persistence.GeneratedValue;
import javax.persistence.GenerationType;
import javax.persistence.Id;
import javax.persistence.JoinColumn;
import javax.persistence.ManyToOne;
import javax.persistence.NamedQueries;
import javax.persistence.NamedQuery;
import javax.persistence.Table;
import javax.validation.constraints.NotNull;
import javax.validation.constraints.Size;

@Entity
@Table(name = "ttt_task")
@NamedQueries({
    @NamedQuery(name = "Task.findAll", query = "SELECT t FROM Task
t"),
    @NamedQuery(name = "Task.findByIdTask", query = "SELECT t FROM
Task t WHERE t.idTask = :idTask"),
    @NamedQuery(name = "Task.findByTaskName", query = "SELECT t FROM
Task t WHERE t.taskName = :taskName")})
public class Task implements Serializable {
    private static final long serialVersionUID = 1L;
    @Id
```

```java
@GeneratedValue(strategy = GenerationType.IDENTITY)
@Basic(optional = false)
@Column(name = "id_task")
private Integer idTask;
@Basic(optional = false)
@NotNull
@Size(min = 1, max = 200)
@Column(name = "task_name")
private String taskName;
@JoinColumn(name = "id_project", referencedColumnName = "id_
project")
@ManyToOne(optional = false)
private Project project;

public Task() {
}

public Task(Integer idTask) {
    this.idTask = idTask;
}

public Task(Integer idTask, String taskName) {
    this.idTask = idTask;
    this.taskName = taskName;
}

public Integer getIdTask() {
    return idTask;
}

public void setIdTask(Integer idTask) {
    this.idTask = idTask;
}

public String getTaskName() {
    return taskName;
}

public void setTaskName(String taskName) {
    this.taskName = taskName;
}

public Project getProject() {
    return project;
```

```
    }

    public void setProject(Project project) {
        this.project = project;
    }

    @Override
    public int hashCode() {
        int hash = 0;
        hash += (idTask != null ? idTask.hashCode() : 0);
        return hash;
    }

    @Override
    public boolean equals(Object object) {
        if (!(object instanceof Task)) {
            return false;
        }
        Task other = (Task) object;
        if ((this.idTask == null && other.idTask != null) || (this.
idTask != null && !this.idTask.equals(other.idTask))) {
            return false;
        }
        return true;
    }

    @Override
    public String toString() {
        return "com.gieman.tttracker.domain.Task[ idTask=" + idTask +
" ]";
    }
}
```

Note the @ManyToOne annotation referencing the Project class using the @JoinColumn definition. The Task object owns this relationship.

The User.java file

The User entity represents the underlying ttt_user table. The generated class has a @OneToMany definition for the relationship to the TaskLog class:

```
@OneToMany(cascade = CascadeType.ALL, mappedBy = "username")
private List<TaskLog> taskLogList;
```

Refactoring in this file will once again **delete** this relationship completely. As noted in the `Tasks.java` section, a `User` entity may also have many thousands of task logs. By understanding the application's requirements and data structure, it is often far cleaner to remove unnecessary relationships completely.

You will also note that the `@Pattern` annotation is commented out by default during the reverse engineering process. The `email` field name indicated to NetBeans that this might be an e-mail field and NetBeans added the annotation for use if required. We will uncomment this annotation to enable e-mail pattern checking for the field and add the required import:

```
import javax.validation.constraints.Pattern;
```

The refactored `User.java` file will now look like the following code snippet:

```
package com.gieman.tttracker.domain;

import java.io.Serializable;
import javax.persistence.Basic;
import javax.persistence.Column;
import javax.persistence.Entity;
import javax.persistence.Id;
import javax.persistence.NamedQueries;
import javax.persistence.NamedQuery;
import javax.persistence.Table;
import javax.validation.constraints.NotNull;
import javax.validation.constraints.Pattern;
import javax.validation.constraints.Size;

@Entity
@Table(name = "ttt_user")
@NamedQueries({
    @NamedQuery(name = "User.findAll", query = "SELECT u FROM User
u"),
    @NamedQuery(name = "User.findByUsername", query = "SELECT u FROM
User u WHERE u.username = :username"),
    @NamedQuery(name = "User.findByFirstName", query = "SELECT u FROM
User u WHERE u.firstName = :firstName"),
    @NamedQuery(name = "User.findByLastName", query = "SELECT u FROM
User u WHERE u.lastName = :lastName"),
    @NamedQuery(name = "User.findByEmail", query = "SELECT u FROM User
u WHERE u.email = :email"),
    @NamedQuery(name = "User.findByPassword", query = "SELECT u FROM
User u WHERE u.password = :password"),
    @NamedQuery(name = "User.findByAdminRole", query = "SELECT u FROM
User u WHERE u.adminRole = :adminRole") })
```

```java
public class User implements Serializable {
    private static final long serialVersionUID = 1L;
    @Id
    @Basic(optional = false)
    @NotNull
    @Size(min = 1, max = 10)
    @Column(name = "username")
    private String username;
    @Basic(optional = false)
    @NotNull
    @Size(min = 1, max = 100)
    @Column(name = "first_name")
    private String firstName;
    @Basic(optional = false)
    @NotNull
    @Size(min = 1, max = 100)
    @Column(name = "last_name")
    private String lastName;
    @Pattern(regexp="[a-z0-9!#$%&'*+/=?^_`{|}~-]+(?:\\.[a-
z0-9!#$%&'*+/=?^_`{|}~-]+)*@(?:[a-z0-9](?:[a-z0-9-]*[a-z0-
9])?\\.)+[a-z0-9](?:[a-z0-9-]*[a-z0-9])?", message="Invalid email")
    @Basic(optional = false)
    @NotNull
    @Size(min = 1, max = 100)
    @Column(name = "email")
    private String email;
    @Basic(optional = false)
    @NotNull
    @Size(min = 1, max = 100)
    @Column(name = "password")
    private String password;
    @Column(name = "admin_role")
    private Character adminRole;

    public User() {
    }

    public User(String username) {
        this.username = username;
    }

    public User(String username, String firstName, String lastName,
String email, String password) {
        this.username = username;
```

```java
        this.firstName = firstName;
        this.lastName = lastName;
        this.email = email;
        this.password = password;
    }

    public String getUsername() {
        return username;
    }

    public void setUsername(String username) {
        this.username = username;
    }

    public String getFirstName() {
        return firstName;
    }

    public void setFirstName(String firstName) {
        this.firstName = firstName;
    }

    public String getLastName() {
        return lastName;
    }

    public void setLastName(String lastName) {
        this.lastName = lastName;
    }

    public String getEmail() {
        return email;
    }

    public void setEmail(String email) {
        this.email = email;
    }

    public String getPassword() {
        return password;
    }

    public void setPassword(String password) {
        this.password = password;
```

```
    }

    public Character getAdminRole() {
        return adminRole;
    }

    public void setAdminRole(Character adminRole) {
        this.adminRole = adminRole;
    }

    @Override
    public int hashCode() {
        int hash = 0;
        hash += (username != null ? username.hashCode() : 0);
        return hash;
    }

    @Override
    public boolean equals(Object object) {
        if (!(object instanceof User)) {
            return false;
        }
        User other = (User) object;
        if ((this.username == null && other.username != null) ||
(this.username != null && !this.username.equals(other.username))) {
            return false;
        }
        return true;
    }

    @Override
    public String toString() {
        return "com.gieman.tttracker.domain.User[ username=" +
username + " ]";
    }
}
```

The TaskLog.java file

The final entry in our application represents the `ttt_task_log` table. The refactoring required here is to rename the `idTask` field to `task` (remember to also rename the get and set methods) and then rename the `username` field to `user`. The file should now look like the following code snippet:

```
package com.tttracker.domain;

import java.io.Serializable;
import java.util.Date;
import javax.persistence.Basic;
import javax.persistence.Column;
import javax.persistence.Entity;
import javax.persistence.GeneratedValue;
import javax.persistence.GenerationType;
import javax.persistence.Id;
import javax.persistence.JoinColumn;
import javax.persistence.ManyToOne;
import javax.persistence.NamedQueries;
import javax.persistence.NamedQuery;
import javax.persistence.Table;
import javax.persistence.Temporal;
import javax.persistence.TemporalType;
import javax.validation.constraints.NotNull;
import javax.validation.constraints.Size;

@Entity
@Table(name = "ttt_task_log")
@NamedQueries({
  @NamedQuery(name = "TaskLog.findAll", query = "SELECT t FROM TaskLog
t"),
  @NamedQuery(name = "TaskLog.findByIdTaskLog", query = "SELECT t FROM
TaskLog t WHERE t.idTaskLog = :idTaskLog"),
  @NamedQuery(name = "TaskLog.findByTaskDescription", query = "SELECT
t FROM TaskLog t WHERE t.taskDescription = :taskDescription"),
  @NamedQuery(name = "TaskLog.findByTaskLogDate", query = "SELECT t
FROM TaskLog t WHERE t.taskLogDate = :taskLogDate"),
  @NamedQuery(name = "TaskLog.findByTaskMinutes", query = "SELECT t
FROM TaskLog t WHERE t.taskMinutes = :taskMinutes")})
public class TaskLog implements Serializable {
  private static final long serialVersionUID = 1L;
  @Id
  @GeneratedValue(strategy = GenerationType.IDENTITY)
  @Basic(optional = false)
  @Column(name = "id_task_log")
  private Integer idTaskLog;
  @Basic(optional = false)
  @NotNull
  @Size(min = 1, max = 2000)
  @Column(name = "task_description")
  private String taskDescription;
```

```java
@Basic(optional = false)
@NotNull
@Column(name = "task_log_date")
@Temporal(TemporalType.DATE)
private Date taskLogDate;
@Basic(optional = false)
@NotNull
@Column(name = "task_minutes")
private int taskMinutes;
@JoinColumn(name = "username", referencedColumnName = "username")
@ManyToOne(optional = false)
private User user;
@JoinColumn(name = "id_task", referencedColumnName = "id_task")
@ManyToOne(optional = false)
private Task task;

public TaskLog() {
}

public TaskLog(Integer idTaskLog) {
  this.idTaskLog = idTaskLog;
}

public TaskLog(Integer idTaskLog, String taskDescription, Date
taskLogDate, int taskMinutes) {
  this.idTaskLog = idTaskLog;
  this.taskDescription = taskDescription;
  this.taskLogDate = taskLogDate;
  this.taskMinutes = taskMinutes;
}

public Integer getIdTaskLog() {
  return idTaskLog;
}

public void setIdTaskLog(Integer idTaskLog) {
  this.idTaskLog = idTaskLog;
}

public String getTaskDescription() {
  return taskDescription;
}

public void setTaskDescription(String taskDescription) {
```

```java
    this.taskDescription = taskDescription;
}

public Date getTaskLogDate() {
  return taskLogDate;
}

public void setTaskLogDate(Date taskLogDate) {
  this.taskLogDate = taskLogDate;
}

public int getTaskMinutes() {
  return taskMinutes;
}

public void setTaskMinutes(int taskMinutes) {
  this.taskMinutes = taskMinutes;
}

public User getUser() {
  return user;
}

public void setUser(User user) {
  this.user = user;
}

public Task getTask() {
  return task;
}

public void setTask(Task task) {
  this.task = task;
}

@Override
public int hashCode() {
  int hash = 0;
  hash += (idTaskLog != null ? idTaskLog.hashCode() : 0);
  return hash;
}

@Override
public boolean equals(Object object) {
```

```
      if (!(object instanceof TaskLog)) {
        return false;
      }
      TaskLog other = (TaskLog) object;
      if ((this.idTaskLog == null && other.idTaskLog != null) || (this.
idTaskLog != null && !this.idTaskLog.equals(other.idTaskLog))) {
        return false;
      }
      return true;
   }

   @Override
   public String toString() {
      return "com.tttracker.domain.TaskLog[ idTaskLog=" + idTaskLog + "
]";
   }
}
```

Introducing the Java Persistence Query Language

Everyone reading this book should be familiar with SQL queries and how they work. Constructing a simple query against the `ttt_company` table to retrieve all records would look something like:

```
select * from ttt_company
```

Restricting the result set to companies starting with G would look like the following code line:

```
select * from ttt_company where company_name like "G%"
```

In JPA, we are dealing with entities and relationships between entities. The **Java Persistence Query Language (JPQL)** is used to formulate queries in a similar way to SQL. The previously mentioned statement will be written in JPQL as follows:

```
SELECT c FROM Company c
```

And the statement that follows is written as such:

```
SELECT c FROM Company c WHERE c.companyName LIKE 'G%'
```

The following are the major differences between SQL and JPQL:

- JPQL class and field names are case sensitive. When we are dealing with classes, the class name must start with an uppercase letter. All the fields must have the exact case as defined in the class. The following statement will not compile as the company entity starts with a lowercase c:

  ```
  SELECT c FROM company c WHERE c.companyName LIKE 'G%'
  ```

- JPQL keywords are case insensitive. The preceding statement could just as well have been written as follows:

  ```
  select c from Company c where c.companyName like 'G%'
  ```

- JPQL uses aliases to define instances and relationships between the instances. In the previous examples, the lowercase c is used as the alias in the SELECT and WHERE clauses.

- JPQL queries may be static (defined in an annotation) or dynamic (built and executed at runtime). Static queries are compiled once and looked up whenever required. This makes static queries faster to use and more performant.

- JPQL queries are translated into SQL; they are then executed against the underlying database. This translation allows for database-specific query optimization in the persistence engine.

- JPQL has a rich set of functions to define conditional expressions. These expressions are translated into the correct SQL for the underlying database. This means that developers no longer need to write database-specific SQL statements. Switching between databases will not require any coding as the JPQL statements abstract the underlying SQL required to execute the statement.

> We strongly recommend you spend time learning about JPQL. There are many excellent books available that are dedicated to JPA and JPQL; they explain advanced usage. There are also many online tutorials and JPQL examples on the Internet. It is beyond the scope of this book to go beyond the basics, and we leave it to you to delve into this rich language further.

Defining named queries

The reverse engineering process generated a set of @NamedQuery annotations in each class, one for each persistent field. The Company class, for example, had the following named queries defined:

```
@NamedQueries({
   @NamedQuery(name = "Company.findAll", query = "SELECT c FROM Company
c"),
   @NamedQuery(name = "Company.findByIdCompany", query = "SELECT c FROM
Company c WHERE c.idCompany = :idCompany"),
   @NamedQuery(name = "Company.findByCompanyName", query = "SELECT c
FROM Company c WHERE c.companyName = :companyName")})
```

Each @NamedQuery name must be unique within the persistence engine; hence, it is prefixed with the name of the class. The first query name, Company.findAll, represents the full list of the Company objects. The second query uses a named parameter, idCompany, as a placeholder for a value provided at runtime. Named parameters are always prefixed with the colon symbol. You should spend some time browsing the queries generated in the Java classes to become familiar with the basic JPQL syntax. We will learn more about named queries and how they are used in the following chapters.

Refactoring Java equals() and hashCode()

Our domain layer entity classes have autogenerated equals and hashCode methods defined. The Company class, for example, defines these methods as shown:

```
Company.java  ×
Source  History

75        @Override
76  □     public int hashCode() {
77            int hash = 0;
78            hash += (idCompany != null ? idCompany.hashCode() : 0);
79            return hash;
80        }
81
82        @Override
83  □     public boolean equals(Object object) {
84            // TODO: Warning - this method won't work in the case the id fields are not set
85            if (!(object instanceof Company)) {
86                return false;
87            }
88            Company other = (Company) object;
89            if ((this.idCompany == null && other.idCompany != null) || (this.idCompany != nu
90                return false;
91            }
92            return true;
93        }
```

It is best practice to always provide correctly implemented `equals` and `hashCode` methods that use the entity ID to calculate the value that is returned. These methods are used by JPA to determine the equality between entities. Our autogenerated `equals` method will work correctly with JPA as the ID entity is used in the comparison for each method. However, the `//TODO: Warning` message on line 83 (see the previous screenshot) indicates an issue that can be avoided if we regenerate the `equals` method with the NetBeans IDE.

Delete the `equals` method and right-click on the `Company.java` file in the editor using the mouse to display the context menu. Select the **Insert Code...** option:

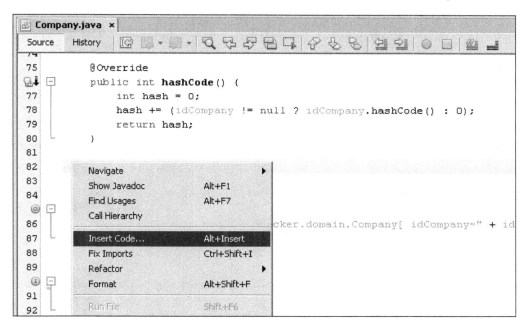

From the pop-up menu, select the **equals()...** option and ensure that the **idCompany : Integer** field is selected in the **Generate equals()** pop up:

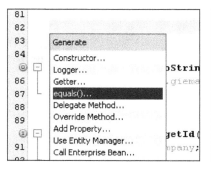
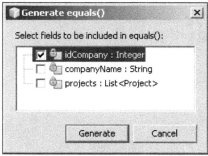

Click on **Generate** to create the new `equals` method:

```
82
83          @Override
            public boolean equals(Object obj) {
85              if (obj == null) {
86                  return false;
87              }
88              if (getClass() != obj.getClass()) {
89                  return false;
90              }
91              final Company other = (Company) obj;
                if (!Objects.equals(this.idCompany, other.idCompany)) {
93                  return false;
94              }
95              return true;
96          }
```

Click on the information icon (circled) over line 92 to display the context information:

```
90              }
91              final Company other = (Company) obj;
                if (!Objects.equals(this.idCompany, other.idCompany)) {
93      ▌ 💡 The if statement is redundant        ▶
94              }
95              return true;
96          }
```

Click on **The if statement is redundant** to clean your code further and replace the `if` statement with the following line:

```
return Objects.equals(this.idCompany, other.idCompany);
```

The `Objects` class was introduced in Java 1.7 and consists of static utility methods for operating on objects. The `Objects.equals` method takes into account `null` values and solves the potential `//TODO: Warning` issue with the autogenerated `equals` method. From the Java 1.7 JavaDoc for the `Objects.equals` method:

Returns `true` if the arguments are equal to each other and `false` otherwise. Consequently, if both the arguments are null, `true` is returned, and if exactly one argument is null, `false` is returned. Otherwise, the equality is determined using the `equals` method of the first argument.

You can now replace the autogenerated `equals` method of the `Project`, `Task`, `User`, and `TaskLog` entity classes in a similar way.

Summary

In this chapter we have reverse engineered the 3T database into a set of Java classes. Each Java class represents a JPA entity with annotations defining the relationship between entities as well as the mapping of database columns to Java fields. We have had a brief introduction to JPQL through named query definitions and introduced key JPA annotations.

Although this chapter has introduced many key concepts, the scope of JPA and JPQL leaves much for you to learn. JPA is a key tool in enterprise application development, allowing for easy enhancements and database-agnostic programming.

The next chapter will introduce the **Data Access Object (DAO)** design pattern and implement a robust data access layer using the domain classes we have just defined. Our JPA journey has just started!

4

Data Access Made Easy

The Data Access Object (DAO) design pattern is a simple and elegant way of abstracting database persistence from application business logic. This design ensures a clear separation of the two core parts of any enterprise application: the data access layer and the service (or business logic) layer. The DAO pattern is a well-understood Java EE programming structure, initially brought to prominence by Sun Microsystems in its Java EE Design Blueprints that has since been adopted by other programming environments such as the .NET framework.

The following image illustrates where the DAO layer sits in the overall application structure:

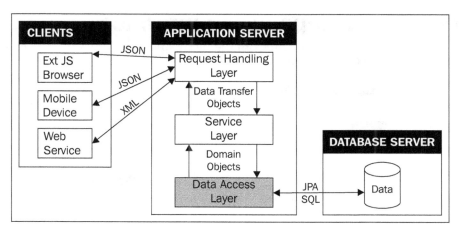

Changing an implementation in the DAO layer should not affect the service layer in any way. This is achieved by defining DAO interfaces to encapsulate the persistence operations that the service layer can access. The DAO implementation itself is hidden to the service layer.

Defining the DAO interfaces

An interface in the Java programming language defines a set of method signatures and constant declarations. Interfaces expose behaviors (or *what* can be done) and define a contract that implementing classes promise to provide (*how* it is done). Our DAO layer will contain one interface and one implementing class per domain object.

The use of interfaces is an often misunderstood pattern in enterprise programming. The argument goes along the line, "Why add another set of Java objects to your codebase when they are not required". Interfaces do add to the number of lines of code that you write, but their beauty will be appreciated as soon as you are asked to refactor an aging project that was written with interfaces from the start. I have migrated an SQL-based persistence layer to a JPA persistence layer. The new DAO implementation replaced the old without any significant change in the service layer, thanks to the use of interfaces. Development was done in parallel to supporting the existing (old) implementation until we were ready to swap in the new implementation. This was a relatively painless process that would not have been as easily achieved without the use of interfaces.

Let's start with the company interface.

Adding the CompanyDao interface

1. Navigate to **File** | **New File** from the menu and select **Java Interface** as shown in the following screenshot:

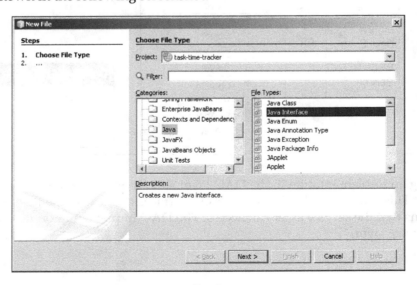

2. Click on the **Next** button and fill in the details as shown in the following screenshot:

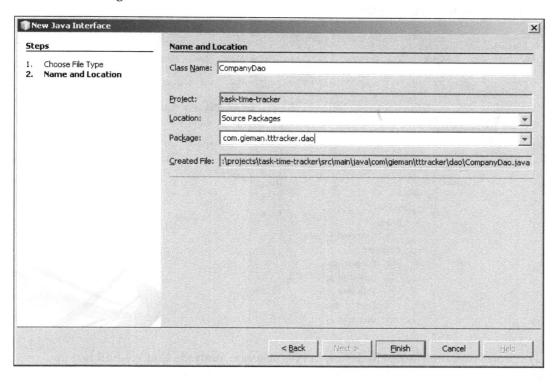

The name of the interface is CompanyDao. We could have named this interface using the uppercase acronym CompanyDAO. In keeping with the newer Java EE naming styles, we have decided to use the camel case form of the acronym. Recent examples of this style include the Html*, Json*, and Xml* classes and interfaces, an example of which is javax.json.JsonObject. We also believe that this form is easier to read. However, this does not prohibit you from using the uppercase acronym; there are many of these examples in Java EE as well (EJB*, JAXB*, and JMS* interfaces and classes to name a few). Whatever you choose, be consistent. Do not mix forms and create CompanyDAO and ProjectDao interfaces!

Note that the package `com.gieman.tttracker.dao` does not exist yet and will be created for you. Click on **Finish** to create your first interface, after which NetBeans will open the file in the editor.

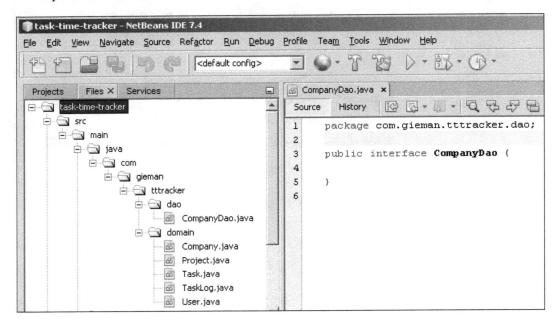

The Company interface will define the persistence methods that we will use in our application. The core methods must include the ability to perform each CRUD operation in addition to any other operations appropriate to our business needs. We will add the following methods to this interface:

- `persist`: This method inserts a new company record
- `merge`: This method updates an existing company record
- `remove`: This method deletes a company record
- `find`: This method selects a company record using a primary key
- `findAll`: This method returns all the company records

Note that the JPA terminologies `persist`, `merge`, `remove`, and `find` are equivalent to the SQL operations `insert`, `update`, `delete`, and `select`. Add the methods to `CompanyDao` as shown in the following code:

```
package com.gieman.tttracker.dao;

import com.gieman.tttracker.domain.Company;
import java.util.List;
```

```
public interface CompanyDao {

    public Company find(Integer idCompany);

    public List<Company> findAll();

    public void persist(Company company);

    public Company merge(Company company);

    public void remove(Company company);
}
```

We have defined a contract that the implementing class must promise to deliver. We will now add the ProjectDao interface.

Adding the ProjectDao interface

The ProjectDao interface will define a similar set of methods to the CompanyDao interface:

```
package com.gieman.tttracker.dao;

import com.gieman.tttracker.domain.Company;
import com.gieman.tttracker.domain.Project;
import java.util.List;

public interface ProjectDao {

    public Project find(Integer idProject);

    public List<Project> findAll();

    public void persist(Project project);

    public Project merge(Project project);

    public void remove(Project project);
}
```

You will note that all method signatures in the `ProjectDao` interface are identical to the `CompanyDao` interface. The only difference is in class types where `Company` is replaced by `project`. The same situation will occur in all the other interfaces that we are going to add (`TaskDao`, `UserDao`, and `TaskLogDao`). Each of the interfaces will require a definition for the `find` method that will look like the following code:

```
public Company find(Integer idCompany); // in CompanyDao
public Project find(Integer idProject); // in ProjectDao
public Task find(Integer idTask); // in TaskDao
public User find(Integer idUser); // in UserDao
public TaskLog find(Integer idTaskLog); // in TaskLogDao
```

As you can see, the only functional difference in each of these methods is the returned type. The same can be said for the `persist`, `merge`, and `remove` methods. This situation lends itself perfectly to the use of Java generics.

Defining a generic DAO interface

This interface will be extended by each of our DAO interfaces. The `GenericDao` interface uses generics to define each method in a way that can be used by each descendent interface. These methods will then be available free of cost to the extending interfaces. Rather than defining a `find(Integer id)` method in each of the `CompanyDao`, `ProjectDao`, `TaskDao`, `UserDao`, and `TaskLogDao` interfaces, the `GenericDao` interface defines the generic method that is then available for all descendants.

 This is a powerful technique for enterprise application programming and should always be considered when designing or architecting an application framework. A well-structured design using Java generics will simplify change requests and maintenance for many years to come.

The generic interface definition looks like this:

```
package com.gieman.tttracker.dao;

public interface GenericDao<T, ID> {

    public T find(ID id);

    public void persist(T obj);

    public T merge(T obj);

    public void remove(T obj);
}
```

We can now refactor the `CompanyDao` interface as follows:

```
package com.gieman.tttracker.dao;

import com.gieman.tttracker.domain.Company;
import java.util.List;

public interface CompanyDao extends GenericDao<Company, Integer>{

    public List<Company> findAll();

}
```

Note the way in which we have extended the `GenericDao` interface using the `<Company, Integer>` types. The type parameters `<T, ID>` in the `GenericDao` interface become placeholders for the types specified in the `CompanyDao` definition. A `T` or `ID` that is found in the `GenericDao` interface will be replaced with `Company` and `Integer` in the `CompanyDao` interface. This automatically adds the `find`, `persist`, `merge`, and `remove` methods to `CompanyDao`.

Generics allow the compiler to check type correctness at compile-time. This improves code robustness. A good explanation of Java generics can be found at `http://docs.oracle.com/javase/tutorial/extra/generics/index.html`.

In a similar way, we can now refactor the `ProjectDao` interface:

```
package com.gieman.tttracker.dao;

import com.gieman.tttracker.domain.Company;
import com.gieman.tttracker.domain.Project;
import java.util.List;

public interface ProjectDao extends GenericDao<Project, Integer>{

    public List<Project> findAll();

}
```

Let's continue with the missing interfaces in the same manner.

The TaskDao interface

Apart from the common generic methods, we will once again need a `findAll` method. This interface looks like the following code:

```
package com.gieman.tttracker.dao;

import com.gieman.tttracker.domain.Project;
import com.gieman.tttracker.domain.Task;
import java.util.List;

public interface TaskDao extends GenericDao<Task, Integer>{

    public List<Task> findAll();
}
```

The UserDao interface

We will need a list of all the users in the system as well as a few finder methods to identify a user by different parameters. These methods will be required when we develop our frontend user interfaces and service layer functionality. The `UserDao` interface looks like the following code:

```
package com.gieman.tttracker.dao;

import com.gieman.tttracker.domain.User;
import java.util.List;

public interface UserDao extends GenericDao<User, String> {

    public List<User> findAll();

    public User findByUsernamePassword(String username, String
password);

    public User findByUsername(String username);

    public User findByEmail(String email);
}
```

Note that the `UserDao` interface extends `GenericDao` with a `String` ID type. This is because the `User` domain entity has a `String` primary key type.

The TaskLogDao interface

The TaskLogDao interface will also need a few additional methods to be defined in order to allow different views into the task log data. These methods will once again be required when we develop our frontend user interfaces and service layer functionality.

```
package com.gieman.tttracker.dao;

import com.gieman.tttracker.domain.Task;
import com.gieman.tttracker.domain.TaskLog;
import com.gieman.tttracker.domain.User;
import java.util.Date;
import java.util.List;

public interface TaskLogDao extends GenericDao<TaskLog, Integer>{

    public List<TaskLog> findByUser(User user, Date startDate,
        Date endDate);

    public long findTaskLogCountByTask(Task task);

    public long findTaskLogCountByUser(User user);
}
```

Note that our finder methods for the TaskLogDao interface have descriptive names that identify the purpose of the method. Each finder method will be used to retrieve a subset of task log entries that are appropriate for the business needs of the application.

This covers all the required interfaces for our application. It is now time to define the implementations for each of our interfaces.

Defining the generic DAO implementation

We will once again use Java generics to define a common ancestor class that will be extended by each of our implementation classes (CompanyDaoImpl, ProjectDaoImpl, TaskDaoImpl, TaskLogDaoImpl, and UserDaoImpl). The GenericDaoImpl and all other implementing classes will be added to the same com.gieman.tttracker.dao package as our DAO interfaces. Key lines of code in GenericDaoImpl are highlighted and will be explained in the following sections:

```
package com.gieman.tttracker.dao;

import java.io.Serializable;
```

```java
import org.slf4j.Logger;
import org.slf4j.LoggerFactory;
import javax.persistence.EntityManager;
import javax.persistence.PersistenceContext;
import org.springframework.transaction.annotation.Propagation;
import org.springframework.transaction.annotation.Transactional;

public class GenericDaoImpl<T, ID extends Serializable> implements
  GenericDao<T, ID> {

    final protected Logger logger =
      LoggerFactory.getLogger(this.getClass());

    @PersistenceContext(unitName = "tttPU")
    protected EntityManager em;

    private Class<T> type;

    public GenericDaoImpl(Class<T> type1) {
        this.type = type1;
    }

    @Override
    @Transactional(readOnly = true, propagation =
      Propagation.SUPPORTS)
    public T find(ID id) {
        return (T) em.find(type, id);
    }

    @Override
    @Transactional(readOnly = false, propagation =
      Propagation.REQUIRED)
    public void persist(T o) {
      em.persist(o);
    }

    @Override
    @Transactional(readOnly = false, propagation =
      Propagation.REQUIRED)
    public T merge(T o) {

        o = em.merge(o);
      return o;
    }
```

```
@Override
@Transactional(readOnly = false, propagation =
    Propagation.REQUIRED)
public void remove(T o) {

    // associate object with persistence context
    o = merge(o);
    em.remove(o);

}
}
```

There are a lot of new concepts in this class! Let's tackle them one at a time.

The Simple Logging Facade for Java

The Simple Logging Facade for Java or SLF4J is a simple abstraction for key logging frameworks including java.util.logging, log4j and logback. SLF4J allows the end user to plug in the desired logging framework at deployment time by simply including the appropriate implementation library. More information about SLF4J can be found at http://slf4j.org/manual.html. Logging not only allows developers to debug code, but it can also provide a permanent record of actions and application state within your application. Examples of application state could be current memory usage, the number of authorized users currently logged on, or the number of pending messages awaiting processing. Log files are usually the first place to look at when analyzing production bugs, and they are an important component of any enterprise application.

Although the default Java logging is adequate for simple uses, it would not be appropriate for more sophisticated applications. The log4J framework (http://logging.apache.org/log4j/1.2) and the logback framework (http://logback.qos.ch) are examples of highly configurable logging frameworks. The logback framework is usually considered the successor of log4j as it offers some key advantages over log4j including better performance, less memory consumption, and automatic reloading of configuration files. We will use logback in our application.

The required SLF4J and logback libraries will be added to the application by adding the following dependency to pom.xml:

```
<dependency>
  <groupId>ch.qos.logback</groupId>
  <artifactId>logback-classic</artifactId>
  <version>${logback.version}</version>
</dependency>
```

You will also need to add the additional `logback.version` property to `pom.xml`:

```
<properties>
 <endorsed.dir>${project.build.directory}/endorsed</endorsed.dir>
 <project.build.sourceEncoding>UTF-
  8</project.build.sourceEncoding>
 <spring.version>3.2.4.RELEASE</spring.version>
 <logback.version>1.0.13</logback.version>
</properties>
```

You can now perform a **Clean and Build Project** to download the `logback-classic`, `logback-core`, and `slf4j-api` JAR files. This will then enable us to add the imports defined in `GenericDaoImpl` as well as the logger definition:

```
final protected Logger logger =
  LoggerFactory.getLogger(this.getClass());
```

All descendent classes will now be able to use the logger (it is declared as `protected`) but will not be able to change it (it is declared as `final`). We will start using the logger in *Chapter 5*, *Testing the DAO Layer with Spring and JUnit*, where we will examine the `logback.xml` configuration file in detail.

The@PersistenceContext(unitName = "tttPU") line

This one line annotating the `EntityManager` interface method is all that's required for Spring Framework to plug in or inject the `EclipseLink` implementation during runtime. The `EntityManager` interface defines methods for interacting with the persistence context such as `persist`, `merge`, `remove`, and `find`. A full listing of the `EntityManager` interface methods can be found at http://docs.oracle.com/javaee/7/api/javax/persistence/EntityManager.html.

Our persistence context is defined in `persistence.xml` in which we have named it as `tttPU`. This is what binds `EntityManager` in `GenericDaoImpl` to the persistence context through the `@PersistenceContext` annotation `unitName` property. A persistence context is a set of entity instances (in our application, these are the `Company`, `Project`, `Task`, `User`, and `TaskLog` objects) in which, for any persistent entity, there is a unique entity instance. Within the persistence context, the entity instances and their lifecycle is managed.

The `EntityManager` API is used to create and remove persistent entity instances, to find entities by their primary key, and to query over entities. In our `GenericDaoImpl` class, the `EntityManager` instance `em` is used to perform the generic CRUD operations. Each descendent class will hence have access to these methods as well as the `em` instance itself (it is declared as protected).

The @Transactional annotation

The `@Transactional` annotation is the cornerstone of Spring's declarative transaction management. It allows you to specify transactional behavior at an individual method level and is very simple to use. This option has the least impact on application code, and it does not require any complex configuration. In fact, it is completely non-invasive as there is no Java coding required for commits and rollbacks.

Spring recommends that you only annotate classes (and methods of classes) with the `@Transactional` annotation as opposed to annotating interfaces (a full explanation can be found at `http://static.springsource.org/spring/docs/3.2.x/spring-framework-reference/html/transaction.html`). For this reason, we will annotate all appropriate methods in the generic and implementing classes with one of the following:

```
@Transactional(readOnly = false, propagation =
    Propagation.REQUIRED)
@Transactional(readOnly = true, propagation =
    Propagation.SUPPORTS)
```

The `@Transactional` annotation is metadata that specifies that a method must have transactional semantics. For example, we could define metadata that defines starting a brand new read-only transaction when this method is invoked, suspending any existing transaction. The default `@Transactional` settings are as follows:

* `propagation` setting is `Propagation.REQUIRED`
* `readOnly` is false

It is a good practice to define all properties including default settings, as we have done previously. Let's examine these properties in detail.

The Propagation.REQUIRED property

It is the default value for transactions that do not specify a `propagation` setting. This property supports a current transaction if one exists or creates a new one if none exists. This ensures that the `Propagation.REQUIRED` annotated method will always have a valid transaction available and should be used whenever the data is modified in the persistence storage. This property is usually combined with `readOnly=false`.

The Propagation.SUPPORTS property

This property supports a current transaction if one exists or executes non-transactionally if none exists. The Propagation.SUPPORTS property should be used if the annotated method does not modify the data (will not execute an insert, update, or delete statement against the database). This property is usually combined with readOnly=true.

The readOnly property

This just serves as a hint for the actual transaction subsystem to allow optimization of executed statements if possible. It may be possible that the transaction manager may not be able to interpret this property. For self-documenting code, however, it is a good practice to include this property.

Other transaction properties

Spring allows us to fine-tune transactional properties with additional options that are beyond the scope of this book. Browse the link that was mentioned earlier to find out more about how transactions can be managed in more complex scenarios including multiple transactional resources.

Defining the DAO implementations

The following DAO implementations will inherit the core CRUD operations from GenericDaoImpl and add their own class-specific methods as defined in the implemented interface. Each method will use the @Transactional annotation to define the appropriate transactional behavior.

The CompanyDaoImpl class

The full listing for our CompanyDaoImpl class is as follows:

```
package com.gieman.tttracker.dao;

import com.gieman.tttracker.domain.Company;
import java.util.List;
import org.springframework.stereotype.Repository;
import org.springframework.transaction.annotation.Propagation;
import org.springframework.transaction.annotation.Transactional;

@Repository("companyDao")
```

```
@Transactional
public class CompanyDaoImpl extends GenericDaoImpl<Company,
    Integer>
    implements CompanyDao {

    public CompanyDaoImpl() {
        super(Company.class);
    }

    @Override
    @Transactional(readOnly = true, propagation =
        Propagation.SUPPORTS)
    public List<Company> findAll() {
        return em.createNamedQuery("Company.findAll")
                .getResultList();
    }
}
```

The first thing to notice is the @Repository("companyDao") annotation. This annotation is used by Spring to automatically detect and process DAO objects when the application is loaded. The Spring API defines this annotation as follows:

 It indicates that an annotated class is a Repository, originally defined by Domain-Driven Design (Evans, 2003) as a mechanism for encapsulating storage, retrieval, and search behavior that emulate a collection of objects.

The purpose of the annotation is to allow Spring to auto detect implementing classes through the classpath scanning and to process this class for data access exception translation (used by Spring to abstract database exception messages from the underlying implementation). The Spring application will then hold a reference to the implementing class under the key companyDao. It is considered as the best practice to match the key value with the name of the implemented interface.

The CompanyDaoImpl class also introduces the use of the JPA named queries that were defined during the reverse engineering process in the previous chapter. The method call em.createNamedQuery("Company.findAll") creates the named query defined by the unique identifier "Company.findAll" in the persistence engine. This named query was defined in the Company class. Calling getResultList() executes the query against the database, returning a java.util.List of Company objects. Let's now review the named query definition in the Company class:

```
@NamedQuery(name = "Company.findAll", query = "SELECT c FROM
    Company c")
```

We will make a minor change to this named query to arrange the results by companyName in ascending order. This will require the addition of an ORDER BY clause in the query statement. The final named queries definition in the Company class will now look like the following code:

```
@NamedQueries({
    @NamedQuery(name = "Company.findAll", query = "SELECT c FROM
Company c ORDER BY c.companyName ASC "),
    @NamedQuery(name = "Company.findByIdCompany", query = "SELECT
        c FROM Company c WHERE c.idCompany = :idCompany"),
    @NamedQuery(name = "Company.findByCompanyName", query =
        "SELECT c FROM Company c WHERE c.companyName =
            :companyName")})
```

The ProjectDaoImpl class

This implementation is defined as:

```
package com.gieman.tttracker.dao;

import com.gieman.tttracker.domain.Company;
import com.gieman.tttracker.domain.Project;
import java.util.List;
import org.springframework.stereotype.Repository;
import org.springframework.transaction.annotation.Propagation;
import org.springframework.transaction.annotation.Transactional;

@Repository("projectDao")
@Transactional
public class ProjectDaoImpl extends GenericDaoImpl<Project,
    Integer>
    implements ProjectDao {

    public ProjectDaoImpl() {
        super(Project.class);
    }

    @Override
    @Transactional(readOnly = true, propagation =
        Propagation.SUPPORTS)
    public List<Project> findAll() {
        return em.createNamedQuery("Project.findAll")
                .getResultList();
    }
}
```

Once again, we will add the ORDER BY clause to the `Project.findAll` named query in the Project class:

```
@NamedQuery(name = "Project.findAll", query = "SELECT p FROM
  Project p ORDER BY p.projectName")
```

The TaskDaoImpl class

This class is defined as:

```
package com.gieman.tttracker.dao;

import com.gieman.tttracker.domain.Project;
import com.gieman.tttracker.domain.Task;
import java.util.List;
import org.springframework.stereotype.Repository;
import org.springframework.transaction.annotation.Propagation;
import org.springframework.transaction.annotation.Transactional;

@Repository("taskDao")
@Transactional
public class TaskDaoImpl extends GenericDaoImpl<Task, Integer>
  implements TaskDao {

    public TaskDaoImpl() {
        super(Task.class);
    }

    @Override
    @Transactional(readOnly = true, propagation = Propagation.
SUPPORTS)
    public List<Task> findAll() {
        return em.createNamedQuery("Task.findAll")
                .getResultList();
    }
}
```

Once again, we will add the ORDER BY clause to the `Task.findAll` named query in the Task class:

```
@NamedQuery(name = "Task.findAll", query = "SELECT t FROM Task t
  ORDER BY t.taskName")
```

The UserDaoImpl class

This `UserDaoImpl` class will require an additional named query in the `User` domain class to test a user's logon credentials (username/password combination). The `UserDaoImpl` class definition follows:

```java
package com.gieman.tttracker.dao;

import com.gieman.tttracker.domain.User;
import java.util.List;
import org.springframework.stereotype.Repository;
import org.springframework.transaction.annotation.Propagation;
import org.springframework.transaction.annotation.Transactional;

@Repository("userDao")
@Transactional
public class UserDaoImpl extends GenericDaoImpl<User, String>
  implements UserDao {

    public UserDaoImpl() {
        super(User.class);
    }

    @Override
    @Transactional(readOnly = true, propagation =
      Propagation.SUPPORTS)
    public List<User> findAll() {
        return em.createNamedQuery("User.findAll")
                .getResultList();
    }

    @Override
    @Transactional(readOnly = true, propagation =
      Propagation.SUPPORTS)
    public User findByUsernamePassword(String username, String
      password) {

        List<User> users =
          em.createNamedQuery("User.findByUsernamePassword")
                .setParameter("username", username)
                .setParameter("password", password)
                .getResultList();

        return (users.size() == 1 ? users.get(0) : null);
    }

    @Override
    @Transactional(readOnly = true, propagation =
      Propagation.SUPPORTS)
    public User findByUsername(String username) {
```

```
        List<User> users =
            em.createNamedQuery("User.findByUsername")
                .setParameter("username", username)
                .getResultList();

        return (users.size() == 1 ? users.get(0) : null);
    }

    @Override
    @Transactional(readOnly = true, propagation =
        Propagation.SUPPORTS)
    public User findByEmail(String email) {

        List<User> users = em.createNamedQuery("User.findByEmail")
                .setParameter("email", email)
                .getResultList();

        return (users.size() == 1 ? users.get(0) : null);
    }
}
```

The missing named query is `User.findByUsernamePassword` that is used to verify a user with the given username and password. The query definition must be added to the `User` class as follows:

```
@NamedQuery(name = "User.findByUsernamePassword", query = "SELECT
    u FROM User u WHERE u.password = :password AND (u.email =
    :username OR u.username = :username)")
```

Note that this definition allows a user to be matched by either the username or e-mail field. As is the common practice in web applications, a user may log on with either their unique logon name (username) or their e-mail address.

The `findByEmail`, `findByUsername`, and `findByUsernamePassword` methods can only ever return `null` (no match found) or a single result as there cannot be more than one record in the database with these unique fields. Instead of using the `getResultList()` method to retrieve a `List` of results and testing for a list size of one, we could have used the code that is similar to the following:

```
public User findByEmail(String email) {

    User user = (User) em.createNamedQuery("User.findByEmail")
            .setParameter("email", email)
            .getSingleResult();

    return user;
}
```

The getSingleResult() method returns exactly one result or throws an exception if a single result could not be found. You will also notice the need to cast the returned result to the required User type. The calling method would also need to catch any exceptions that would be thrown from the getSingleResult() method unless the sample code given previously is changed to catch the exception.

```
public User findByEmail(String email) {

    User user = null;

    try {
      user = (User) em.createNamedQuery("User.findByEmail")
        .setParameter("email", email)
        .getSingleResult();

    } catch(NoResultException nre){

    }
    return user;
}
```

We believe that the code in our UserDaoImpl interface is cleaner than the previous example that uses the try/catch function to wrap the getSingleResult() method. In both cases, however, the method returns null if the record cannot be found.

> Exceptions should be used judiciously in enterprise programming and only for truly exceptional circumstances. Throwing exceptions should be avoided unless the exception indicates a situation that the calling code cannot recover from. It is far cleaner to return null (or perhaps true/false in appropriate scenarios) to indicate that a situation is not as expected.

We do not consider being unable to find a record by ID, or by e-mail or by e-mail address as an exceptional circumstance; it is possible that a different user has deleted the record, or there is simply no record with the e-mail specified. Returning null clearly identifies that the record was not found without the need to throw an exception.

Regardless of whether you throw exceptions to indicate a record that cannot be found or use null as is our preference, your API should be documented to indicate the behavior. The UserDaoImpl.findByUsernamePassword method could, for example, be documented as follows:

```
/**
 * Find a User with the username/password combination or return null
 * if a valid user could not be found.
 * @param username
```

```
 * @param password
 * @return valid User object or null if not found.
 */
```

Users of your API will then understand the expected behavior and code their interactions accordingly.

The TaskLogDaoImpl class

The final DAO class in our application follows:

```java
package com.gieman.tttracker.dao;

import com.gieman.tttracker.domain.Task;
import com.gieman.tttracker.domain.TaskLog;
import com.gieman.tttracker.domain.User;
import java.util.Date;
import java.util.List;
import javax.persistence.TemporalType;

public class TaskLogDaoImpl extends GenericDaoImpl<TaskLog,
    Integer> implements TaskLogDao {

    public TaskLogDaoImpl() {
        super(TaskLog.class);
    }

    @Override
    public List<TaskLog> findByUser(User user, Date startDate,
      Date endDate) {
        return em.createNamedQuery("TaskLog.findByUser")
                .setParameter("user", user)
                .setParameter("startDate", startDate,
                  TemporalType.DATE)
                .setParameter("endDate", endDate,
                  TemporalType.DATE)
                .getResultList();
    }

    @Override
    public long findTaskLogCountByTask(Task task) {
        Long count = (Long)
          em.createNamedQuery("TaskLog.findTaskLogCountByTask")
                .setParameter("task", task)
                .getSingleResult();
```

```
            return count;
        }

        @Override
        public long findTaskLogCountByUser(User user) {
            Long count = (Long)
                em.createNamedQuery("TaskLog.findTaskLogCountByUser")
                    .setParameter("user", user)
                    .getSingleResult();

            return count;
        }
    }
```

This time, we will refactor the `TaskLog` named queries as follows:

```
@NamedQueries({
    @NamedQuery(name = "TaskLog.findByUser", query = "SELECT tl
        FROM TaskLog tl WHERE tl.user = :user AND tl.taskLogDate
        BETWEEN :startDate AND :endDate order by tl.taskLogDate
        ASC"),
    @NamedQuery(name = "TaskLog.findTaskLogCountByTask", query =
        "SELECT count(tl) FROM TaskLog tl WHERE tl.task = :task "),
    @NamedQuery(name = "TaskLog.findTaskLogCountByUser", query =
        "SELECT count(tl) FROM TaskLog tl WHERE tl.user = :user ")
})
```

We have removed several queries that will not be required and added three new
ones as shown. The `TaskLog.findByUser` query will be used to list task logs
assigned to a user for the given date range. Note the use of the BETWEEN key word
to specify the date range. Also note the use of the `TemporalType.DATE` when setting
the parameter in the `TaskLogDaoImpl.findByUser` method. This will ensure a strict
date comparison, ignoring any time component, if present, in the arguments.

The `TaskLog.findTaskLogCountByTask` and `TaskLog.findTaskLogCountByUser`
named queries will be used in our service layer to test if deletions are permitted. We
will implement checks to ensure that a user or a task may not be deleted if valid task
logs are assigned.

A better domain layer

Let's now revisit the domain layer created in *Chapter 3, Reverse Engineering the Domain
Layer with JPA*. Defining an ancestor class for all entities in this layer is not only the
best practice but will also make our domain layer far easier to enhance in the future.
Our ancestor class is defined as follows:

```
package com.gieman.tttracker.domain;

import java.io.Serializable;

public abstract class AbstractEntity implements Serializable{

}
```

Although this class has an empty implementation, we will add functionality in subsequent chapters.

We will also define an appropriate interface that has one generic method to return the ID of the entity:

```
package com.gieman.tttracker.domain;

public interface EntityItem<T> {

    public T getId();

}
```

Our domain layer can now extend our base AbstractEntity class and implement the EntityItem interface. The changes required to our Company class follows:

```
public class Company extends AbstractEntity implements
  EntityItem<Integer> {

// many more lines of code here

    @Override
    public Integer getId() {
        return idCompany;
    }
}
```

In a similar way, we can change the remaining domain classes:

```
public class Project extends AbstractEntity implements
  EntityItem<Integer> {

// many more lines of code here

    @Override
    public Integer getId() {
        return idProject;
    }
```

```
    }
    public class Task extends AbstractEntity implements
      EntityItem<Integer> {

    // many more lines of code here

        @Override
        public Integer getId() {
            return idTask;
        }
    }
    public class User extends AbstractEntity implements
      EntityItem<String> {

    // many more lines of code here

        @Override
        public String getId() {
            return username;
        }
    }
    public class TaskLog extends AbstractEntity implements
      EntityItem<Integer> {

    // many more lines of code here

        @Override
        public Integer getId() {
            return idTaskLog;
        }
    }
```

We will now be well prepared for future changes in the domain layer.

Exercise – a simple change request

This simple exercise will again demonstrate the power of generics. Each record inserted into the database should now be logged at using `logger.info()` with the message:

```
The "className" record with ID=? has been inserted
```

In addition, records that are deleted should be logged using `logger.warn()` with the message:

```
The "className" record with ID=? has been deleted
```

In both cases, the `?` token should be replaced with the ID of the entity being inserted or deleted while the `className` token should be replaced with the class name of the entity being inserted or deleted. This is a trivial change when using generics, as the code can be added to the `persist` and `remove` methods of the `GenericDaoImpl` class. Without the use of generics, each of the `CompanyDaoImpl`, `ProjectDaoImpl`, `TaskDaoImpl`, `UserDaoImpl`, and `TaskLogDaoImpl` classes would need to have this change made. When you consider that enterprise applications may have 20, 30, 40, or more tables represented in the DAO layer, such a trivial change may not be so trivial without the use of generics.

Your task is to implement the change request as outlined previously. Note that this exercise will introduce you to the `instanceof` operator.

Summary

This chapter has introduced the Data Access Object design pattern and defined a set of interfaces that will be used in our 3T application. The DAO design pattern clearly separates the persistence layer operations from the business logic of the application. As will be introduced in the next chapter, this clear separation ensures that the data access layer is easy to test and maintain.

We have also introduced Java Generics as a technique to simplify application design by moving common functionality to an ancestor. The `GenericDao` interface and the `GenericDaoImpl` class define and implement methods that will be available free of cost to the extending components. Our implementations also introduced SLF4J, transactional semantics, and working with JPA named queries.

Our journey will now continue with *Chapter 5, Testing the DAO Layer with Spring and JUnit*, where we will configure a testing environment and develop test cases for several of our DAO implementations.

5
Testing the DAO Layer with Spring and JUnit

Everyone would agree that software testing should be a fundamental part of the development process. Thorough testing will ensure that the business requirements are met, the software works as expected, and that the defects are discovered before your client finds them. Although testing can never completely identify all the bugs, it is commonly believed that the earlier an issue is found, the cheaper it is to fix. It is far quicker to fix a `NullPointerException` in a block of code during development than when the system has been deployed to your client's production server. When developing enterprise systems, it becomes even more critical to deliver high-quality code. The reputation of your company is at stake; identifying and fixing issues before delivery is an important reason to make testing a critical part of the development lifecycle.

There are many different types of testing, including but not limited to, unit testing, integration testing, regression testing, black/white box testing, and acceptance testing. Each of these testing strategies could warrant a chapter in their own right but are beyond the scope of this book. An excellent article covering software testing in general can be found here: https://en.wikipedia.org/wiki/Software_testing. We will focus on **unit testing**.

Unit testing overview

Unit testing is a strategy for testing discrete units of source code. From a programmer's perspective, a unit is the smallest testable part of an application. A unit of source code is usually defined as a **public method** that is callable within the application and has a specific purpose. Unit testing of the DAO layer will ensure that each public method has at least one appropriate test case. In practice, we will need many more test cases than just a single one for each public method. For example, every DAO `find(ID)` method requires at least two test cases: one with an outcome returning a valid found object and one with an outcome that does not find a valid object. As a result, for every line of code written, developers often need several lines of test code.

Unit testing is an art form that takes time to master. Our goal is to establish a set of tests that cover as many scenarios as possible. This is inherently opposite to what we are trying to achieve as developers, where our goal is to ensure that a task is performed to meet the precise functional requirements. Consider the following business requirement: take the cost value in cents and convert it to the euro equivalent according to the exchange rate of the day.

The solution may seem self-explanatory, but what happens if the exchange rate is not available? Or the date is in the future? Or the cost value is null? What is the expected behavior if the value cannot be calculated? These are all valid scenarios that should be considered when crafting test cases.

With unit testing we define **how** the program should behave. Each unit test should tell a well-documented story of how that part of the program should act in a specific scenario. The tests become a contract that describes what should happen from the client code's point of view under the various reproducible conditions.

The benefits of unit testing

Unit testing gives us confidence that the code we have written works correctly. The unit testing process also encourages us to think about how our code will be used and what conditions need to be met. There are many benefits including:

- **Identifying problems early:** Unit tests will help identify coding issues early in the development lifecycle when it is far easier to fix.

- **Higher quality:** We don't want customers to find bugs, resulting in downtime and expensive release cycles. We want to build software that has as few bugs as possible in the first place.

- **Confidence:** Developers are reluctant to touch code that is fragile. Well-tested code with solid test cases can be approached with confidence.

- **Regression proofing:** Test cases build and evolve with the application. Enhancements and new functionalities may break the old code silently, but a well-written test suite will go a long way in identifying such scenarios.

Enterprise applications, with many programmers doing parallel development across different modules, are even more vulnerable. Coding side effects may result in far-reaching consequences if not caught early.

A helper method was used to trim a Java String passed in as an argument. The argument was tested for null and the method returned an empty string " " if this was the case. The helper method was used everywhere in the application. One day, a developer changed the helper method to return null if the passed-in argument was null (they needed to identify the difference between null and an empty string). A simple test case would have ensured that this change did not get checked in to version control. The sheer number of null pointer exceptions when using the application was amazing!

Configuring the test environment

Our strategy for unit testing is to create a set of test cases that can be run in an automated manner at any time during the development lifecycle. "Automated" means that no developer interaction is required; the tests can be run as part of the build process and do not require user input. The entire process is managed seamlessly through the use of Maven, JUnit, and Spring. Maven convention expects a test directory structure under the `src` directory with testing resources and Java test cases in subdirectories as shown in the following screenshot:

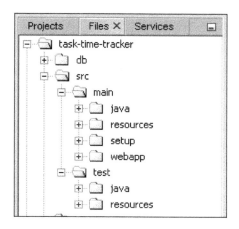

Note how Maven uses the same directory structure for both source and testing layouts. All resources required to execute test cases will be found in the `src/test/resources` directory. Likewise, all the resources required for deployment will be found in the `src/main/resources` directory. The "convention over configuration" paradigm once again reduces the number of decisions that the developer needs to make. Maven-based testing will work without the need for any further configuration as long as this directory structure is followed. If you do not already have this directory structure, then you will need to create it manually by right-clicking on the required folder:

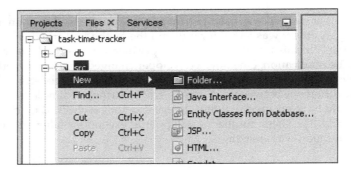

After adding the directory structure, we can create individual files as shown:

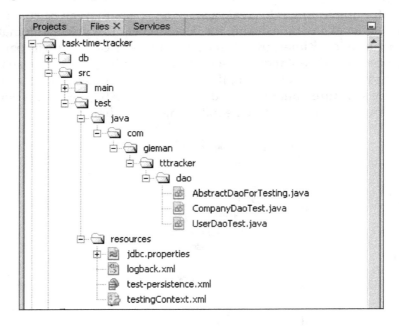

We will start by using NetBeans to create the `jdbc.properties` file.

The jdbc.properties file

Right-click on the `test/resources` folder and navigate to **New | Other**. The **New File** wizard will open where you can select **Other** from **Categories** and **Properties File** as shown:

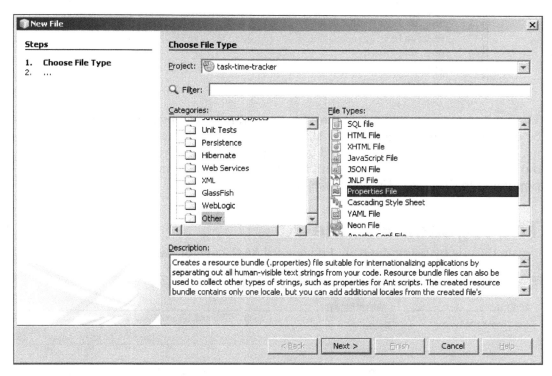

Select **Next** and type in `jdbc` as the filename:

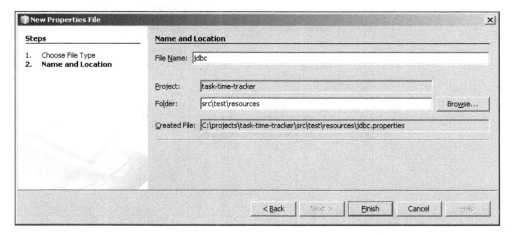

Click on the **Finish** button to create the `jdbc.properties` file. NetBeans will then open the file in the editor where you can add the following code:

The `jdbc.properties` file is used to define the database connection details that will be used by Spring to configure our DAO layer for unit testing. Enterprise projects usually have one or more dedicated test databases that are prefilled with appropriate data for all testing scenarios. We will use the database that was generated and populated in *Chapter 2, The Task Time Tracker Database*.

The logback.xml file

Create this file by using the **New File** wizard **XML** category as shown:

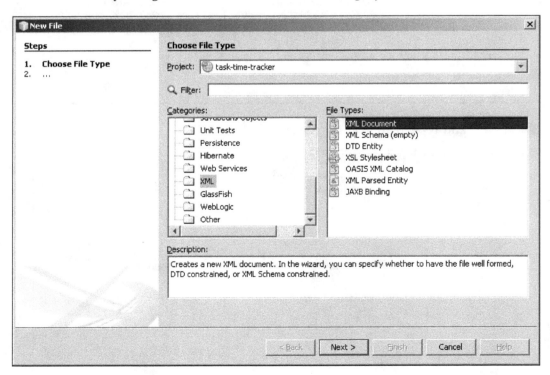

After creating the `logback.xml` file, you can enter the following content:

```xml
<?xml version="1.0" encoding="UTF-8"?>
<configuration scan="true" scanPeriod="30 seconds" >
    <contextName>TaskTimeTracker</contextName>
    <appender name="STDOUT" class="ch.qos.logback.core.
ConsoleAppender">
        <encoder>
            <pattern>%d{HH:mm:ss.SSS} [%thread] %-5level %logger{5} -
%msg%n</pattern>
        </encoder>
    </appender>

    <logger name="com.gieman.tttracker" level="DEBUG"
additivity="false">
        <appender-ref ref="STDOUT" />
    </logger>
    <logger name="com.gieman.tttracker.dao" level="DEBUG"
additivity="false">
        <appender-ref ref="STDOUT" />
    </logger>
    <logger name="com.gieman.tttracker.domain" level="DEBUG"
additivity="false">
        <appender-ref ref="STDOUT" />
    </logger>
    <logger name="com.gieman.tttracker.service" level="DEBUG"
additivity="false">
        <appender-ref ref="STDOUT" />
    </logger>
    <logger name="com.gieman.tttracker.web" level="DEBUG"
additivity="false">
        <appender-ref ref="STDOUT" />
    </logger>

    <root level="INFO">
        <appender-ref ref="STDOUT" />
    </root>
</configuration>
```

For those who are familiar with log4j, the syntax of the logback logger definitions is very similar. We have set the root log level to INFO, which will cover all the loggers that are not explicitly defined (note that the default level is DEBUG but this will usually result in extensive logging at the root level). Each individual logger, with the name matching a com.gieman.tttracker package, is set to log level DEBUG. This configuration gives us considerable flexibility and control over package-level logging properties. In production we would normally deploy a WARN level for all loggers to minimize logging. If an issue is encountered, we would then selectively enable logging in different packages to help identify any problems. Unlike log4j, this dynamic reloading of logger properties can be done on the fly thanks to logback's scan="true" scanPeriod="30 seconds" option in the <configuration> node. More information about the logback configuration can be found here: http://logback.qos.ch/manual/configuration.html.

The test-persistence.xml file

Follow the **New File** steps outlined in the previous section to create the test-persistence.xml file. Enter the following persistence context definition:

```xml
<?xml version="1.0" encoding="UTF-8"?>
<persistence version="2.1" xmlns="http://java.sun.com/xml/ns/
persistence" xmlns:xsi="http://www.w3.org/2001/XMLSchema-instance"
xsi:schemaLocation="http://java.sun.com/xml/ns/persistence http://
java.sun.com/xml/ns/persistence/persistence_2_1.xsd">
  <persistence-unit name="tttPU" transaction-type="RESOURCE_LOCAL">
    <provider>org.eclipse.persistence.jpa.PersistenceProvider</
provider>
    <class>com.gieman.tttracker.domain.Company</class>
    <class>com.gieman.tttracker.domain.Project</class>
    <class>com.gieman.tttracker.domain.Task</class>
    <class>com.gieman.tttracker.domain.TaskLog</class>
    <class>com.gieman.tttracker.domain.User</class>
    <exclude-unlisted-classes>true</exclude-unlisted-classes>
    <properties>
      <property name="eclipselink.logging.level" value="WARNING"/>
    </properties>
  </persistence-unit>
</persistence>
```

This persistence unit definition is slightly different from the one created in *Chapter 3, Reverse Engineering the Domain Layer with JPA*:

```xml
<?xml version="1.0" encoding="UTF-8"?>
<persistence version="2.1" xmlns="http://xmlns.jcp.org/xml/ns/
persistence" xmlns:xsi="http://www.w3.org/2001/XMLSchema-instance"
xsi:schemaLocation="http://xmlns.jcp.org/xml/ns/persistence http://
xmlns.jcp.org/xml/ns/persistence/persistence_2_1.xsd">
    <persistence-unit name="tttPU" transaction-type="JTA">
        <provider>org.eclipse.persistence.jpa.PersistenceProvider</
provider>
        <jta-data-source>jdbc/tasktimetracker</jta-data-source>
        <exclude-unlisted-classes>false</exclude-unlisted-classes>
        <properties/>
    </persistence-unit>
</persistence>
```

Note that the testing `persistence-unit` transaction type is `RESOURCE_LOCAL` rather than `JTA`. Our testing environment uses a local (Spring-managed) transaction manager rather than the one provided by our GlassFish server container (which is `JTA`). In both cases, the `tttPU` persistence unit name matches the `@PersistenceContext` `unitName` annotation of the `EntityManager` field in the `GenericDaoImpl`:

```java
@PersistenceContext(unitName = "tttPU")
protected EntityManager em;
```

The second difference is the way the classes are discovered. During testing our domain entities are explicitly listed and we exclude any classes that are not defined. This simplifies processing and ensures that only the required entities are loaded for testing *without scanning the classpath*. This is an important point for Windows users; on some Windows versions, there's a limit to the length of the command-line statement, and therefore, a limit on how long you can make your classpath argument. Using classpath scanning, the loading of domain entities for testing may not work, resulting in strange errors such as:

```
org.springframework.dao.InvalidDataAccessApiUsageException: Object:
com.tttracker.domain.Company[ idCompany=null ] is not a known entity
type.; nested exception is java.lang.IllegalArgumentException: Object:
com.tttracker.domain.Company[ idCompany=null ] is not a known entity
type.
```

Always ensure that your testing persistence XML definitions include all domain classes in your application.

Introducing the Spring IoC container

The modern Spring Framework is an extensive suite of framework "stacks" based on architectural concepts that go back to the start of the century. The Spring Framework first came to prominence with *Expert One-on-One J2EE Design and Development, Rod Johnson*, in 2002. Spring's implementation of the **Inversion of Control (IoC)** principle, sometimes also known as **Dependency Injection (DI)**, was a breakthrough in enterprise application design and development. The Spring IoC container provided a simple way of configuring objects (JavaBeans) and injecting dependencies through constructor arguments, factory methods, object properties, or setter methods. We have already seen the `@PersistenceContext` annotation in our DAO layer that is used by Spring to identify whether an `EntityManager` object should be injected into the `GenericDaoImpl` class. The sophisticated configuration options available make the Spring Framework a very flexible foundation for enterprise development.

It is beyond the scope of this book to cover more than the basics of the Spring Framework configuration as is required by our project needs. However, we recommend that you browse through the detailed description of how the IoC container works at `http://docs.spring.io/spring/docs/3.2.x/spring-framework-reference/html/beans.html#beans-definition` to enhance their knowledge of the core principles.

Exploring the testingContext.xml file

This is the main configuration file used by Spring to configure and load the IoC bean container. The XML-based configuration has been the default way to configure Spring applications since the very start, but with Spring 3 Framework, it became possible to use the Java-based configuration. Both options achieve the same result—a fully configured Spring container. We will use the XML approach as it does not require any Java coding and is more intuitive and simple to use.

There have been many articles written over the years about the "complexities" of the Spring XML configuration. Prior to Java 1.5 and the introduction of annotations, there could have been a case made for such comments. Configuration files were lengthy and daunting for new users. This is no longer the case. Configuring a Spring container with XML is now a trivial process. Be wary of anyone who tells you otherwise!

The `testingContext.xml` configuration file completely defines the Spring environment required for testing the DAO layer. The full file listing is:

```xml
<?xml version="1.0" encoding="UTF-8"?>
<beans xmlns="http://www.springframework.org/schema/beans"
xmlns:xsi="http://www.w3.org/2001/XMLSchema-instance"
       xmlns:p="http://www.springframework.org/schema/p"
       xmlns:context="http://www.springframework.org/schema/context"
       xmlns:tx="http://www.springframework.org/schema/tx"
       xsi:schemaLocation="
       http://www.springframework.org/schema/beans http://www.
springframework.org/schema/beans/spring-beans-3.0.xsd
       http://www.springframework.org/schema/context http://www.
springframework.org/schema/context/spring-context-3.0.xsd
        http://www.springframework.org/schema/tx http://www.
springframework.org/schema/tx/spring-tx-3.0.xsd">

    <bean id="propertyConfigurer"
        class="org.springframework.beans.factory.config.
PropertyPlaceholderConfigurer"
        p:location="classpath:jdbc.properties" />

    <bean id="tttDataSource"
        class="org.springframework.jdbc.datasource.
DriverManagerDataSource"
        p:driverClassName="${jdbc.driverClassName}"
        p:url="${jdbc.url}"
        p:username="${jdbc.username}"
        p:password="${jdbc.password}"/>

    <bean id="loadTimeWeaver" class="org.springframework.instrument.
classloading.InstrumentationLoadTimeWeaver" />

    <bean id="jpaVendorAdapter" class="org.springframework.orm.jpa.
vendor.EclipseLinkJpaVendorAdapter"
        p:showSql="true"
        p:databasePlatform="org.eclipse.persistence.platform.database.
MySQLPlatform" />
```

```
    <bean id="entityManagerFactory" class="org.springframework.orm.
jpa.LocalContainerEntityManagerFactoryBean"
        p:dataSource-ref="tttDataSource"
        p:jpaVendorAdapter-ref="jpaVendorAdapter"
        p:persistenceXmlLocation="test-persistence.xml"
    />

    <!-- Transaction manager for a single JPA EntityManagerFactory
(alternative to JTA) -->
    <bean id="transactionManager" class="org.springframework.orm.jpa.
JpaTransactionManager"
        p:dataSource-ref="tttDataSource"
        p:entityManagerFactory-ref="entityManagerFactory"/>

    <!-- checks for annotated configured beans -->
    <context:annotation-config/>

    <!-- Scan for Repository/Service annotations -->
    <context:component-scan base-package="com.gieman.tttracker.dao" />

    <!-- enable the configuration of transactional behavior based on
annotations -->
    <tx:annotation-driven />

</beans>
```

Let's look at each section in detail.

The Spring XML namespaces

For those not familiar with XML, you can simply ignore the xmlns definitions and schema location URLs. Consider them as "shortcuts" or "qualifiers" in the configuration file that provide the ability to validate the entries. Spring understands what <tx:annotation-driven /> means in the context of loading the Spring environment.

Each Spring application configuration file will have multiple namespace declarations depending on the resources your application needs. Defining the schema location in addition to the namespaces will allow NetBeans to provide helpful hints on configuration options:

```
15    <bean id="tttDataSource"
16          class="org.springframework.jdbc.datasource.Drive
17          p:driverClassName="${jdbc.driverClassName}"
18          p:url="${jdbc.url}"
19          p:username="${jdbc.username}"
20          p:password="${jdbc.password}"
21          p:▌
22          ┌─────────────────────────────────────────────────┐
        ▲ │ p:connectionProperties        Properties         │
23    <be│ p:connectionProperties-ref Properties framework.i │
24    ▼ │ p:driverClassName-ref          String    gframework│
25    <be│ p:logWriter                    PrintWriter         │
26    │ p:logWriter-ref                   PrintWriter         │
27    │ p:loginTimeout                          int ence.platfo│
28    │ p:loginTimeout-ref                      int          │
29    <be│ p:password-ref                      String springframe│
30    │ p:url-ref                           String          │
31    │ p:username-ref                      String ;"        │
32          p:persistenceXmlLocation="test-persistence.xml"
33    />
```

The list of valid properties for different namespaces is very useful when new to
Spring configuration.

The property file configuration

The following bean loads the `jdbc.properties` file and makes it available for use in
the configuration file:

```
<bean id="propertyConfigurer"
    class="org.springframework.beans.factory.config.
PropertyPlaceholderConfigurer"
    p:location="classpath:jdbc.properties" />
```

The `${}` syntax can then be used anywhere in the `testingContext.xml` file to
replace the token with the required `jdbc` property.

Creating the JDBC DataSource

DAO testing requires a connection to the MySQL database. The following Spring
bean definition instantiates and makes available a fully configured DataSource:

```
<bean id="tttDataSource"
    class="org.springframework.jdbc.datasource.
DriverManagerDataSource"
    p:driverClassName="${jdbc.driverClassName}"
    p:url="${jdbc.url}"
    p:username="${jdbc.username}"
    p:password="${jdbc.password}"
    />
```

The placeholders are automatically set with the properties loaded from the `jdbc.properties` file:

```
jdbc.driverClassName=com.mysql.jdbc.Driver
jdbc.url=jdbc:mysql://localhost:3306/task_time_tracker
jdbc.username=root
jdbc.password=adminadmin
```

This very simple Spring configuration snippet replaces many lines of equivalent Java code if we had to implement the DataSource instantiation ourselves. Note how simple it would be to change any of the database properties for different testing scenarios, or for example, even change the database server from MySQL to Oracle. This flexibility makes the Spring IoC container very powerful for enterprise use.

You should note that the `org.springframework.jdbc.datasource.DriverManagerDataSource` should only be used for testing purposes and is not for use in a production environment. The GlassFish server will provide a connection-pooled `DataSource` for production use.

Defining helper beans

The `loadTimeWeaver` and `jpaVendorAdapter` bean definitions help configure the `entityManagerFactory` bean that is used to load the persistence context. Note the way in which we identify the database platform (MySQL) and JPA implementation (EclipseLink) by using specific Spring bean classes:

```
<bean id="jpaVendorAdapter"
class="org.springframework.orm.jpa.vendor.EclipseLinkJpaVendorAdapter"
  p:showSql="true"
  p:databasePlatform="org.eclipse.persistence.platform.database.
MySQLPlatform" />
```

Spring provides a large number of database and JPA implementations as can be seen when using autocomplete in NetBeans (the *Ctrl* + Space bar combination in NetBeans triggers the autocomplete options):

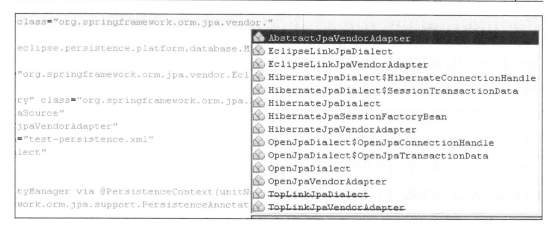

Helper beans are used to define implementation-specific properties. It is very easy to swap implementation strategies for different enterprise environments. For example, developers may use MySQL databases running locally on their own environment for development purposes. Production enterprise servers may use an Oracle database running on a different physical server. Only very minor changes are required to the Spring XML configuration file to implement such differences for the application environment.

Defining the EntityManagerFactory class

This Spring bean defines the EntityManagerFactory class that is used to create and inject the EntityManager instance into the GenericDaoImpl class:

```
<bean id="entityManagerFactory"
  class="org.springframework.orm.jpa.
LocalContainerEntityManagerFactoryBean"
  p:dataSource-ref="tttDataSource"
  p:jpaVendorAdapter-ref="jpaVendorAdapter"
  p:persistenceXmlLocation="test-persistence.xml"
/>
```

This definition references the tttDataSource and jpaVendorAdapter beans that are already configured, as well as the test-persistence.xml persistence context definition file. Once again, Spring does a lot of work in the background by creating and configuring the EntityManager instance and making it available for use in our code.

Configuring the transaction manager

The Spring bean used to manage transactions is defined as follows:

```
<bean id="transactionManager"
  class="org.springframework.orm.jpa.JpaTransactionManager"
  p:dataSource-ref="tttDataSource"
  p:entityManagerFactory-ref="entityManagerFactory"/>
```

This bean wires together the `tttDataSource` and `entityManagerFactory` instance to enable transactional behavior in our application. This behavior is applied to all classes with `@Transactional` annotations; in our current situation this applies to all the DAO objects. Spring scans for this annotation and applies a transactional wrapper to each annotated method when the following line is included in the configuration file:

```
<tx:annotation-driven />
```

Which classes are scanned for the `@Transactional` annotation? The following line defines that Spring should scan the `com.gieman.tttracker.dao` package:

```
<context:component-scan base-package="com.gieman.tttracker.dao"/>
```

Autowiring beans

Autowiring is a Spring term used to automatically inject a resource into a managed bean. The following line enables autowiring in beans that have the `@Autowired` annotation:

```
<context:annotation-config/>
```

We do not have any autowired annotations as of yet in our code; the next section will introduce how this annotation is used.

Thanks for the plumbing!

The Spring configuration file, when loaded by the Spring container, will do an enormous amount of work in the background configuring and wiring together the many supporting classes required by our application. The tedious and often error-prone "plumbing" code is done for us. Never again will we need to commit a transaction, open a database connection, or close a JDBC resource. These low-level operations will be handled very elegantly for us by the Spring Framework.

As enterprise application developers we can and should focus most of our time and energy on core application concerns: business logic, user interfaces, requirements, testing, and, of course, our customers. Spring makes sure we can stay focused on these tasks.

Enabling the Maven environment for testing

The Maven build process includes the ability to execute test suites. We will now need to add this functionality to the pom.xml file. The required changes to the existing file are highlighted in the following code snippet:

```xml
<?xml version="1.0" encoding="UTF-8"?>
<project xmlns="http://maven.apache.org/POM/4.0.0" xmlns:xsi="http://
www.w3.org/2001/XMLSchema-instance" xsi:schemaLocation="http://maven.
apache.org/POM/4.0.0 http://maven.apache.org/xsd/maven-4.0.0.xsd">
    <modelVersion>4.0.0</modelVersion>

    <groupId>com.gieman</groupId>
    <artifactId>task-time-tracker</artifactId>
    <version>1.0</version>
    <packaging>war</packaging>

    <name>task-time-tracker</name>

    <properties>
        <endorsed.dir>${project.build.directory}/endorsed</endorsed.
dir>
        <project.build.sourceEncoding>UTF-8</project.build.
sourceEncoding>
        <spring.version>3.2.4.RELEASE</spring.version>
        <logback.version>1.0.13</logback.version>
    </properties>

    <dependencies>
        <dependency>
            <groupId>org.eclipse.persistence</groupId>
            <artifactId>javax.persistence</artifactId>
            <version>2.1.0-SNAPSHOT</version>
            <scope>provided</scope>
        </dependency>
        <dependency>
            <groupId>org.eclipse.persistence</groupId>
            <artifactId>eclipselink</artifactId>
```

```xml
                <version>2.5.0-SNAPSHOT</version>
                <scope>provided</scope>
        </dependency>
        <dependency>
                <groupId>org.eclipse.persistence</groupId>
                <artifactId>org.eclipse.persistence.jpa.modelgen.
processor</artifactId>
                <version>2.5.0-SNAPSHOT</version>
                <scope>provided</scope>
        </dependency>
        <dependency>
                <groupId>javax</groupId>
                <artifactId>javaee-web-api</artifactId>
                <version>7.0</version>
                <scope>provided</scope>
        </dependency>
        <dependency>
                <groupId>ch.qos.logback</groupId>
                <artifactId>logback-classic</artifactId>
                <version>${logback.version}</version>
        </dependency>
        <dependency>
                <groupId>junit</groupId>
                <artifactId>junit</artifactId>
                <version>4.11</version>
                <scope>test</scope>
        </dependency>
        <dependency>
                <groupId>mysql</groupId>
                <artifactId>mysql-connector-java</artifactId>
                <version>5.1.26</version>
                <scope>provided</scope>
        </dependency>
        <dependency>
                <groupId>org.springframework</groupId>
                <artifactId>spring-context</artifactId>
                <version>${spring.version}</version>
        </dependency>
        <dependency>
                <groupId>org.springframework</groupId>
                <artifactId>spring-context-support</artifactId>
                <version>${spring.version}</version>
        </dependency>
        <dependency>
```

```
            <groupId>org.springframework</groupId>
            <artifactId>spring-tx</artifactId>
            <version>${spring.version}</version>
        </dependency>
        <dependency>
            <groupId>org.springframework</groupId>
            <artifactId>spring-jdbc</artifactId>
            <version>${spring.version}</version>
        </dependency>
        <dependency>
            <groupId>org.springframework</groupId>
            <artifactId>spring-orm</artifactId>
            <version>${spring.version}</version>
        </dependency>
        <dependency>
            <groupId>org.springframework</groupId>
            <artifactId>spring-instrument</artifactId>
            <version>${spring.version}</version>
        </dependency>
        <dependency>
            <groupId>org.springframework</groupId>
            <artifactId>spring-webmvc</artifactId>
            <version>${spring.version}</version>
        </dependency>
        <dependency>
            <groupId>org.springframework</groupId>
            <artifactId>spring-test</artifactId>
            <version>${spring.version}</version>
<scope>test</scope>
        </dependency>

    </dependencies>

    <build>
        <plugins>
            <plugin>
                <groupId>org.apache.maven.plugins</groupId>
                <artifactId>maven-compiler-plugin</artifactId>
                <version>3.1</version>
                <configuration>
                    <source>1.7</source>
                    <target>1.7</target>
                    <compilerArguments>
                        <endorseddirs>${endorsed.dir}</endorseddirs>
```

```
                </compilerArguments>
            </configuration>
        </plugin>
        <plugin>
            <groupId>org.apache.maven.plugins</groupId>
            <artifactId>maven-war-plugin</artifactId>
            <version>2.3</version>
            <configuration>
                <warName>${project.build.finalName}</warName>
                <failOnMissingWebXml>false</failOnMissingWebXml>
            </configuration>
        </plugin>
        <plugin>
            <groupId>org.apache.maven.plugins</groupId>
            <artifactId>maven-dependency-plugin</artifactId>
            <version>2.6</version>
            <executions>
                <execution>
                    <id>copy-endorsed</id>
                    <phase>validate</phase>
                    <goals>
                        <goal>copy</goal>
                    </goals>
                    <configuration>
                        <outputDirectory>${endorsed.dir}</
outputDirectory>
                        <silent>true</silent>
                        <artifactItems>
                            <artifactItem>
                                <groupId>javax</groupId>
                                <artifactId>javaee-endorsed-api</
artifactId>
                                <version>7.0</version>
                                <type>jar</type>
                            </artifactItem>
                        </artifactItems>
                    </configuration>
                </execution>
                <execution>
                    <id>copy-all-dependencies</id>
                    <phase>compile</phase>
                    <goals>
                        <goal>copy-dependencies</goal>
```

```
                </goals>
                <configuration>
                    <outputDirectory>${project.build.
directory}/lib</outputDirectory>
                    <includeScope>compile</includeScope>
                </configuration>
            </execution>

        </executions>
    </plugin>
    <plugin>
        <groupId>org.apache.maven.plugins</groupId>
        <artifactId>maven-surefire-plugin</artifactId>
        <version>2.14.1</version>
        <configuration>
            <skipTests>false</skipTests>
            <includes>
                <include>**/dao/*Test.java</include>
            </includes>
            <argLine>-javaagent:target/lib/spring-instrument-
${spring.version}.jar</argLine>
        </configuration>
    </plugin>

    </plugins>
  </build>
  <repositories>
    <repository>
        <url>http://download.eclipse.org/rt/eclipselink/maven.
repo/</url>
        <id>eclipselink</id>
        <layout>default</layout>
        <name>Repository for library EclipseLink (JPA 2.1)</name>
    </repository>
  </repositories>
</project>
```

The first two changes add the `mysql-connector-java` and `junit` dependencies.
Without these we will not be able to connect to the database or write test cases.
These dependencies will download the appropriate Java libraries for inclusion
into our project.

The most important settings are in the Maven plugin that performs the actual work. Adding the `maven-surefire-plugin` will allow the test case execution based on the contents of the `main/src/test` directory structure. This clearly separates the testing classes from our application classes. The main configuration properties for this plugin are:

- `<skipTests>`: This property can be `true` (to disable testing) or `false` (to enable testing).

- `<includes>`: This property includes a list of file sets during testing. The setting `<include>**/dao/*Test.java</include>` specifies that all the classes in any `dao` subdirectory with the filename ending in `Test.java` should be loaded and included in the testing process. You may specify any number of file sets.

- `<argLine>-javaagent:target/lib/spring-instrument-${spring.version}.jar</argLine>`: This property is used to configure the Java Agent for the testing JVM and is required by Spring for the load-time weaving of classes, a discussion of which is beyond the scope of this text.

Now that we have configured the Spring and Maven testing environments, we can start writing test cases.

Defining a test case superclass

The first step is to create a superclass that all of our DAO test cases will inherit. This abstract class looks like the following code snippet:

```
package com.gieman.tttracker.dao;

import org.slf4j.Logger;
import org.slf4j.LoggerFactory;

import org.springframework.beans.factory.annotation.Autowired;
import org.springframework.test.context.ContextConfiguration;
import org.springframework.test.context.junit4.
AbstractTransactionalJUnit4SpringContextTests;

@ContextConfiguration("/testingContext.xml")
public abstract class AbstractDaoForTesting extends
AbstractTransactionalJUnit4SpringContextTests {

    protected final Logger logger = LoggerFactory.getLogger(this.
getClass());
```

```
    @Autowired(required = true)
    protected CompanyDao companyDao;
    @Autowired(required = true)
    protected ProjectDao projectDao;
    @Autowired(required = true)
    protected TaskDao taskDao;
    @Autowired(required = true)
    protected UserDao userDao;
    @Autowired(required = true)
    protected TaskLogDao taskLogDao;
}
```

The `AbstractDaoForTesting` class is marked as abstract so that it cannot be
instantiated directly. It provides member variables that are accessible to all the
subclasses, thus removing the need to replicate code in the descendents. As a result,
each subclass will have access to the DAO instances as well as the SLF4J `logger`.
There are two new Spring annotations:

- `@ContextConfiguration`: This annotation defines the Spring application
  context used to load the bean container. The `testingContext.xml` file has
  been covered in detail in the previous sections.

- `@Autowired`: This annotation indicates to Spring that the container-managed
  bean with matching type should be dependency injected into the class.
  For example, the `CompanyDao companyDao` definition will result in Spring
  querying the container for an object with type `CompanyDao`. There is only
  one object with this type: the `CompanyDaoImpl` class that was discovered
  and configured by Spring when scanning the `com.gieman.tttracker.dao`
  package via the `<context:component-scan base-package="com.gieman.
  tttracker.dao"/>` entry in the `testingContext.xml` file.

The final important thing to notice is that the `AbstractDaoForTesting` class extends
the Spring `AbstractTransactionalJUnit4SpringContextTests` class. Apart
from being a very long class name, this class provides transparent transactional
rollbacks at the end of each test method. This means the database state at the
end of any DAO testing operations (including any insert, update, or delete) will
be the same as at the start of testing. If this behavior is not required, you should
extend `AbstractJUnit4SpringContextTests` instead. In this case any testing
database operations can be examined and confirmed after the tests have been run.
It is also possible to mark a single method with `@Rollback(false)` when using
`AbstractTransactionalJUnit4SpringContextTests` to commit changes
if required.

Let's now write our first test case for the `CompanyDao` operation.

Defining the CompanyDao test case

Each CompanyDao method should have at least one test method defined. We will include exactly one test method per implemented CompanyDao method. In enterprise applications, we would expect many more scenarios to be covered than the ones identified in the code snippet that follows.

We have also included minimum logging, just enough to split the output when running the test cases. You may wish to add more logging to help analyze the results. The test code assumes that the ttt_company table has appropriate data. In *Chapter 2, The Task Time Tracker Database,* we added three rows so that we know there is data available. Additional checks would need to be done if we do not have a database with consistent testing data. The file listing is:

```java
package com.gieman.tttracker.dao;

import com.gieman.tttracker.domain.Company;
import java.util.List;
import static org.junit.Assert.assertTrue;
import org.junit.Test;

public class CompanyDaoTest extends AbstractDaoForTesting {

    public CompanyDaoTest(){}

    @Test
    public void testFind() throws Exception {

        logger.debug("\nSTARTED testFind()\n");
        List<Company> allItems = companyDao.findAll();

        assertTrue(allItems.size() > 0);

        // get the first item in the list
        Company c1 = allItems.get(0);

        int id = c1.getId();

        Company c2 = companyDao.find(id);

        assertTrue(c1.equals(c2));
        logger.debug("\nFINISHED testFind()\n");
    }

    @Test
```

```
    public void testFindAll() throws Exception {

        logger.debug("\nSTARTED testFindAll()\n");
        int rowCount = countRowsInTable("ttt_company");

        if(rowCount > 0){

            List<Company> allItems = companyDao.findAll();
            assertTrue("Company.findAll list not equal to row count of
table ttt_company", rowCount == allItems.size());

        } else {
            throw new IllegalStateException("INVALID TESTING SCENARIO:
Company table is empty");
        }
        logger.debug("\nFINISHED testFindAll()\n");
    }

    @Test
    public void testPersist() throws Exception {

        logger.debug("\nSTARTED testPersist()\n");
        Company c = new Company();
        final String NEW_NAME = "Persist Test Company name";
        c.setCompanyName(NEW_NAME);

        companyDao.persist(c);

        assertTrue(c.getId() != null);
        assertTrue(c.getCompanyName().equals(NEW_NAME));

        logger.debug("\nFINISHED testPersist()\n");
    }

    @Test
    public void testMerge() throws Exception {

        logger.debug("\nSTARTED testMerge()\n");
        final String NEW_NAME = "Merge Test Company New Name";

        Company c = companyDao.findAll().get(0);
        c.setCompanyName(NEW_NAME);

        c = companyDao.merge(c);
```

```
            assertTrue(c.getCompanyName().equals(NEW_NAME));

            logger.debug("\nFINISHED testMerge()\n");

        }

        @Test
        public void testRemove() throws Exception {

            logger.debug("\nSTARTED testRemove()\n");
            Company c = companyDao.findAll().get(0);

            companyDao.remove(c);

            List<Company> allItems = companyDao.findAll();

            assertTrue("Deleted company may not be in findAll List",
    !allItems.contains(c) );

            logger.debug("\nFINISHED testRemove()\n");
        }
    }
```

Running the JUnit test cases with Maven

The `pom.xml` configuration file will automatically run the test cases using
`<skipTests>false</skipTests>` when doing **Clean and Build Project
(task-time-tracker)** by clicking on the toolbar icon:

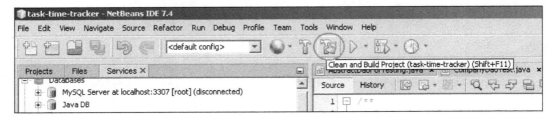

It is also possible to only run the testing phase of the project by navigating to
Run | Test Project (task-time-tracker):

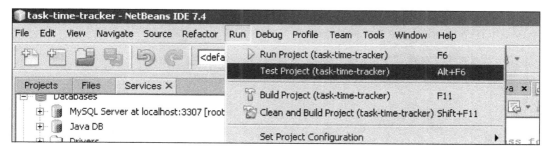

The results of the testing process can now be examined in the **Output – task-time-tracker** panel. Note that you may need to dock the output panel to the bottom of the IDE if it is minimized, as shown in the following screenshot (the minimized panel is usually in the bottom-left corner of the NetBeans IDE). The [surefire:test] plugin output is displayed at the start of the testing process. There are many lines of output for configuring Spring, connecting to the database, and loading the persistence context:

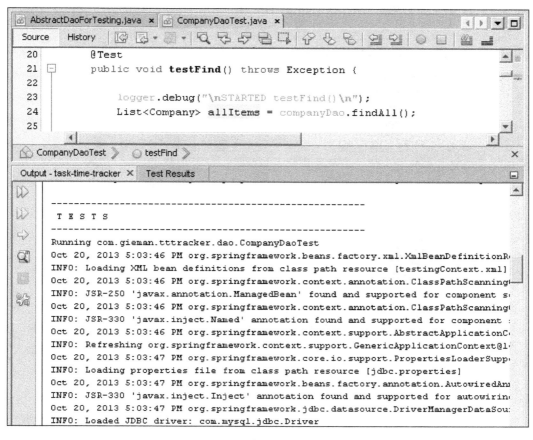

We will examine the key testing output in detail soon. Scroll through the output until you reach the end of the test section:

```
Output - task-time-tracker  ✕    Test Results

    Results :

    Tests run: 5, Failures: 0, Errors: 0, Skipped: 0

    ---------------------------------------------------

    BUILD SUCCESS
    ---------------------------------------------------
    Total time: 4.156s
    Finished at: Sun Oct 20 17:11:46 EST 2013
    Final Memory: 5M/15M
    ---------------------------------------------------
    |
```

There were five tests executed in total with no errors—a great start!

Running the CompanyDaoTest.java file

You can execute a single test case file by right-clicking on the file displayed in the editor and selecting the **Test File** option:

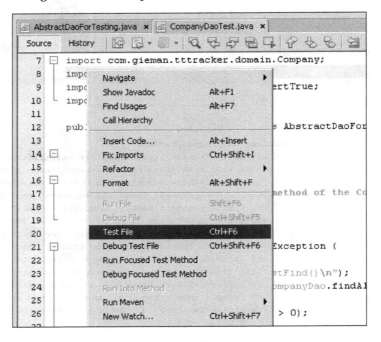

This will execute the file's test cases, producing the same testing output as shown previously, and present you with the results in the **Test Results** panel. This panel should appear under the file editor but may not be docked (it may be floating at the bottom of the NetBeans IDE; you can change the position and docking as required). The individual file testing results can then be examined:

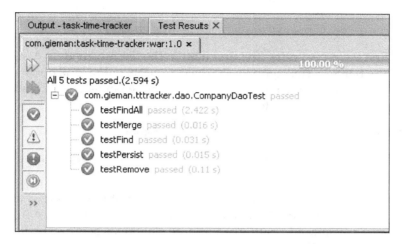

Single test file execution is a practical and quick way of debugging and developing code. We will continue to execute and examine single files during the rest of the chapter.

Let's now examine the results of each test case in detail.

 In all of the following testing outputs, the SLF4J-specific messages have been removed. This will include timestamps, threads, and session information. We will only focus on the generated SQL.

The results for the CompanyDaoTests. testMerge test case

The output for this test case is:

```
STARTED testMerge()
SELECT id_company, company_name FROM ttt_company ORDER BY company_name
ASC
FINISHED testMerge()
```

A `merge` call is used to update a persistent entity. The `testMerge` method is very simple:

```
final String NEW_NAME = "Merge Test Company New Name";
Company c = companyDao.findAll().get(0);
c.setCompanyName(NEW_NAME);
c = companyDao.merge(c);
assertTrue(c.getCompanyName().equals(NEW_NAME));
```

We find the first `Company` entity (the first item in the list returned by `findAll`) and then update the name of the company to the `NEW_NAME` value. The `companyDao.merge` call then updates the `Company` entity state in the persistence context. This is tested using the `assertTrue()` test.

Note that the testing output only has **one** SQL statement:

```
SELECT id_company, company_name FROM ttt_company ORDER BY company_name
ASC
```

This output corresponds to the `findAll` method call. Note that there is no SQL update statement executed! This may seem strange because the entity manager's `merge` call should result in an update statement being issued against the database. However, the JPA implementation is **not** required to execute such statements immediately and may cache statements when possible, for performance and optimization purposes. The cached (or queued) statements are then executed only when an explicit `commit` is called. In our example, Spring executes a `rollback` immediately after the `testMerge` method returns (remember, we are running transactional test cases thanks to our `AbstractTransactionalJUnit4SpringContextTests` extension), and hence the persistence context never needs to execute the update statement.

We can force a flush to the database by making a slight change to the `GenericDaoImpl` class:

```
@Override
@Transactional(readOnly = false, propagation = Propagation.REQUIRED)
public T merge(T o) {
  o = em.merge(o);
  em.flush();
  return o;
}
```

The `em.flush()` method results in an **immediate** update statement being executed; the entity manager is flushed with all pending changes. Changing this code in the `GenericDaoImpl` class and executing the test case again will result in the following testing output:

```
SELECT id_company, company_name FROM ttt_company ORDER BY company_name
ASC
UPDATE ttt_company SET company_name = ? WHERE (id_company = ?)
  bind => [Merge Test Company New Name, 2]
```

The update statement now appears as expected. If we now check the database directly after executing the test case, we find:

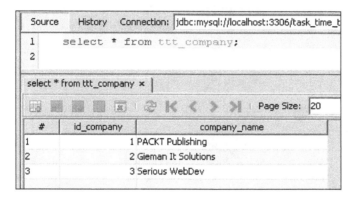

As expected, Spring has rolled back the database at the end of the `testMerge` method call, and the company name of the first record has not changed.

> In enterprise applications, it is recommended not to call `em.flush()` explicitly and to allow the JPA implementation to optimize statements according to their transactional behavior. There may be situations, however, where an immediate flush is required but these are rare.

The results for the CompanyDaoTests. testFindAll test case

The output for this test case is:

```
STARTED testFindAll()
SELECT id_company, company_name FROM ttt_company ORDER BY company_name
ASC
FINISHED testFindAll()
```

Even though the `testMerge` method uses the `findAll` method to retrieve the first item in the list, we should always include a separate `findAll` test method to compare the size of the result set with the database table. This is easy when using the Spring helper method `countRowsInTable`:

```
int rowCount = countRowsInTable("ttt_company");
```

We can then compare the size of the `findAll` result list with `rowCount` using the `assertTrue` statement:

```
assertTrue("Company.findAll list not equal to row count of table ttt_
company", rowCount == allItems.size());
```

Note how the `assertTrue` statement is used; the message is displayed if the assertion is `false`. We can test the statement by slightly modifying the assertion so that it fails:

```
assertTrue("Company.findAll list not equal to row count of table ttt_
company", rowCount+1 == allItems.size());
```

It will now fail and result in the following output when the test case is executed:

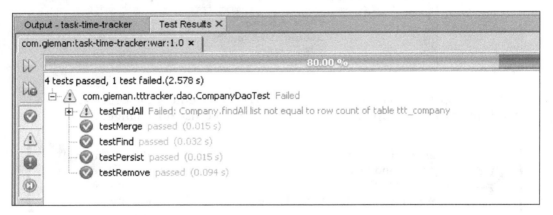

The results for the CompanyDaoTests. testFind test case

The output for this test case is:

```
STARTED testFind()
SELECT id_company, company_name FROM ttt_company ORDER BY company_name
ASC
FINISHED testFind()
```

This may seem a bit surprising for those new to JPA. The SELECT statement is executed from the code:

```
List<Company> allItems = companyDao.findAll();
```

But where is the expected SELECT statement when calling the find method using the id attribute?

```
int id = c1.getId(); // find ID of first item in list
Company c2 = companyDao.find(id);
```

JPA does not need to execute the SELECT statement using the primary key statement on the database as the entity with the required ID has already been loaded in the persistence context. There will be three entities loaded as a result of the findAll method with IDs 1, 2, and 3. When asked to find the entity using the ID of the first item in the list, JPA will return the entity it has already loaded in the persistence context with the matching ID, avoiding the need to execute a database select statement.

This is often a trap in understanding the behavior of JPA-managed applications. When an entity is loaded into the persistence context it will remain there until it expires. The definition of what constitutes "expires" will depend on the implementation and caching properties. It is possible that small sets of data will never expire; in our Company example with only a few records, this will most likely be the case. Performing an update statement directly on the underlying table, for example, changing the company name of the first record, may never be reflected in the JPA persistence context as the persistence context entity will never be refreshed.

> If an enterprise application expects data modification from multiple sources (for example, through stored procedures or web service calls via a different entity manager), a caching strategy to expire stale entities will be required. JPA does not automatically refresh the entity state from the database and will assume that the persistence context is the only mechanism for managing persistent data. EclipseLink provides several caching annotations to solve this problem. An excellent guide can be found here: http://wiki.eclipse.org/EclipseLink/Examples/JPA/Caching.

Results for the CompanyDaoTests.testPersist test case

We have added a few minor changes to the `GenericDaoImpl.persist` method as a result of the exercises from the previous chapter. The modified `persist` method in the `GenericDaoImpl` implementation is:

```
em.persist(o);

em.flush();

if (o instanceof EntityItem) {
  EntityItem<ID> item = (EntityItem<ID>) o;
  ID id = item.getId();
  logger.info("The " + o.getClass().getName() + " record with ID=" +
id + " has been inserted");
}
```

You will notice the `em.flush()` method in `GenericDaoImpl` after the `em.persist()` method. Without this flush to the database ,we cannot guarantee that a valid primary key has been set on the new `Company` entity. The output for this test case is:

```
STARTED testPersist()
INSERT INTO ttt_company (company_name) VALUES (?)
  bind => [Persist Test Company name]
SELECT LAST_INSERT_ID()
The com.gieman.tttracker.domain.Company record with ID=4 has been
inserted
FINISHED testPersist()
```

Note that the logging outputs the newly generated primary key value of 4. This value is retrieved when JPA queries MySQL using the `SELECT LAST_INSERT_ID()` statement. In fact, removing the `em.flush()` method from `GenericDaoImpl` and executing the test case would result in the following output:

```
STARTED testPersist()
The com.gieman.tttracker.domain.Company record with ID=null has been
inserted
```

The assertion `assertTrue(c.getId() != null)` will fail and we will not even display the `FINISHED testPersist()` message. Our test case fails before the debug message is reached.

Once again we see the JPA optimization in action. Without the `em.flush()` method, JPA will wait until a transaction is committed in order to execute any changes in the database. As a result, the primary key may not be set as expected for any subsequent code using the newly created entity object within the same transaction. This is another trap for the unwary developer, and the `persist` method identifies the only situation where an entity manager `flush()` to the database may be required.

Results for the CompanyDaoTests. testRemove test case

This is probably the most interesting test case so far. The output is:

```
STARTED testRemove()

SELECT id_company, company_name FROM ttt_company ORDER BY company_name
ASC
SELECT id_project, project_name, id_company FROM ttt_project WHERE
(id_company = ?)
   bind => [2]
SELECT id_task, task_name, id_project FROM ttt_task WHERE (id_project
= ?)
   bind => [4]
SELECT id_task, task_name, id_project FROM ttt_task WHERE (id_project
= ?)
   bind => [5]
SELECT id_task, task_name, id_project FROM ttt_task WHERE (id_project
= ?)
   bind => [6]
The com.gieman.tttracker.domain.Company record with ID=2 has been
deleted
DELETE FROM ttt_task WHERE (id_task = ?)
   bind => [10]
DELETE FROM ttt_task WHERE (id_task = ?)
   bind => [12]
DELETE FROM ttt_task WHERE (id_task = ?)
   bind => [11]
DELETE FROM ttt_task WHERE (id_task = ?)
   bind => [13]
DELETE FROM ttt_project WHERE (id_project = ?)
   bind => [4]
DELETE FROM ttt_project WHERE (id_project = ?)
   bind => [6]
```

```
DELETE FROM ttt_project WHERE (id_project = ?)
  bind => [5]
DELETE FROM ttt_company WHERE (id_company = ?)
  bind => [2]
SELECT id_company, company_name FROM ttt_company ORDER BY company_name
ASC

FINISHED testRemove()
```

The first SELECT statement is executed as a result of finding the first company in the list:

```
Company c = companyDao.findAll().get(0);
```

The second SELECT statement may not be as obvious:

```
SELECT id_project, project_name, id_company FROM ttt_project WHERE
(id_company = ?)
  bind => [2]
```

Why does deleting a company result in a SELECT statement on the ttt_project table? The reason is that each Company entity may have one or more related Projects entities as defined in the Company class definition:

```
@OneToMany(cascade = CascadeType.ALL, mappedBy = "company")
private List<Project> projects;
```

JPA understands that deleting a Company requires a check against the ttt_project table to see if there are any dependent Projects. In the @OneToMany annotation, the cascade = CascadeType.ALL property defines the behavior if a Company is deleted; the change should be cascaded to any dependent entities. In this example, deleting a company record will require the deletion of all related project records. Each Project entity in turn owns a collection of Task entities as defined in the Project class definition:

```
@OneToMany(cascade = CascadeType.ALL, mappedBy = "project")
private List<Task> tasks;
```

The result of removing a Company entity has far-reaching consequences as all related Projects and their related Tasks are deleted from the underlying tables. A cascade of DELETE statements in the testing output is the result of the final deletion being that of the company itself. This may not be suitable behavior for enterprise applications; in fact, such a cascading of deletions is usually **never** implemented without extensive checks to ensure data integrity. A simple change in the cascade annotation in the Company class will ensure that the deletion is not propagated:

```
@OneToMany(cascade = {CascadeType.MERGE, CascadeType.PERSIST},
mappedBy ="company")
private List<Project> projects;
```

Now only the MERGE and PERSIST operations on the Company entity will be cascaded to the related Project entities. Running the test case again after making this change will result in:

```
Internal Exception: com.mysql.jdbc.exceptions.jdbc4.
MySQLIntegrityConstraintViolationException: Cannot delete or update a
parent row: a foreign key constraint fails (`task_time_tracker`.`ttt_
project`, CONSTRAINT `ttt_project_ibfk_1` FOREIGN KEY (`id_company`)
REFERENCES `ttt_company` (`id_company`))
```

As the cascade type for REMOVE was not included, JPA does not check for related rows in the ttt_project table and simply attempts to execute the DELETE statement on the ttt_company table. This will fail, as there are related records on the ttt_project table. It will now only be possible to remove a Company entity if there are no related Project entities (the projects field is an empty list).

> Changing the CascadeType as outlined in this section adds **business logic** to the DAO layer. You will no longer be able to perform certain actions through the persistence context. There may, however, be a legitimate situation where you **do** want a cascading delete of a Company entity and this will no longer be possible. CascadeType.ALL is the most flexible option, allowing all possible scenarios. Business logic such as deletion strategies should be implemented in the service layer, which is the subject of the next chapter.

We will continue to use the cascade = CascadeType.ALL property and allow JPA-managed deletions to propagate. The business logic to restrict these actions will be implemented in the service layer.

JPA traps for the unwary

There are some JPA traps worthy of special examination. We will start by creating the following test case:

```
package com.gieman.tttracker.dao;

import com.gieman.tttracker.domain.Company;
import com.gieman.tttracker.domain.Project;
import com.gieman.tttracker.domain.User;
import static org.junit.Assert.assertTrue;
import org.junit.Test;

public class JpaTrapTest extends AbstractDaoForTesting {
```

```
    @Test
    public void testManyToOne() throws Exception {

        logger.debug("\nSTARTED testManyToOne()\n");

        Company c = companyDao.findAll().get(0);
        Company c2 = companyDao.findAll().get(1);

        Project p = c.getProjects().get(0);

        p.setCompany(c2);
        p = projectDao.merge(p);

        assertTrue("Original company still has project in its
collection!",
                    !c.getProjects().contains(p));
        assertTrue("Newly assigned company does not have project in
its collection",
                    c2.getProjects().contains(p));

        logger.debug("\nFINISHED testManyToOne()\n");

    }

    @Test
    public void testFindByUsernamePassword() throws Exception {

        logger.debug("\nSTARTED testFindByUsernamePassword()\n");

        // find by username/password combination
        User user = userDao.findByUsernamePassword("bjones", "admin");

        assertTrue("Unable to find valid user with correct username/
password combination",
                    user != null);

        user = userDao.findByUsernamePassword("bjones", "ADMIN");

        assertTrue("User found with invalid password",
                    user == null);

        logger.debug("\nFINISHED testFindByUsernamePassword()\n");
    }
}
```

Running this test case may surprise you:

The first failure arises from the `userDao.findByUsernamePassword` statement, which uses the uppercase password:

```
user = userDao.findByUsernamePassword("bjones", "ADMIN");
```

Why was the user found with an obviously incorrect password? The reason is very simple and is a trap for the unwary developer. Most databases, by default, are case insensitive when matching text fields. In this situation the uppercase ADMIN will match the lowercase admin in the password field. Not exactly what we want when checking passwords! The database term that describes this behavior is collation; we need to modify the password column to use a case-sensitive collation. This can be achieved in MySQL with the following SQL command:

```
ALTER TABLE ttt_user MODIFY
    password VARCHAR(100)
        COLLATE latin1_general_cs;
```

Other databases will have similar semantics. This will change the collation on the password field to be case sensitive (note the _cs appended in `latin1_general_cs`). Running the test case will now result in expected behavior for case-sensitive password checking:

The `testManyToOne` failure is another interesting case. In this test case, we are reassigning the project to a different Company. The `p.setCompany(c2);` line will change the assigned company to the second one in the list. We would expect that after calling the `merge` method on the project, the collection of projects in the `c2` company would contain the newly reassigned project. In other words, the following code line should equate to `true`:

```
c2.getProjects().contains(p)
```

Likewise, the old company should no longer contain the newly reassigned project and hence should be `false`:

```
c.getProjects().contains(p)
```

This is obviously not the case and identifies a trap for developers new to JPA.

Although the persistence context understands the relationship between entities using `@OneToMany` and `@ManyToOne`, the Java representation of the relationship needs to be handled by the developer when collections are concerned. The simple changes required are as follows:

```
p.setCompany(c2);
p = projectDao.merge(p);

c.getProjects().remove(p);
c2.getProjects().add(p);
```

When the `projectDao.merge(p)` line is executed, the persistence context has no way of knowing the **original** parent company (if there is one at all; this may be a newly inserted project). The original `Company` entity in the persistence context still has a collection of projects assigned. This collection will never be updated during the lifetime of the `Company` entity within the persistence context. The additional two lines of code are used to remove the project (using `remove`) from the original company's project list and we add (using `add`) the project to the new company to ensure that the persistence context entities are updated to the correct state.

Exercises

1. Add test assertions to the `CompanyDaoTest.find()` method to test for the following scenarios:

- Attempting to find a company with a null primary key
- Attempting to find a company with a negative primary key

What do you consider to be the expected results?

2. Create the missing test case files for the `ProjectDao`, `TaskDao`, `UserDao`, and `TaskLogDao` implementations.

3. Create a test case to determine if removing (deleting) a project will automatically remove the project from the owning company's project collection.

Summary

We have once again covered a lot of territory. Unit testing is a critical part of enterprise application development, and the combination of NetBeans, Maven, JUnit, and Spring provides us with a solid platform to launch both automated and single file test cases. Writing comprehensive test cases is an art form that is always appreciated and valued in any high-quality development team; never underestimate the confidence gained from working with well-tested code with a solid suite of test cases!

In the next chapter, we will examine the role of the service layer in enterprise application development. Our 3T business logic will then be implemented using the **Data Transfer Objects (DTO)** design pattern.

6
Back to Business – The Service Layer

The service layer is the nucleus of the application; it is where the business logic resides. The business logic encapsulates the rules that define the working application and it is where a significant amount of development time is spent. Enhancements, changing requirements, and ongoing maintenance will usually require modifications to the service layer. Business rules may include such operations as restricting access to specific roles, security constraints, calculations, validations, compliance checks, and logging, to name a few.

Some typical business logic examples could include the following:

- Only administrators can change the country assigned to a user
- Administrators can only change a user to a country in their own geographical region
- If payment is made in a currency other that USD, an exchange rate premium of 5 percent must be added
- An Australian zip code must be exactly four digits
- Reassigning an invoice to the Canadian affiliate can only be performed during East Coast business hours
- Each new invoice must be logged onto a separate file, if not originating from one of the five largest business clients

The core business rules we will be implementing in this chapter are far simpler:

- A user must be authenticated prior to accessing any resources
- Only a 3T administrator can maintain the 3T configuration
- Users may only update and add task logs for themselves

Service layer considerations

It is important to have clearly defined entry points for service layer operations. This will again be achieved through Java interfaces that define the operations exposed by the service layer. Clients of the service layer will interact with the business logic through these interfaces, not the implementing classes.

For similar reasons, it is important that the service layer itself is decoupled from the underlying DAO implementation. We have already achieved this by ensuring that our DAO layer exposes its persistence operations through interfaces. The service layer should know nothing about how the persistence layer is implemented and there should not be any persistence operations coded within the service layer classes.

Enterprise application clients come in many different forms, most commonly web browsers and web services. However, there may be other types of clients; for example, standalone servers using RMI. In all cases, the service layer must be as independent as possible of the client implementation. As such, the service layer should never incorporate presentation logic and should know nothing about how the data is used. The following diagram illustrates where the service layer sits in the overall application structure:

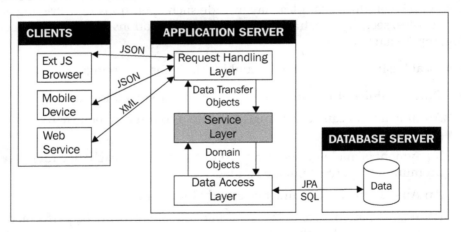

The service layer interacts with the data access layer via domain objects. There is a clear demarcation of roles with this design. The DAO layer is responsible for interacting with the database and the service layer has no knowledge of how this is done. Likewise, the DAO layer has no interest in how the domain objects are consumed. This is the role of the service layer where business logic controls decide what can and should be done with the domain objects.

A well-architected service layer should have a simple interface that allows any type of request handling layer to work with the underlying application business logic. If a list of Company entities are requested from the service layer, the exposed interface method that provides this functionality does not need to know whether the list is being used to render a web page, to execute a web service call, or to send an e-mail with an attached Excel spreadsheet. The request handling layer will be discussed in detail in the following chapter.

Building the service layer

The service layer classes and interfaces will follow the same naming conventions of our DAO layer, where Service simply replaces the Dao equivalent name:

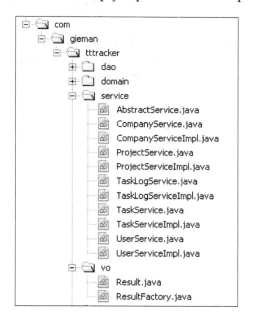

Our first definition will be for the Result class.

The Result Data Transfer Object

The service layer will communicate with the request handling tier through interfaces that return `Result` **Data Transfer Objects (DTO)**. The DTO design pattern is commonly used in enterprise application programming to transfer data between different layers or subsystems. Our `Result` DTO will have the following three properties:

- `boolean success`: This property is used if the action was successful and an appropriate data payload is available
- `String msg`: This is a message that may be used by the client for logging or informational purposes
- `<T> data`: This is a generically typed data payload that will be consumed by the request handling layer

The `Result` class is also a **Value Object (VO)**, an immutable object whose state cannot be changed after creation. Each instance variable is marked `final` and we will use an appropriate `ResultFactory` method to create the value object instance. Value objects are a concept used in Domain-Driven Design to represent data without any conceptual identity. You can find out more about Domain-Driven Design at `http://en.wikipedia.org/wiki/Domain-driven_design`. The definition of the `Result` class follows:

```
package com.gieman.tttracker.vo;

import java.io.Serializable;
import java.util.List;
import java.util.Objects;

public class Result<T> implements Serializable {

    final private boolean success;
    final private T data;
    final private String msg;

    Result(boolean success, T data) {
        this.success = success;
        this.data = data;
        this.msg = null;
    }

    Result(boolean success, String msg) {
        this.success = success;
        this.data = null;
```

```java
        this.msg = msg;
    }

    public boolean isSuccess() {
        return success;
    }

    public T getData() {
        return data;
    }

    public String getMsg() {
        return msg;
    }

    @Override
    public String toString() {

        StringBuilder sb = new StringBuilder("\"Result{\"");
        sb.append("success=").append(success);
        sb.append(", msg=").append(msg);

        sb.append(", data=");

        if(data == null){

            sb.append("null");

        } else if(data instanceof List){

            List castList = (List) data;
            if(castList.isEmpty()){

                sb.append("empty list");

            } else {
                Object firstItem = castList.get(0);

                sb.append("List of
                  ").append(firstItem.getClass());
            }

        } else {
```

```
            sb.append(data.toString());
        }

        sb.append("}");

        return sb.toString();

    }

    @Override
    public int hashCode() {
        int hash = 7;
        hash = 89 * hash + (this.success ? 1 : 0);
        hash = 89 * hash + Objects.hashCode(this.data);
        return hash;
    }

    @Override
    public boolean equals(Object obj) {
        if (obj == null) {
            return false;
        }
        if (getClass() != obj.getClass()) {
            return false;
        }
        final Result<?> other = (Result<?>) obj;
        if (this.success != other.success) {
            return false;
        }
        return Objects.deepEquals(this.data, other.data);
    }
}
```

You will notice that the Result constructors are package-private (cannot be created by classes outside of the package). The Result value object instantiation will be managed by the ResultFactory class:

```
package com.gieman.tttracker.vo;

public class ResultFactory {

    public static <T> Result<T> getSuccessResult(T data) {
        return new Result(true, data);
    }
```

```
public static <T> Result<T> getSuccessResult(T data, String
    msg) {
        return new Result(true, msg);
}

public static <T> Result<T> getSuccessResultMsg(String msg) {
        return new Result(true, msg);
}

public static <T> Result<T> getFailResult(String msg) {
        return new Result(false, msg);
}
}
```

The static utility methods will create and return Result instances configured for the appropriate purpose in our service layer.

In our design, a failure is considered to be a recoverable state of the application. Attempting to log in with an invalid username/password combination would be an example of a failed action. Not having permission to perform a delete would be another possible failure action. The client of the service layer can recover from such actions and present graceful messages to the user by examining the msg of the Result. An alternate design pattern for handling failures is through Java-checked exceptions; an exception is thrown when a failure is encountered. Implementing such a design pattern forces the client to catch the exception, determine the cause of the exception, and handle processing accordingly. We prefer our design for handling failures and recommend you to not use checked exceptions unless a truly exceptional situation has occurred. The resulting code is cleaner to read and we can avoid the overhead of working with exceptions.

The AbstractService.java class

All service layer implementations will extend the AbstractService class to provide common functionality. We will simply define a logger, @Autowire, the UserDao implementation, and add a convenience method for checking if a user is valid.

```
package com.gieman.tttracker.service;

import com.gieman.tttracker.dao.UserDao;
import com.gieman.tttracker.domain.User;
import org.slf4j.Logger;
import org.slf4j.LoggerFactory;
import org.springframework.beans.factory.annotation.Autowired;
```

```
public abstract class AbstractService {

    final protected Logger logger =
      LoggerFactory.getLogger(this.getClass());

    @Autowired
    protected UserDao userDao;

    protected  final String USER_INVALID = "Not a valid user";
    protected  final String USER_NOT_ADMIN = "Not an admin user";

    protected boolean isValidUser(String username){

        User user = userDao.findByUsername(username);
        return user != null;
    }
}
```

As discussed in the previous chapter, Spring injects the container-managed bean with matching type for each of the `@Autowired` annotated fields. Each service layer implementation that extends the `AbstractService` class will hence have access to the `UserDao` instance.

Our service layer will implement very basic security to differentiate between normal users and administrator users. The `admin_role` column in the `ttt_user` table is used to identify if a user has administrator privileges. Enterprise applications will most likely have LDAP realms with appropriate roles configured for different user groups but the principle is the same; we need to be able to identify if a user is allowed to perform an action. The administrator role will be the only role on our 3T application and we will now add a helper method to the `User` class to identify whether the user is an administrator:

```
public boolean isAdmin(){
    return adminRole == null ? false : adminRole.equals('Y');
}
```

The service layer implementations will use this new method to test if the user is an administrator.

The service layer interfaces

The service layer interfaces define methods that will be exposed to clients. These methods define the core actions required by our 3T application. Each method has a `String actionUsername` argument to identify the user executing this request. The `actionUsername` can be used in the implementation for logging purposes or to ensure a valid user is requesting data. The definition of valid will depend on the action being performed. Each interface will use generic types to define the returned `Result` value object.

The `CompanyService` interface will return a data payload that is either a Company object (`Result<Company>`) or a list of Company objects (`Result<List<Company>>`). The definition of this interface follows:

```
package com.gieman.tttracker.service;

import java.util.List;
import com.gieman.tttracker.domain.Company;
import com.gieman.tttracker.vo.Result;

public interface CompanyService {

    public Result<Company> store(
        Integer idCompany,
        String companyName,
        String actionUsername);

    public Result<Company> remove(Integer idCompany, String
      actionUsername);
    public Result<Company> find(Integer idCompany, String
      actionUsername);
    public Result<List<Company>> findAll(String actionUsername);

}
```

Note we have defined a single `store` method that will be used to save data to persistent storage. The implementing method will decide if a `persist` or `merge` is required. In a similar way, we can define the remaining interfaces (package and import definitions have been removed).

```
public interface ProjectService {

    public Result<Project> store(
        Integer idProject,
        Integer idCompany,
```

```
            String projectName,
            String actionUsername);

    public Result<Project> remove(Integer idProject, String
        actionUsername);
    public Result<Project> find(Integer idProject, String
        actionUsername);
    public Result<List<Project>> findAll(String actionUsername);


}
public interface TaskService {

    public Result<Task> store(
        Integer idTask,
        Integer idProject,
        String taskName,
        String actionUsername);

    public Result<Task> remove(Integer idTask, String
        actionUsername);
    public Result<Task> find(Integer idTask, String
        actionUsername);
    public Result<List<Task>> findAll(String actionUsername);
}
public interface TaskLogService {

    public Result<TaskLog> store(
        Integer idTaskLog,
        Integer idTask,
        String username,
        String taskDescription,
        Date taskLogDate,
        int taskMinutes,
        String actionUsername);

    public Result<TaskLog> remove(Integer idTaskLog, String
        actionUsername);
    public Result<TaskLog> find(Integer idTaskLog, String
        actionUsername);
    public Result<List<TaskLog>> findByUser(String username, Date
        startDate, Date endDate, String actionUsername);
}
public interface UserService {
```

```
    public Result
        String username,
        String firstName,
        String lastName,
        String email,
        String password,
        Character adminRole,
        String actionUsername);

    public Result remove(String username, String
      actionUsername);
    public Result find(String username, String
      actionUsername);
    public Result<List<User>> findAll(String actionUsername);
    public Result<User> findByUsernamePassword(String username,
      String password);
}
```

Implementing the service layer

Each interface defined previously will have an appropriate implementation. The implementing classes will follow our DAO naming conventions by adding `Impl` to the interface names resulting in `CompanyServiceImpl`, `ProjectServiceImpl`, `TaskServiceImpl`, `TaskLogServiceImpl`, and `UserServiceImpl`. We will define the `CompanyServiceImpl`, `TaskServiceImpl`, and `TaskLogServiceImpl` classes and leave the `ProjectServiceImpl` and `UserServiceImpl` as an exercise.

The service layer implementations will process business logic with one or more calls to the DAO layer, validating parameters, and confirming user authorization as required. The 3T application security is very simple as mentioned in the following list:

- A valid user is required for all actions. The `actionUsername` must represent a valid user in the database.
- Only an administrator can modify the `Company`, `Project`, or `Task` data.
- Only an administrator can modify or add users.

Our service layer implementation will use the `isValidUser` method in the `AbstractService` class to check if the user is valid.

Authentication, authorization, and security

Application security is a critical part of enterprise application development and it is important to understand the difference between authentication and authorization.

- Authentication verifies who you are. It involves verifying the username/ password combination and is performed once during the initial login to the 3T application.

- Authorization verifies what you are allowed to do. 3T administrators are allowed to perform more actions than normal users.

A 3T user must have a valid record in the `ttt_user` table; the service layer will simply test if the provided username represents a valid user. The actual authorization of the user will be covered in the next chapter when we develop the request handling layer.

Securing an enterprise application is beyond the scope of this book but no discussion of this topic would be complete without mentioning Spring Security, an overview of which can be found at `http://static.springframework.org/spring-security/site/index.html`. Spring Security has become the de facto standard for securing Spring-based applications and an excellent book called *Spring Security 3*, by Packt Publishing, that covers all concepts can be found here at `http://www.springsecuritybook.com`. We recommend you learn more about Spring Security to understand the many different ways you can authenticate users and secure your service layer.

The CompanyService implementation

The `CompanyServiceImpl` class is defined as:

```
package com.gieman.tttracker.service;

import com.gieman.tttracker.dao.CompanyDao;
import java.util.List;
import com.gieman.tttracker.domain.*;
import org.springframework.stereotype.Service;
import org.springframework.transaction.annotation.Propagation;
import org.springframework.transaction.annotation.Transactional;
import com.gieman.tttracker.vo.Result;
import com.gieman.tttracker.vo.ResultFactory;
import org.springframework.beans.factory.annotation.Autowired;
```

```
@Transactional
@Service("companyService")
public class CompanyServiceImpl extends AbstractService implements
  CompanyService {

    @Autowired
    protected CompanyDao companyDao;

    public CompanyServiceImpl() {
        super();
    }

    @Transactional(readOnly = true, propagation =
      Propagation.SUPPORTS)
    @Override
    public Result<Company> find(Integer idCompany, String
      actionUsername) {

        if (isValidUser(actionUsername)) {
            Company company = companyDao.find(idCompany);
            return ResultFactory.getSuccessResult(company);

        } else {
            return ResultFactory.getFailResult(USER_INVALID);
        }
    }

    @Transactional(readOnly = false, propagation =
      Propagation.REQUIRED)
    @Override
    public Result<Company> store(
            Integer idCompany,
            String companyName,
            String actionUsername) {

        User actionUser = userDao.find(actionUsername);

        if (!actionUser.isAdmin()) {
            return ResultFactory.getFailResult(USER_NOT_ADMIN);
        }

        Company company;
```

```
            if (idCompany == null) {
                company = new Company();
            } else {

                company = companyDao.find(idCompany);

                if (company == null) {
                    return ResultFactory.getFailResult("Unable to find
                        company instance with ID=" + idCompany);
                }
            }

            company.setCompanyName(companyName);

            if (company.getId() == null) {
                companyDao.persist(company);
            } else {
                company = companyDao.merge(company);
            }

            return ResultFactory.getSuccessResult(company);

    }

    @Transactional(readOnly = false, propagation =
        Propagation.REQUIRED)
    @Override
    public Result<Company> remove(Integer idCompany, String
        actionUsername) {

        User actionUser = userDao.find(actionUsername);

        if (!actionUser.isAdmin()) {
            return ResultFactory.getFailResult(USER_NOT_ADMIN);
        }

        if (idCompany == null) {
            return ResultFactory.getFailResult("Unable to remove
                Company [null idCompany]");
        }

        Company company = companyDao.find(idCompany);
```

```
        if (company == null) {
            return ResultFactory.getFailResult("Unable to load
                Company for removal with idCompany=" + idCompany);
        } else {

            if (company.getProjects() == null ||
                company.getProjects().isEmpty()) {

                companyDao.remove(company);

                String msg = "Company " + company.getCompanyName()
                    + " was deleted by " + actionUsername;
                logger.info(msg);
                return ResultFactory.getSuccessResultMsg(msg);
            } else {
                return ResultFactory.getFailResult("Company has
                    projects assigned and could not be deleted");
            }
        }

    }


    @Transactional(readOnly = true, propagation =
        Propagation.SUPPORTS)
    @Override
    public Result<List<Company>> findAll(String actionUsername) {

        if (isValidUser(actionUsername)) {
            return
                ResultFactory.getSuccessResult
                    (companyDao.findAll());
        } else {
            return ResultFactory.getFailResult(USER_INVALID);
        }
    }
}
```

Each method returns a `Result` object that is created by the appropriate `ResultFactory`
static method. Each method confirms the `actionUsername` method that identifies
a valid user for the action. Methods that modify the `Company` entity require an
administrative user (the `store` and `remove` methods). Other methods that retrieve
data (the `find*` method) simply require a valid user; one that exists in the
`ttt_user` table.

Note the reuse of the `if(isValidUser(actionUsername))` and `if(!actionUser.isAdmin())` code blocks in each method. This is not considered a good practice as this logic should be part of the security framework and not replicated on a per method basis. Using Spring Security, for example, you can apply security to a service layer bean by using annotations.

```
@Secured("ROLE_USER")
public Result<List<Company>> findAll(String actionUsername) {
// application specific code here

@Secured("ROLE_ADMIN")
public Result<Company> remove(Integer idCompany, String
  actionUsername) {
// application specific code here
```

The `@Secured` annotation is used to define a list of security configuration attributes that are applicable to the business methods. A user would then be linked to one or more roles by the security framework. Such a design pattern is less intrusive, easier to maintain, and easier to enhance.

> We once again recommend you learn more about Spring Security for use in real-world enterprise applications.

Any action that cannot be performed as expected is considered to have "failed". In this case, the `ResultFactory.getFailResult` method is called to create the failure `Result` object.

A few points to note:

- Each service layer class uses the `@Service` annotation to identify this as a Spring-managed bean. The Spring Framework will be configured to scan for this annotation using `<context:component-scan base-package="com.gieman.tttracker.service"/>` in the application context configuration file. Spring will then load the `CompanyServiceImpl` class into the bean container under the `companyService` name.

- The `store` method is used to both `persist` and `merge` a Company entity. The service layer client has no need to know if this will be an `insert` statement or an `update` statement. The appropriate action is selected in the `store` method based on the existence of the primary key.

- The `remove` method checks if the company has projects assigned. The business rule implemented will only allow a company deletion if there are no projects assigned and then check if `company.getProjects().isEmpty()` is true. If projects are assigned, the `remove` method fails.

- Transactional attributes depend on the action being implemented. If data is being modified, we use `@Transactional(readOnly = false, propagation = Propagation.REQUIRED)` to ensure a transaction is created if not already available. If data is not being modified in the method, we use `@Transactional(readOnly = true, propagation = Propagation.SUPPORTS)`.

All service layer implementations will follow a similar pattern.

The TaskService implementation

The `TaskServiceImpl` class is defined as follows:

```
package com.gieman.tttracker.service;

import com.gieman.tttracker.dao.ProjectDao;
import com.gieman.tttracker.dao.TaskDao;
import com.gieman.tttracker.dao.TaskLogDao;
import java.util.List;
import com.gieman.tttracker.domain.*;
import org.springframework.stereotype.Service;
import org.springframework.transaction.annotation.Propagation;
import org.springframework.transaction.annotation.Transactional;
import com.gieman.tttracker.vo.Result;
import com.gieman.tttracker.vo.ResultFactory;
import org.springframework.beans.factory.annotation.Autowired;

@Transactional
@Service("taskService")
public class TaskServiceImpl extends AbstractService implements
  TaskService {

    @Autowired
    protected TaskDao taskDao;
    @Autowired
    protected TaskLogDao taskLogDao;
    @Autowired
    protected ProjectDao projectDao;

    public TaskServiceImpl() {
        super();
    }
```

```
@Transactional(readOnly = true, propagation =
  Propagation.SUPPORTS)
@Override
public Result<Task> find(Integer idTask, String
  actionUsername) {

    if(isValidUser(actionUsername)) {
        return
          ResultFactory.getSuccessResult
            (taskDao.find(idTask));
    } else {
        return ResultFactory.getFailResult(USER_INVALID);
    }

}

@Transactional(readOnly = false, propagation =
  Propagation.REQUIRED)
@Override
public Result<Task> store(
    Integer idTask,
    Integer idProject,
    String taskName,
    String actionUsername) {

    User actionUser = userDao.find(actionUsername);

    if (!actionUser.isAdmin()) {
        return ResultFactory.getFailResult(USER_NOT_ADMIN);
    }

    Project project = projectDao.find(idProject);

    if(project == null){
        return ResultFactory.getFailResult("Unable to store
          task without a valid project [idProject=" +
            idProject + "]");
    }

    Task task;

    if (idTask == null) {
```

```
            task = new Task();
            task.setProject(project);
            project.getTasks().add(task);

      } else {

            task = taskDao.find(idTask);

            if(task == null) {

                  return ResultFactory.getFailResult("Unable to find
                      task instance with idTask=" + idTask);

            } else {

                  if(! task.getProject().equals(project)){

                        Project currentProject = task.getProject();
                        // reassign to new project
                        task.setProject(project);
                        project.getTasks().add(task);
                        // remove from previous project
                        currentProject.getTasks().remove(task);
                  }
            }
      }

      task.setTaskName(taskName);

      if(task.getId() == null) {
            taskDao.persist(task);
      } else {
            task = taskDao.merge(task);
      }

      return ResultFactory.getSuccessResult(task);
}

@Transactional(readOnly = false, propagation =
   Propagation.REQUIRED)
@Override
public Result<Task> remove(Integer idTask, String
   actionUsername){
```

```
User actionUser = userDao.find(actionUsername);

if (!actionUser.isAdmin()) {
    return ResultFactory.getFailResult(USER_NOT_ADMIN);
}

if(idTask == null){

    return ResultFactory.getFailResult("Unable to remove
      Task [null idTask]");

} else {

    Task task = taskDao.find(idTask);
    long taskLogCount =
      taskLogDao.findTaskLogCountByTask(task);

    if(task == null) {

        return ResultFactory.getFailResult("Unable to load
          Task for removal with idTask=" + idTask);

    } else if(taskLogCount > 0) {

        return ResultFactory.getFailResult("Unable to
          remove Task with idTask=" + idTask + " as valid
            task logs are assigned");

    } else {

        Project project = task.getProject();

        taskDao.remove(task);

        project.getTasks().remove(task);

        String msg = "Task " + task.getTaskName() + " was
          deleted by " + actionUsername;
        logger.info(msg);
        return ResultFactory.getSuccessResultMsg(msg);
    }
}
```

```
@Transactional(readOnly = true, propagation =
    Propagation.SUPPORTS)
@Override
public Result<List<Task>> findAll(String actionUsername){

    if(isValidUser(actionUsername)){
        return
            ResultFactory.getSuccessResult(taskDao.findAll());
    } else {
        return ResultFactory.getFailResult(USER_INVALID);
    }
}
}
```

This class implements the following business rules:

- Removing a task is not allowed if task logs are assigned
- Only administrators can modify a task

Note that in the `remove` method we check if task logs are assigned to the task using the code:

```
long taskLogCount = taskLogDao.findTaskLogCountByTask (task);
```

The `taskLogDao.findTaskLogCountByTask` method uses the `getSingleResult()` method on the `Query` interface to return a `long` value as defined in the `TaskLogDaoImpl`. It would have been possible to code a method as follows to find the `taskLogCount`:

```
List<TaskLog> allTasks = taskLogDao.findByTask(task);
long taskLogCount = allTasks.size();
```

However this option would result in JPA loading all `TaskLog` entities assigned to the task into memory. This is not an efficient use of resources as there could be millions of `TaskLog` records in a large system.

The TaskLogService implementation

The `TaskLogService` implementation will be the final class we will go through in detail.

```
package com.gieman.tttracker.service;

import com.gieman.tttracker.dao.TaskDao;
import com.gieman.tttracker.dao.TaskLogDao;
import java.util.List;
```

```
import com.gieman.tttracker.domain.*;
import java.util.Date;
import org.springframework.stereotype.Service;
import org.springframework.transaction.annotation.Propagation;
import org.springframework.transaction.annotation.Transactional;
import com.gieman.tttracker.vo.Result;
import com.gieman.tttracker.vo.ResultFactory;
import org.springframework.beans.factory.annotation.Autowired;

@Transactional
@Service("taskLogService")
public class TaskLogServiceImpl extends AbstractService implements
  TaskLogService {

    @Autowired
    protected TaskLogDao taskLogDao;
    @Autowired
    protected TaskDao taskDao;

    public TaskLogServiceImpl() {
        super();
    }

    @Transactional(readOnly = true, propagation =
      Propagation.SUPPORTS)
    @Override
    public Result<TaskLog> find(Integer idTaskLog, String
      actionUsername) {

        User actionUser = userDao.find(actionUsername);

        if(actionUser == null) {
            return ResultFactory.getFailResult(USER_INVALID);
        }

        TaskLog taskLog = taskLogDao.find(idTaskLog);

        if(taskLog == null){
            return ResultFactory.getFailResult("Task log not found
              with idTaskLog=" + idTaskLog);
        } else if( actionUser.isAdmin() ||
          taskLog.getUser().equals(actionUser)){
```

```
            return ResultFactory.getSuccessResult(taskLog);
        } else {
            return ResultFactory.getFailResult("User does not have
              permission to view this task log");
        }
    }


    @Transactional(readOnly = false, propagation =
      Propagation.REQUIRED)
    @Override
    public Result<TaskLog> store(
        Integer idTaskLog,
        Integer idTask,
        String username,
        String taskDescription,
        Date taskLogDate,
        int taskMinutes,
        String actionUsername) {

        User actionUser = userDao.find(actionUsername);
        User taskUser = userDao.find(username);

        if(actionUser == null || taskUser == null) {
            return ResultFactory.getFailResult(USER_INVALID);
        }

        Task task = taskDao.find(idTask);

        if(task == null) {
            return ResultFactory.getFailResult("Unable to store
              task log with null task");
        }

        if( !actionUser.isAdmin() && ! taskUser.equals(actionUser)
          ){
            return ResultFactory.getFailResult("User performing
              save must be an admin user or saving their own
                record");
        }

        TaskLog taskLog;
```

```java
        if (idTaskLog == null) {
            taskLog = new TaskLog();
        } else {
            taskLog = taskLogDao.find(idTaskLog);
            if(taskLog == null) {
                return ResultFactory.getFailResult("Unable to find
                    taskLog instance with ID=" + idTaskLog);
            }
        }

        taskLog.setTaskDescription(taskDescription);
        taskLog.setTaskLogDate(taskLogDate);
        taskLog.setTaskMinutes(taskMinutes);
        taskLog.setTask(task);
        taskLog.setUser(taskUser);

        if(taskLog.getId() == null) {
            taskLogDao.persist(taskLog);
        } else {
            taskLog = taskLogDao.merge(taskLog);
        }

        return ResultFactory.getSuccessResult(taskLog);

    }

    @Transactional(readOnly = false, propagation =
        Propagation.REQUIRED)
    @Override
    public Result<TaskLog> remove(Integer idTaskLog, String
        actionUsername){

        User actionUser = userDao.find(actionUsername);

        if(actionUser == null) {
            return ResultFactory.getFailResult(USER_INVALID);
        }

        if(idTaskLog == null){
            return ResultFactory.getFailResult("Unable to remove
                TaskLog [null idTaskLog]");
        }
```

```
TaskLog taskLog = taskLogDao.find(idTaskLog);

if(taskLog == null) {
    return ResultFactory.getFailResult("Unable to load
        TaskLog for removal with idTaskLog=" + idTaskLog);
}

// only the user that owns the task log may remove it
// OR an admin user
if(actionUser.isAdmin() ||
  taskLog.getUser().equals(actionUser)){
    taskLogDao.remove(taskLog);
    return ResultFactory.getSuccessResultMsg("taskLog
        removed successfully");
} else {
    return ResultFactory.getFailResult("Only an admin user
        or task log owner can delete a task log");
}
}

@Transactional(readOnly = true, propagation =
  Propagation.SUPPORTS)
@Override
public Result<List<TaskLog>> findByUser(String username, Date
  startDate, Date endDate, String actionUsername){

    User taskUser = userDao.findByUsername(username);
    User actionUser = userDao.find(actionUsername);

    if(taskUser == null || actionUser == null) {
        return ResultFactory.getFailResult(USER_INVALID);
    }

    if(startDate == null || endDate == null){
        return ResultFactory.getFailResult("Start and end date
            are required for findByUser ");
    }

    if(actionUser.isAdmin() || taskUser.equals(actionUser)){
        return
            ResultFactory.getSuccessResult(taskLogDao.findByUser
                (taskUser, startDate, endDate));
```

```
        } else {
            return ResultFactory.getFailResult("Unable to find
                task logs. User does not have permission with
                    username=" + username);
        }
    }
}
```

Once again there is a lot of business logic in this class. The main business rules implemented are:

- Only the owner of the `TaskLog` or an administrator can find a task log
- An administrator can add a task log for any other user
- A normal user can only add a task log for themselves
- Only the owner of a task log or an administrator can remove a task log
- A normal user can only retrieve their own task logs
- An administrator can retrieve anyone's task logs
- The `findByUser` method requires a valid start and end date

We leave the remaining service layer classes (`UserServiceImpl` and `ProjectServiceImpl`) for you to implement as exercises.

It is now time to configure the testing environment for our service layer.

Testing the service layer

Service layer testing is a critical part of the enterprise application development. As mentioned previously, the service layer encapsulates the business rules that define the working application and is where a significant amount of development time is spent. Business logic evolves as the application is enhanced, new modules are added, and business rules change. The test cases for the service layer will therefore represent the evolution of the application. Well-documented test cases will enhance the knowledge base of the application lifecycle, define changes, and explain the purpose of the change. The service layer test cases will become a repository of information appreciated by all developers working on the project.

The only change required to enable service layer testing is to add the following to the `testingContext.xml` file defined in the previous chapter:

```
<context:component-scan base-
    package="com.gieman.tttracker.service" />
```

Test case classes added to the directory `src/test/java/com/gieman/tttracker/service` will then be available for testing. We will add the following classes to the service package:

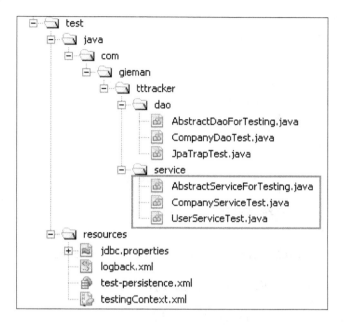

The `AbstractServiceForTesting` superclass will once again extend `AbstractTransactionalJUnit4SpringContextTests`, define the `@ContextConfiguration` configuration file, and override the default Spring logger with the `slf4j` logger.

```
package com.gieman.tttracker.service;

import org.slf4j.Logger;
import org.slf4j.LoggerFactory;

import org.springframework.test.context.ContextConfiguration;
import
  org.springframework.test.context.junit4.
    AbstractTransactionalJUnit4SpringContextTests;

@ContextConfiguration("/testingContext.xml")
public abstract class AbstractServiceForTesting extends
  AbstractTransactionalJUnit4SpringContextTests {
```

```
      final protected Logger logger =
        LoggerFactory.getLogger(this.getClass());


}
```
The CompanyServiceTest class is defined as:
```
package com.gieman.tttracker.service;

import com.gieman.tttracker.dao.ProjectDao;
import com.gieman.tttracker.domain.Company;
import com.gieman.tttracker.domain.Project;
import com.gieman.tttracker.vo.Result;
import java.util.List;
import static org.junit.Assert.assertTrue;
import org.junit.Test;
import org.springframework.beans.factory.annotation.Autowired;

public class CompanyServiceTest extends AbstractServiceForTesting
  {

    protected final String TEST_USERNAME = "bjones";
    @Autowired
    protected CompanyService companyService;
    @Autowired
    protected ProjectDao projectDao;

    @Test
    public void testFind() throws Exception {

        logger.debug("\nSTARTED testFind()\n");
        Result<List<Company>> allItems =
          companyService.findAll(TEST_USERNAME);

        assertTrue(allItems.getData().size() > 0);

        // get the first item in the list
        Company c1 = allItems.getData().get(0);

        int id = c1.getId();

        Result<Company> c2= companyService.find(id,
          TEST_USERNAME);
```

```
        assertTrue(c1.equals(c2.getData()));
        logger.debug("\nFINISHED testFind()\n");
    }


    @Test
    public void testFindAll() throws Exception {

        logger.debug("\nSTARTED testFindAll()\n");
        int rowCount = countRowsInTable("ttt_company");

        if(rowCount > 0){

            Result<List<Company>> allItems =
                companyService.findAll(TEST_USERNAME);
            assertTrue("Company.findAll list not equal to row
                count of table ttt_company", rowCount ==
                    allItems.getData().size());

        } else {
            throw new IllegalStateException("INVALID TESTING
                SCENARIO: Company table is empty");
        }
        logger.debug("\nFINISHED testFindAll()\n");
    }


    @Test
    public void testAddNew() throws Exception {

        logger.debug("\nSTARTED testAddNew()\n");
        //Company c = new Company();
        final String NEW_NAME = "New Test Company name";
        //c.setCompanyName(NEW_NAME);

        Result<Company> c2 = companyService.store(null, NEW_NAME,
            TEST_USERNAME);

        assertTrue(c2.getData().getId() != null);
        assertTrue(c2.getData().getCompanyName()
            .equals(NEW_NAME));

        logger.debug("\nFINISHED testAddNew()\n");
    }
```

```java
@Test
public void testUpdate() throws Exception {

    logger.debug("\nSTARTED testUpdate()\n");
    final String NEW_NAME = "Update Test Company New Name";

    Result<List<Company>> ar1 =
      companyService.findAll(TEST_USERNAME);
    Company c = ar1.getData().get(0);

    companyService.store(c.getIdCompany(), NEW_NAME,
      TEST_USERNAME);

    Result<Company> ar2 =
      companyService.find(c.getIdCompany(), TEST_USERNAME);

    assertTrue(ar2.getData().
      getCompanyName().equals(NEW_NAME));

    logger.debug("\nFINISHED testMerge()\n");

}


@Test
public void testRemove() throws Exception {

    logger.debug("\nSTARTED testRemove()\n");
    Result<List<Company>> ar1 =
      companyService.findAll(TEST_USERNAME);
    Company c = ar1.getData().get(0);

    Result<Company> ar =
      companyService.remove(c.getIdCompany(), TEST_USERNAME);
    Result<Company> ar2 =
      companyService.find(c.getIdCompany(), TEST_USERNAME);

    // should fail as projects are assigned
    assertTrue(! ar.isSuccess());
    // finder still works
    assertTrue(ar2.getData() != null);
```

```
logger.debug("\ntestRemove() - UNABLE TO DELETE TESTS
  PASSED\n");
// remove all the projects
c = ar2.getData();

for(Project p : c.getProjects()){
    projectDao.remove(p);

}
c.getProjects().clear();

logger.debug("\ntestRemove() - removed all projects\n");

ar = companyService.remove(c.getIdCompany(),
  TEST_USERNAME);
// remove should have succeeded
assertTrue(ar.isSuccess());

ar2 = companyService.find(c.getIdCompany(),
  TEST_USERNAME);
// should not have been found
assertTrue(ar2.getData() == null);
assertTrue(ar2.isSuccess());

logger.debug("\nFINISHED testRemove()\n");
    }
}
```

Running this test case by right-clicking on the file in the editor and selecting the **Test File** option should result in the following output:

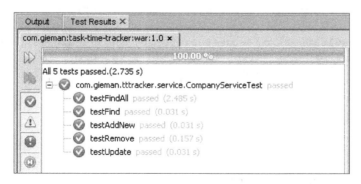

The `UserServiceTest` class is defined as:

```
package com.gieman.tttracker.service;

import com.gieman.tttracker.dao.TaskLogDao;
import com.gieman.tttracker.dao.UserDao;
import com.gieman.tttracker.domain.TaskLog;
import com.gieman.tttracker.domain.User;
import com.gieman.tttracker.vo.Result;
import java.util.Calendar;
import java.util.List;
import static org.junit.Assert.assertTrue;
import org.junit.Test;
import org.springframework.beans.factory.annotation.Autowired;

public class UserServiceTest extends AbstractServiceForTesting {

    @Autowired
    protected UserService userService;
    @Autowired
    protected TaskLogDao taskLogDao;
    @Autowired
    protected UserDao userDao;
    private final String TEST_USERNAME = "jsmith";

    @Test
    public void testAddNew() throws Exception {

        String ADMIN_USERNAME = "bjones";

        logger.debug("\nSTARTED testAddNew()\n");

        Result<User> ar = userService.store("nusername", "David",
            "Francis", "df@tttracker.com", "admpwd", 'N',
                ADMIN_USERNAME);

        // should succeed
        logger.debug(ar.getMsg());
        assertTrue(ar.isSuccess());

        ar = userService.store(this.TEST_USERNAME, "David",
            "Francis", "df@tttracker.com", "admpwd", 'Y',
                ADMIN_USERNAME);
```

```
        logger.debug(ar.getMsg());
        assertTrue("Cannot assign email that is currently assigned
            to other user", !ar.isSuccess());

        ar = userService.store("user100", "David", "Francis",
            "user100@tttracker.com", "", 'Y', ADMIN_USERNAME);

        logger.debug(ar.getMsg());
        assertTrue("Cannot set empty password for user",
            !ar.isSuccess());

        ar = userService.store("user101", "David", "Francis", "
            ", "validpwd", 'Y', ADMIN_USERNAME);

        logger.debug(ar.getMsg());
        assertTrue("Cannot set empty email for user",
            !ar.isSuccess());

        ar = userService.store(this.TEST_USERNAME, "David",
            "Francis", "diff@email.com", "validpwd", 'Y',
                ADMIN_USERNAME);

        logger.debug(ar.getMsg());
        assertTrue("Assigning new email to user is allowed",
            ar.isSuccess());

        logger.debug("\nFINISHED testAddNew()\n");
    }


    @Test
    public void testRemove() throws Exception {

        String ADMIN_USERNAME = "bjones";
        Calendar DEFAULT_START_DATE = Calendar.getInstance();
        Calendar DEFAULT_END_DATE = Calendar.getInstance();
        DEFAULT_START_DATE.set(Calendar.YEAR, 1900);
        DEFAULT_END_DATE.set(Calendar.YEAR, 3000);

        logger.debug("\nSTARTED testRemove()\n");

        User user1 = userDao.find(TEST_USERNAME);

        List<TaskLog> logs = taskLogDao.findByUser(user1,
            DEFAULT_START_DATE.getTime(),
                DEFAULT_END_DATE.getTime());
```

```
Result<User> ar;

if (logs.isEmpty()) {

    ar = userService.remove(TEST_USERNAME,
      ADMIN_USERNAME);
    logger.debug(ar.getMsg());
    assertTrue("Delete of user should be allowed as no
      task logs assigned!", ar.isSuccess());

} else {

    // this user has task log assigned
    ar = userService.remove(TEST_USERNAME,
      ADMIN_USERNAME);
    logger.debug(ar.getMsg());
    assertTrue("Cascading delete of user to task logs not
      allowed!", !ar.isSuccess());

}

logs = taskLogDao.findByUser(user1,
  DEFAULT_START_DATE.getTime(),
    DEFAULT_END_DATE.getTime());
if (logs.isEmpty()) {

    ar = userService.remove(TEST_USERNAME,
      ADMIN_USERNAME);
    logger.debug(ar.getMsg());
    assertTrue("Delete of user should be allowed as empty
      task log list!", ar.isSuccess());

} else {

    // this user has task log assigned
    ar = userService.remove(TEST_USERNAME,
      ADMIN_USERNAME);
    logger.debug(ar.getMsg());
    assertTrue("Cascading delete of user to task logs not
      allowed!", !ar.isSuccess());

}
```

```
        ar = userService.remove(ADMIN_USERNAME, ADMIN_USERNAME);
        logger.debug(ar.getMsg());
        assertTrue("Should not be able to delete yourself",
            !ar.isSuccess());

        logger.debug("\nFINISHED testRemove()\n");
    }

    @Test
    public void testLogon() {

        Result<User> ar =
            userService.findByUsernamePassword("jsmith", "admin");

        assertTrue("Valid user could not be found for valid
            user/pwd", ar.getData() != null);
        assertTrue(ar.isSuccess());

        ar = userService.findByUsernamePassword("jsmith",
            "ADMIN");

        assertTrue("Invalid logic - valid user found with
            UPPERCASE password", ar.getData() == null);
        assertTrue(!ar.isSuccess());

        ar =
            userService.findByUsernamePassword("JS@tttracker.com",
                "admin");

        assertTrue("Valid user could not be found for valid
            email/pwd", ar.getData() != null);
        assertTrue(ar.isSuccess());

        ar = userService.findByUsernamePassword("jsmith",
            "invalidadmin");
        assertTrue("Invalid user verified with wrong password",
            ar.getData() == null);
        assertTrue(!ar.isSuccess());

        ar = userService.findByUsernamePassword("blah", "blah");
        assertTrue("Invalid user verified with wrong username and
            password", ar.getData() == null);
        assertTrue(!ar.isSuccess());
    }
}
```

Note we have not yet defined the implementation of the `UserService` interface but we have already written test cases. Thanks to the use of Java interfaces, we are able to define test cases before the implementation has been coded. This is one of the key concepts of **Test-driven Development (TDD)**, where developers write test cases that define the desired behavior before writing the actual code that passes the tests. This strategy is also part of the test-first programming concept of Extreme Programming (`http://en.wikipedia.org/wiki/Extreme_programming`), where test cases are written before the implementation coding starts.

Executing the `UserServiceTest` test file when the `UserServiceImpl` has been coded should result in the following output:

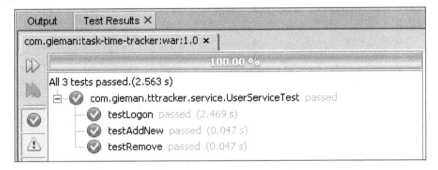

Automating the service layer tests

Updating the `pom.xml` as follows will include the service layer test cases during the Maven build process:

```
<plugin>
  <groupId>org.apache.maven.plugins</groupId>
  <artifactId>maven-surefire-plugin</artifactId>
    <version>2.14.1</version>
  <configuration>
    <skipTests>false</skipTests>
    <includes>
      <include>**/dao/*Test.java</include>
      <include>**/service/*Test.java</include>
    </includes>
    <argLine>-javaagent:target/lib/spring-instrument-
      ${spring.version}.jar</argLine>
  </configuration>
</plugin>
```

Selecting **Run | Test Project** from the **NetBeans** menu will then execute all test cases from both the `dao` and `service` packages, resulting in the following output:

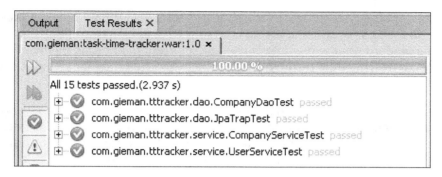

We leave it to you to add test cases for the remaining service layer implementations.

Exercises

Implement the `ProjectServiceImpl` and `UserServiceImpl` interfaces as required by their interface definitions. Business logic to consider when implementing the `UserServiceImpl` are as follows:

- Only an admin user may modify data
- The `email` address may not be empty
- The `password` may not be zero length
- The `adminRole` flag must be either `Y` or `N`
- Users are not allowed to delete themselves
- Users cannot be deleted if they have task logs assigned

Confirm your `UserServiceImpl` implementation by executing the `UserServiceTest` test case.

Summary

The service layer is the most valuable asset an enterprise application possesses. It is the core of all business logic processing and is the layer that holds the most detailed code. Our service layer has no coupling with the DAO implementation and is independent of how the data is used. It is purely focused on business logic operations, delivering data through a simple, generically typed value object using the data transfer object design pattern.

Our service layer implementation has clearly defined entry points for business logic operations. This is achieved through Java interfaces that define all publicly accessible methods. The use of interfaces also enables us to write test cases prior to coding the implementations — a core principle of test-driven development and extreme programming. In the following chapter, we will use these interfaces to define a request handling layer for web clients.

7
The Web Request
Handling Layer

The request handling layer is the glue that binds the HTTP client to the services provided by your application. It is the interpretation of requests and the transfer of data that is the realm of this layer. Our focus will be on the data that is consumed and submitted by Ext JS 4 clients. This data is in JSON format and we will hence discuss JSON parsing and generation using the Java API for JSON Processing. It is important to note, however, that any type of data can be exposed by an appropriate request handling implementation. It is just as easy to implement an RMI or RESTful interface, if required.

A brief history of Web MVC

It may seem strange to discuss the **Model-View-Controller** (**MVC**) paradigm in a historical context, as a majority of web applications still use this technology today. The MVC design pattern first came to prominence in the early 2000's with the open source Struts framework. This framework encouraged the use of MVC architecture to promote a clear demarcation of responsibilities when processing and serving requests. The MVC paradigm for server-side Java development has been around ever since in a variety of formats, culminating in the well-designed and powerful Spring MVC framework.

The rationale for using an MVC approach is quite simple. The web layer implementing interactions between the clients and the application can be divided into the following three different kinds of objects:

- Model objects that represent the data
- View objects that have the responsibility of displaying the data
- Controller objects that respond to actions and provide model data for the view object to process

Each MVC object would behave independently with loose coupling. For example, the view technology was of no concern to the controller. It did not matter if the view was generated by a FreeMarker template, an XSLT transformation, or a combination of Tiles and JSPs. The controller would simply pass on the responsibility to the view object to process the model data.

One important point to note in this historical discussion is that all of the MVC processing was performed *on the server*. With the rise in the number of JavaScript frameworks, in particular for Ext JS 4, the MVC paradigm has been moved from the server to the client browser. This is a fundamental change to how web applications are being developed and is the very reason that you are reading this book!

Request handling for enterprise web applications

The following diagram clearly identifies where the request handling layer resides in the overall application architecture:

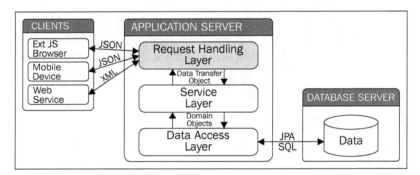

The request handling layer accepts client requests and forwards the respective action to the appropriate service layer method. The returned DTO (or Value Object as it is also known in Domain-Driven Design) is examined and an appropriate response is then sent to the client. Unlike the historical server-side MVC programming, the request handling layer has no knowledge of presentation and simply acts as a request-processing interface to the application.

Building the request handling layer

The web request handling layer for Ext JS 4 clients is a JSON-generating proxy to the service layer interfaces. The domain entities are converted into JSON representations within this layer; so our first step is to create some helper code to make this task easier.

There are several excellent open source JSON generation projects that can assist in this task including Jackson (`http://jackson.codehaus.org`) and Google Gson (`http://code.google.com/p/google-gson/`). Such libraries parse POJOs into an appropriate JSON representation via their declared fields. With the release of Java EE 7, we no longer have a need for third-party libraries. The Java API for JSON Processing (JSR-353) is available in all Java EE 7-compliant application servers including GlassFish 4. We will leverage this API for generating and parsing JSON data.

 If you are unable to use a Java EE 7 application server, you will need to select an alternate JSON-generating strategy, such as Jackson or Google Gson.

Preparing for JSON generation

Our first addition is a new domain interface:

```
package com.gieman.tttracker.domain;

import javax.json.JsonObject;
import javax.json.JsonObjectBuilder;

public interface JsonItem{

    public JsonObject toJson();
    public void addJson(JsonObjectBuilder builder);

}
```

This very simple interface defines two methods to help with JSON generation. The `toJson` method creates a `JsonObject` that represents the entity. The `addJson` method adds the entity properties to a `JsonObjectBuilder` interface. We will see how these two methods are used very soon.

Each of our domain entities will need to implement the `JsonItem` interface, and this can be achieved by simply adding the interface to the abstract superclass of all the domain entities:

```
package com.gieman.tttracker.domain;

import java.io.Serializable;
import java.text.SimpleDateFormat;
import javax.json.Json;
import javax.json.JsonObject;
import javax.json.JsonObjectBuilder;
```

```java
public abstract class AbstractEntity implements JsonItem,
Serializable{

    @Override
    public JsonObject toJson() {

        JsonObjectBuilder builder = Json.createObjectBuilder();
        addJson(builder);
        return builder.build();
    }

}
```

The `JsonObjectBuilder` interface defines a set of methods that add the name/value pairs to the JSON object associated with the builder. The `builder` instance adds the fields defined in the descendent classes that implement the `addJson` method. We will start with the `Company` object.

Implementing the Company addJson method

The `addJson` method that needs to be added to the `Company` class is as follows:

```java
@Override
public void addJson(JsonObjectBuilder builder) {
  builder.add("idCompany", idCompany)
     .add("companyName", companyName);
}
```

The `JsonObject` representation of the `Company` instance is created by calling the `builder.build()` method in the superclass. The generated `JsonObject` can then be written by a `JsonWriter` instance to an output source.

Implementing the Project addJson method

The `addJson` method that needs to be added to the `Project` class is as follows:

```java
@Override
public void addJson(JsonObjectBuilder builder) {

  builder.add("idProject", idProject)
     .add("projectName", projectName);

  if(company != null){
     company.addJson(builder);
  }
}
```

Note that it is always a good practice to perform `null` object tests before accessing the object methods. It is possible to create a `project` object without a `company` instance and hence we perform the `company != null` test prior to adding the `company` JSON properties to the project `builder` instance. We could have used the following code to add the `company` properties to the project `builder` instance directly:

```
builder.add("idProject", idProject)
     .add("projectName", projectName)
.add("idCompany", company.getIdCompany() )
     .add("companyName", company.getCompanyName() );
```

However, we would now have replicated the `builder.add("idCompany"...)` code across two classes (`Company.addJson` and `Project.addJson`), thus making the future maintenance prone to errors. Changing the JSON property name from `idCompany` to `companyId`, for example, would require the scanning of code to check for possible usage across all classes, not just the `Company` class. The creation of `Company` JSON should belong with the `Company` class as we have implemented.

Implementing the Task addJson method

This `Task` class will implement the `addJson` method as follows:

```
@Override
public void addJson(JsonObjectBuilder builder) {

   builder .add("idTask", idTask)
       .add("taskName", taskName);

   if(project != null){
      project.addJson(builder);

      Company company = project.getCompany();
      company.addJson(builder);
   }
}
```

Note once again how we chain the call to `addJson` for both the `project` and `company` classes to add their JSON properties to the task's `builder` instance.

Implementing the User addJson method

The `User.addJson` method is defined as follows:

```
@Override
public void addJson(JsonObjectBuilder builder) {

    builder.add("username", username)
        .add("firstName", firstName)
        .add("lastName", lastName)
        .add("email", email)
        .add("adminRole", adminRole + "")
        .add("fullName", firstName + " " + lastName);
}
```

The `fullName` property is for convenience only; we can just as easily create a `fullName` field that concatenates the `firstName` and `lastName` fields in our Ext JS code. However, keeping this code at the source of the JSON generation allows for easier maintenance. Consider the business change request "add a `middleName` field to the `User` entity". The `fullName` inclusion of the new `middleName` field is then a trivial exercise and would be available to the Ext JS client without any further changes.

Implementing the TaskLog addJson method

The `addJson` method adds all of the `TaskLog` fields to the `builder` instance. The `DATE_FORMAT_yyyyMMdd` constant is used to format the `taskLogDate` to an 8-digit representation of the year/month/day and is added to the `TaskLog` class as follows:

```
static final SimpleDateFormat DATE_FORMAT_yyyyMMdd = new
SimpleDateFormat("yyyyMMdd");
```

The `addJson` method will use the `SimpleDateFormat` instance to format the `taskLogDate` field:

```
public void addJson(JsonObjectBuilder builder) {

    builder.add("idTaskLog", idTaskLog)
      .add("taskDescription", taskDescription)
      .add("taskLogDate", taskLogDate == null ? "" : DATE_FORMAT_
yyyyMMdd.format(taskLogDate))
      .add("taskMinutes", taskMinutes);

    if (user != null) {
      user.addJson(builder);
    }
    if (task != null) {
      task.addJson(builder);
    }
}
```

The `taskLogDate` field is being formatted in a way that cannot be misunderstood when converting to a JavaScript `Date` object in Ext JS clients. Without the use of the `SimpleDateFormat` instance, the `builder` instance would call the default `toString` method on the `taskLogDate` object to retrieve the String representation, resulting in an output similar to the following:

```
Wed Aug 14 00:00:00 EST 2013
```

Using the `SimpleDateFormat` instance configured with a date pattern of `yyyyMMdd` will ensure that such a date is formatted to `20130814`.

> Date formatting in enterprise applications can cause many issues if not approached with a standard strategy. This is even more applicable when we are developing applications to be used worldwide, with multiple timezones and different languages. The dates should always be formatted in a way that can be interpreted in the same way regardless of language, timezone, and user preferences.

A note on JSON

We will be using JSON to transmit data between the GlassFish server and the Ext JS client. The transfer is bidirectional; the server will send the JSON data to the Ext JS client, and the Ext JS client will be sending the data in the JSON format back to the server. The server and client will consume *and* produce the JSON data.

There are no rules for structuring the JSON data as long as it conforms to the specifications (`http://tools.ietf.org/html/rfc4627`). Ext JS 4 models allow any form of valid JSON structure through the use of associations; our approach keeps the JSON structure to its simplest form. The previously defined `addJson` methods return simple, flat data structures without nesting or arrays. As an example, a `task` instance could be serialized into the following JSON object (formatting included for readability):

```
{
    success: true,
    data: {
        "idTask": 1,
        "taskName": "Write Chapter 7",
        "idProject": 1,
        "projectName": "My Book Project",
        "idCompany": 1,
        "companyName": "PACKT Publishing"
    }
}
```

The `data` payload represents the `task` object that will be consumed by the Ext JS 4 client. We could have defined the JSON representation of the `task` object as follows:

```
{
    success: true,
    data: {
        "idTask": 1,
        "taskName": "Write Chapter 7",
        "project": {
            "idProject": 1,
            "projectName": "My Book Project ",
            "company": {
                "idCompany": 1,
                "companyName": "PACKT Publishing"
            }
        }
    }
}
```

In this structure we see that the `task` instance belongs to a `project`, which in turn belongs to a `company`. Both these JSON representations are legal; they both contain the same `task` data in valid JSON format. However, which of these two will be easier to parse? Which will be easier to debug? As an enterprise application developer we should always keep the KISS principle in mind. The **Keep It Simple, Stupid (KISS)** principle states that most systems work best if they are kept simple and unnecessary complexities should be avoided.

> Keep your JSON simple! We know that complex structures are possible; this is achieved only through additional complexities when defining the Ext JS 4 models along with the associated data processing when reading or writing JSON data. A simple JSON structure is easier to understand and maintain.

Creating the request handlers

We will now build the handlers that are used to serve the HTTP requests from our Ext JS client. These handlers will be added to a new `web` directory, as shown in the following screenshot:

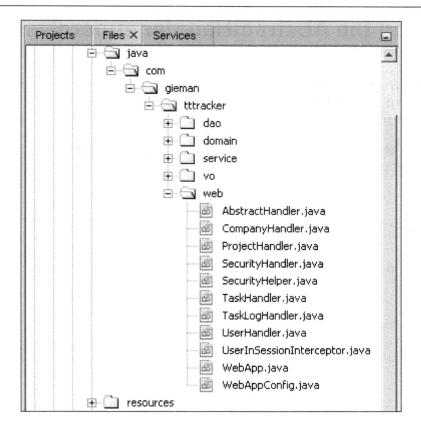

Each handler will use the Spring Framework @Controller annotation to indicate that the class serves the role of a "controller". Strictly speaking, the handlers that we will be defining are *not* controllers in the traditional sense of a Spring MVC application. We will only be using a very small portion of the available Spring controller functionality to process requests. This will ensure that our request handling layer is very lightweight and easy to maintain. As always, we will start by creating a base class that all the handlers will implement.

Defining the AbstractHandler superclass

The AbstractHandler superclass defines several important methods that are used to simplify JSON generation. As we are working toward integration with Ext JS 4 clients, the structure of the JSON object generated by our handlers is specific to data structures expected by Ext JS 4 components. We will always generate a JSON object with a success property that holds a Boolean true or false value. Likewise, we will always generate a JSON object with a payload property named data. This data property will have a valid JSON object as its value, either as a simple JSON object or as a JSON array.

> Remember that all of the generated JSON objects will be in a format that can be consumed by Ext JS 4 components without the need for additional configuration.

The definition of the AbstractHandler class is as follows:

```
package com.gieman.tttracker.web;

import com.gieman.tttracker.domain.JsonItem;
import java.io.StringReader;
import java.io.StringWriter;
import java.util.List;
import javax.json.Json;
import javax.json.JsonArrayBuilder;
import javax.json.JsonNumber;
import javax.json.JsonObject;
import javax.json.JsonObjectBuilder;
import javax.json.JsonReader;
import javax.json.JsonValue;
import javax.json.JsonWriter;
import org.slf4j.Logger;
import org.slf4j.LoggerFactory;

public abstract class AbstractHandler {

    protected final Logger logger = LoggerFactory.getLogger(this.
getClass());

    public static String getJsonSuccessData(List<? extends JsonItem>
results) {

        final JsonObjectBuilder builder = Json.createObjectBuilder();
        builder.add("success", true);
```

```
        final JsonArrayBuilder arrayBuilder = Json.
createArrayBuilder();

        for (JsonItem ji : results) {

            arrayBuilder.add(ji.toJson());
        }

        builder.add("data", arrayBuilder);

        return toJsonString(builder.build());
    }

    public static String getJsonSuccessData(JsonItem jsonItem) {

        final JsonObjectBuilder builder = Json.createObjectBuilder();
        builder.add("success", true);
        builder.add("data", jsonItem.toJson());

        return toJsonString(builder.build());

    }

    public static String getJsonSuccessData(JsonItem jsonItem, int
totalCount) {

        final JsonObjectBuilder builder = Json.createObjectBuilder();
        builder.add("success", true);
        builder.add("total", totalCount);
        builder.add("data", jsonItem.toJson());

        return toJsonString(builder.build());
    }

    public static String getJsonErrorMsg(String theErrorMessage) {

        return getJsonMsg(theErrorMessage, false);

    }

    public static String getJsonSuccessMsg(String msg) {

        return getJsonMsg(msg, true);
    }
```

```java
public static String getJsonMsg(String msg, boolean success) {

    final JsonObjectBuilder builder = Json.createObjectBuilder();
    builder.add("success", success);
    builder.add("msg", msg);

    return toJsonString(builder.build());

}

public static String toJsonString(JsonObject model) {

    final StringWriter stWriter = new StringWriter();

    try (JsonWriter jsonWriter = Json.createWriter(stWriter)) {
        jsonWriter.writeObject(model);
    }

    return stWriter.toString();
}

protected JsonObject parseJsonObject(String jsonString) {

    JsonReader reader = Json.createReader(new
StringReader(jsonString));
    return reader.readObject();

}
protected Integer getIntegerValue(JsonValue jsonValue) {

    Integer value = null;

    switch (jsonValue.getValueType()) {

        case NUMBER:
            JsonNumber num = (JsonNumber) jsonValue;
            value = num.intValue();
            break;
        case NULL:
            break;
    }

    return value;
}
}
```

The overloaded `getJsonSuccessData` methods will each generate a JSON string with the `success` property set to `true` and an appropriate `data` JSON payload. The `getJsonXXXMsg` variants will also generate a JSON String with an appropriate `success` property (either `true` for a successful action or `false` for a failed action) and an `msg` property that holds the appropriate message for consumption by the Ext JS component.

The `parseJsonObject` method will parse a JSON string *into* a `JsonObject` using the `JsonReader` instance. The `toJsonString` method will *write* a `JsonObject` to its JSON string representation using the `JsonWriter` instance. These classes are part of the Java EE 7 `javax.json` package, and they make working with JSON very easy.

The `getIntegerValue` method is used to parse a `JsonValue` object into an `Integer` type. A `JsonValue` object may be of several different types as defined by the `javax.json.jsonValue.ValueType` constants, and appropriate checks are performed on the value prior to attempting to parse the `JsonValue` object into an `Integer`. This will allow us to send JSON data from Ext JS clients in the following form:

```
{
    success: true,
    data: {
        "idCompany":null,
        "companyName": "New Company"
    }
}
```

Note that the `idCompany` property has a value of `null`. The `getIntegerValue` method allows us to parse integers that *may* be `null`, something that is not possible when using the default `JsonObject.getInt(key)` method (which throws an exception if a `null` value is encountered).

Let's now define our first handler class that will process user authentication.

Defining the SecurityHandler class

We first define a simple helper class that can be used to verify whether a user session is active:

```
package com.gieman.tttracker.web;

import com.gieman.tttracker.domain.User;
import javax.servlet.http.HttpServletRequest;
import javax.servlet.http.HttpSession;

public class SecurityHelper {
```

```
        static final String SESSION_ATTRIB_USER = "sessionuser";

    public static User getSessionUser(HttpServletRequest request) {
        User user = null;
        HttpSession session = request.getSession(true);
        Object obj = session.getAttribute(SESSION_ATTRIB_USER);

        if (obj != null && obj instanceof User) {
            user = (User) obj;
        }
        return user;
    }
}
```

The static constant SESSION_ATTRIB_USER will be used as the name of the session property that holds the authenticated user. All handler classes will call the SecurityHelper.getSessionUser method to retrieve the authenticated user from the session. A user session may time out due to inactivity, and the HTTP session will then be removed by the application server. When this happens, the SecurityHelper.getSessionUser method will return null, and the 3T application must handle this gracefully.

The SecurityHandler class is used to authenticate the user credentials. If a user is successfully authenticated, the user object is stored in the HTTP session using the SESSION_ATTRIB_USER attribute. It is also possible for the user to log out of the 3T application by clicking on the **Log Out** button. In this case the user is removed from the session.

The verification and logout functionalities are implemented as follows:

```
package com.gieman.tttracker.web;

import com.gieman.tttracker.domain.User;
import com.gieman.tttracker.service.UserService;
import com.gieman.tttracker.vo.Result;
import static com.gieman.tttracker.web.AbstractHandler.
getJsonErrorMsg;
import static com.gieman.tttracker.web.SecurityHelper.SESSION_ATTRIB_
USER;
import javax.servlet.http.HttpServletRequest;
import javax.servlet.http.HttpSession;
import org.springframework.beans.factory.annotation.Autowired;
import org.springframework.stereotype.Controller;
import org.springframework.web.bind.annotation.RequestMapping;
import org.springframework.web.bind.annotation.RequestMethod;
```

```
import org.springframework.web.bind.annotation.RequestParam;
import org.springframework.web.bind.annotation.ResponseBody;

@Controller
@RequestMapping("/security")
public class SecurityHandler extends AbstractHandler {

    @Autowired
    protected UserService userService;

    @RequestMapping(value = "/logon", method = RequestMethod.POST,
produces = {"application/json"})
    @ResponseBody
    public String logon(
            @RequestParam(value = "username", required = true) String
username,
            @RequestParam(value = "password", required = true) String
password,
            HttpServletRequest request) {

        Result<User> ar = userService.findByUsernamePassword(username,
password);

        if (ar.isSuccess()) {
            User user = ar.getData();
            HttpSession session = request.getSession(true);
            session.setAttribute(SESSION_ATTRIB_USER, user);
            return getJsonSuccessData(user);
        } else {
            return getJsonErrorMsg(ar.getMsg());
        }
    }

    @RequestMapping(value = "/logout", produces = {"application/
json"})
    @ResponseBody
    public String logout(HttpServletRequest request) {

        HttpSession session = request.getSession(true);
        session.removeAttribute(SESSION_ATTRIB_USER);
        return getJsonSuccessMsg("User logged out...");
    }
}
```

The `SecurityHandler` class introduces many new Spring annotations and concepts that need to be explained in detail.

The @Controller and @RequestMapping annotations

The `@Controller` annotation indicates that this class serves the role of a Spring controller. The `@Controller` annotated classes are autodetected by Spring component scanning, the configuration of which is defined later in this chapter. But what exactly is a controller?

A Spring controller is part of the Spring MVC framework and usually acts with models and views to process requests. We have no need for either models or views; in fact, our processing lifecycle is managed entirely by the controller itself. Each controller is responsible for a URL mapping as defined in the class-level `@RequestMapping` annotation. This mapping maps a URL path to the controller. In our 3T application, any URL starting with `/security/` will be directed to the `SecurityHandler` class for further processing. Any subpath will then be used to match a method-level `@RequestMapping` annotation. We have two methods defined, each with their own unique mapping. This results in the following URL path-to-method mappings:

- `/security/logon` will map to the `logon` method
- `/security/logout` will map to the `logout` method

Any other URL starting with `/security/` will not match the defined methods and would produce a `404` error.

The name of the method is not important; it is the `@RequestMapping` annotation that defines the method used to serve a request.

There are two additional properties defined in the `logon` `@RequestMapping` annotation. The `method=RequestMethod.POST` property specifies that the logon request URL `/security/logon` must be submitted as a `POST` request. If any other request type was used for the `/security/logon` submission, a `404` error would be returned. Ext JS 4 stores and models using AJAX will submit `POST` requests by default. Actions that read data, however, will be submitted using a `GET` request unless configured otherwise. The other possible methods used in RESTful web services include `PUT` and `DELETE`, but we will only define the `GET` and `POST` requests in our application.

It is considered a best practice to ensure that each @RequestMapping method has an appropriate RequestMethod defined. The actions that modify data should always be submitted using a POST request. The actions that hold sensitive data (for example, passwords) should also be submitted using a POST request to ensure that the data is not sent in a URL-encoded format. The read actions may be sent as either a GET or a POST request depending on your application needs.

The produces = {"application/json"} property defines the producible media types of the mapped request. All of our requests will produce JSON data that has the media type application/json. Each HTTP request submitted by a browser has an Accept header, such as:

```
text/html,application/xhtml+xml,application/xml;q=0.9,*/*;q=0.8
```

If the Accept request does not include the produces property media type, then the following 406 Not Acceptable error is returned by the GlassFish 4 server:

```
The resource identified by this request is only capable of generating
responses with characteristics not acceptable according to the request
"accept" headers.
```

All modern browsers will accept the application/json content type.

The @ResponseBody annotation

This annotation is used by Spring to identify the methods that should return the content directly to the HTTP response output stream (not placed in a model or interpreted as a view name, which is the default Spring MVC behavior). How this is achieved will depend on the return type of the method. All of our request handling methods will return Java Strings, and Spring will internally use a StringHttpMessageConverter instance to write the String to the HTTP response output stream with a Content-Type of value text/plain. This is a very easy way of returning JSON data object String to an HTTP client and thus makes request handling a trivial process.

The @RequestParam annotation

This annotation on a method argument maps a request parameter to the argument itself. In the logon method we have the following definition:

```
@RequestParam(value = "username", required = true) String
username,
@RequestParam(value = "password", required = true) String
password,
```

Assuming that the `logon` method was of the type GET (it is set to POST in the `SecurityHandler` class, and hence the following URL encoding would not work), a URL such as the following would call the method with a `username` value of `bjones` and a `password` value of `admin`:

`/security/logon.json?username=bjones&password=admin`

We could just as easily have written this method with the following definition:

```
@RequestParam(value = "user", required = true) String username,
@RequestParam(value = "pwd", required = true) String password,
```

This would then map a URL of the following form:

`/security/logon.json?user=bjones&pwd=admin`

Note that it is the `value` property of the `@RequestParam` annotation that maps to the request parameter name.

The `required` property of the `@RequestParam` annotation defines if this parameter is a required field. The following URL would result in an exception:

`/security/logon.json?username=bjones`

The password parameter is obviously missing, which does not adhere to the `required=true` definition.

Note that the `required=true` property only checks for the existence of a request parameter that matches the `value` of the `@RequestParam` annotation. It is entirely valid to have a request parameter that is empty. The following URL would not throw an exception:

`/security/logon.json?username=bjones&password=`

Optional parameters may be defined by using the `required=false` property and may also include a `defaultValue`. Consider the following method argument:

```
@RequestParam(value = "address", required = false, defaultValue =
"Unknown address") String address
```

Also consider the following three URLs:

- `/user/address.json?address=Melbourne`
- `/user/address.json?address=`
- `/user/address.json?`

The first URL will result in an address value `Melbourne`, the second URL will have a null address, and the third URL will have an "unknown address". Note that the `defaultValue` will only be used if the request does not have a valid address parameter, and not if the address parameter is empty.

Authenticating a user

The `logon` method in our `SecurityHandler` class is very simple thanks to our implementation of the service-layer business logic. We call the `userService.findByUsernamePassword(username, password)` method and check the returned `Result`. If the `Result` is successful, the `SecurityHandler.logon` method will return a JSON representation of the authenticated user. This is achieved by the line `getJsonSuccessData(user)`, which will result in the following output being written to the HTTP response:

```
{
    "success": true,
    "data": {
        "username": "bjones",
        "firstName": "Betty",
        "lastName": "Jones",
        "email": "bj@tttracker.com",
        "adminRole": "Y",
        "fullName": "Betty Jones"
    }
}
```

Note that the preceding formatting is for readability only. The actual response will be a stream of characters. The authenticated user is then added to the HTTP session with the attribute `SESSION_ATTRIB_USER`. We are then able to identify the authenticated user by calling `SecurityHelper.getSessionUser(request)` in our request handlers.

A `Result` instance that has failed will call the `getJsonErrorMsg(ar.getMsg())` method, which will result in the following JSON object being returned in the HTTP response:

```
{
    "success": false,
    "msg": "Unable to verify user/password combination!"
}
```

The `msg` text is set on the `Result` instance in the `UserServiceImpl.findByUsernamePassword` method. The Ext JS frontend will process each result differently depending on the `success` property.

Logging out

The logic in this method is very simple: remove the user from the session and return a successful JSON message. The Ext JS frontend will then take an appropriate action. There is no `RequestMethod` defined in the `@RequestMapping` annotation as no data is being sent. This means that any `RequestMethod` may be used to map this URL (`GET`, `POST`, and so on). The JSON object returned from this method is as follows:

```
{
    "success": true,
    "msg": "User logged out..."
}
```

Defining the CompanyHandler class

This handler processes company actions and is mapped to the `/company/` URL pattern.

```java
package com.gieman.tttracker.web;

import com.gieman.tttracker.domain.*;
import com.gieman.tttracker.service.CompanyService;
import com.gieman.tttracker.service.ProjectService;

import com.gieman.tttracker.vo.Result;
import static com.gieman.tttracker.web.SecurityHelper.getSessionUser;

import java.util.List;
import javax.json.JsonObject;
import javax.servlet.http.HttpServletRequest;
import org.springframework.beans.factory.annotation.Autowired;

import org.springframework.stereotype.Controller;
import org.springframework.web.bind.annotation.RequestMapping;
import org.springframework.web.bind.annotation.RequestMethod;
import org.springframework.web.bind.annotation.ResponseBody;
import org.springframework.web.bind.annotation.RequestParam;

@Controller
@RequestMapping("/company")
public class CompanyHandler extends AbstractHandler {

    @Autowired
    protected CompanyService companyService;
    @Autowired
    protected ProjectService projectService;
```

```
    @RequestMapping(value = "/find", method = RequestMethod.GET,
produces = {"application/json"})
    @ResponseBody
    public String find(
            @RequestParam(value = "idCompany", required = true)
Integer idCompany,
            HttpServletRequest request) {

        User sessionUser = getSessionUser(request);
        if (sessionUser == null) {
            return getJsonErrorMsg("User is not logged on");
        }

        Result<Company> ar = companyService.find(idCompany,
sessionUser.getUsername());

        if (ar.isSuccess()) {

            return getJsonSuccessData(ar.getData());

        } else {

            return getJsonErrorMsg(ar.getMsg());

        }
    }

    @RequestMapping(value = "/store", method = RequestMethod.POST,
produces = {"application/json"})
    @ResponseBody
    public String store(
            @RequestParam(value = "data", required = true) String
jsonData,
            HttpServletRequest request) {

        User sessionUser = getSessionUser(request);
        if (sessionUser == null) {
            return getJsonErrorMsg("User is not logged on");
        }

        JsonObject jsonObj = parseJsonObject(jsonData);

        Result<Company> ar = companyService.store(
                getIntegerValue(jsonObj.get("idCompany")),
                jsonObj.getString("companyName"),
```

```
                        sessionUser.getUsername());

        if (ar.isSuccess()) {

            return getJsonSuccessData(ar.getData());

        } else {

            return getJsonErrorMsg(ar.getMsg());

        }
    }

    @RequestMapping(value = "/findAll", method = RequestMethod.GET,
produces = {"application/json"})
    @ResponseBody
    public String findAll(HttpServletRequest request) {

        User sessionUser = getSessionUser(request);
        if (sessionUser == null) {
            return getJsonErrorMsg("User is not logged on");
        }

        Result<List<Company>> ar = companyService.findAll(sessionUser.
getUsername());

        if (ar.isSuccess()) {

            return getJsonSuccessData(ar.getData());

        } else {

            return getJsonErrorMsg(ar.getMsg());

        }
    }

    @RequestMapping(value = "/remove", method = RequestMethod.POST,
produces = {"application/json"})
    @ResponseBody
    public String remove(
            @RequestParam(value = "data", required = true) String
jsonData,
            HttpServletRequest request) {
```

```
    User sessionUser = getSessionUser(request);
    if (sessionUser == null) {
        return getJsonErrorMsg("User is not logged on");
    }

    JsonObject jsonObj = parseJsonObject(jsonData);

    Result<Company> ar = companyService.remove(
            getIntegerValue(jsonObj.get("idCompany")),
            sessionUser.getUsername());

    if (ar.isSuccess()) {

        return getJsonSuccessMsg(ar.getMsg());

    } else {

        return getJsonErrorMsg(ar.getMsg());

    }
  }
}
```

Each method is mapped to a different sub URL as defined by the method-level `@RequestMapping` annotation. The `CompanyHandler` class will hence be mapped to the following URLs:

- `/company/find` will map it to the `find` method using a GET request
- `/company/store` will map it to the `store` method using a POST request
- `/company/findAll` will map it to the `findAll` method using a GET request
- `/company/remove` will map it to the `remove` method using a POST request

The following are a few things to note:

- Each handler method is defined with either a `RequestMethod.POST` or `RequestMethod.GET`. The GET method is used for finder methods, and the POST method is used for data-modifying methods. These method types are the defaults used by Ext JS for each action.
- Each method retrieves the user from the HTTP session by calling `getSessionUser(request)` and then tests if the `user` value is `null`. If the user is not in session, the message `"User is not logged on"` is returned in the JSON-encoded HTTP response.

- The POST methods have a single request parameter that holds the JSON data submitted by the Ext JS client. This JSON string is then parsed into a JsonObject before calling the appropriate service layer method using the required parameters.

A typical JSON data payload for adding a new company would look like the following:

```
{"idCompany":null,"companyName":"New Company"}
```

Note that the idCompany value is null. If you are modifying an existing company record, the JSON data payload must contain a valid idCompany value:

```
{"idCompany":5,"companyName":"Existing Company"}
```

Note also that the JSON data holds exactly one company record. It is possible to configure Ext JS clients to submit multiple records per request by submitting a JSON array similar to the following array:

```
[
    {"idCompany":5,"companyName":"Existing Company"},
    {"idCompany":4,"companyName":"Another Existing Company"}
]
```

However, we will restrict our logic to processing a single record per request.

Defining the ProjectHandler class

The ProjectHandler class processes the project actions and is mapped to the /project/ URL pattern as follows:

```
package com.gieman.tttracker.web;

import com.gieman.tttracker.domain.*;
import com.gieman.tttracker.service.ProjectService;
import com.gieman.tttracker.vo.Result;
import static com.gieman.tttracker.web.SecurityHelper.getSessionUser;

import java.util.List;
import javax.json.JsonObject;
import javax.servlet.http.HttpServletRequest;
import org.springframework.beans.factory.annotation.Autowired;

import org.springframework.stereotype.Controller;
import org.springframework.web.bind.annotation.RequestMapping;
import org.springframework.web.bind.annotation.RequestMethod;
import org.springframework.web.bind.annotation.ResponseBody;
```

```
import org.springframework.web.bind.annotation.RequestParam;

@Controller
@RequestMapping("/project")
public class ProjectHandler extends AbstractHandler {

    @Autowired
    protected ProjectService projectService;

    @RequestMapping(value = "/find", method = RequestMethod.GET,
produces = {"application/json"})
    @ResponseBody
    public String find(
            @RequestParam(value = "idProject", required = true)
Integer idProject,
            HttpServletRequest request) {

        User sessionUser = getSessionUser(request);
        if (sessionUser == null) {
            return getJsonErrorMsg("User is not logged on");
        }

        Result<Project> ar = projectService.find(idProject,
sessionUser.getUsername());

        if (ar.isSuccess()) {
            return getJsonSuccessData(ar.getData());
        } else {
            return getJsonErrorMsg(ar.getMsg());
        }
    }

    @RequestMapping(value = "/store", method = RequestMethod.POST,
produces = {"application/json"})
    @ResponseBody
    public String store(
            @RequestParam(value = "data", required = true) String
jsonData,
            HttpServletRequest request) {

        User sessionUser = getSessionUser(request);
        if (sessionUser == null) {
            return getJsonErrorMsg("User is not logged on");
        }
```

```
        JsonObject jsonObj = parseJsonObject(jsonData);

        Result<Project> ar = projectService.store(
                getIntegerValue(jsonObj.get("idProject")),
                getIntegerValue(jsonObj.get("idCompany")),
                jsonObj.getString("projectName"),
                sessionUser.getUsername());

        if (ar.isSuccess()) {
            return getJsonSuccessData(ar.getData());
        } else {
            return getJsonErrorMsg(ar.getMsg());
        }
    }

    @RequestMapping(value = "/remove", method = RequestMethod.POST,
produces = {"application/json"})
    @ResponseBody
    public String remove(
            @RequestParam(value = "data", required = true) String
jsonData,
            HttpServletRequest request) {

        User sessionUser = getSessionUser(request);
        if (sessionUser == null) {
            return getJsonErrorMsg("User is not logged on");
        }

        JsonObject jsonObj = parseJsonObject(jsonData);

        Result<Project> ar = projectService.remove(
                getIntegerValue(jsonObj.get("idProject")),
                sessionUser.getUsername());

        if (ar.isSuccess()) {
            return getJsonSuccessMsg(ar.getMsg());
        } else {
            return getJsonErrorMsg(ar.getMsg());
        }
    }

    @RequestMapping(value = "/findAll", method = RequestMethod.GET,
produces = {"application/json"})
    @ResponseBody
```

```
public String findAll(
        HttpServletRequest request) {

    User sessionUser = getSessionUser(request);
    if (sessionUser == null) {
        return getJsonErrorMsg("User is not logged on");
    }

        Result<List<Project>> ar = projectService.findAll(sessionUser.
getUsername());

    if (ar.isSuccess()) {
        return getJsonSuccessData(ar.getData());
    } else {
        return getJsonErrorMsg(ar.getMsg());
    }
    }
}
```

The `ProjectHandler` class will hence be mapped to the following URLs:

*   `/project/find` will map to the `find` method using a GET request
*   `/project/store` will map to the `store` method using a POST request
*   `/project/findAll` will map to the `findAll` method using a GET request
*   `/project/remove` will map to the `remove` method using a POST request

Note that in the `store` method, we are once again retrieving the required data from the parsed `JsonObject`. The structure of the JSON `data` payload when adding a new project is in the following format:

```
{"idProject":null,"projectName":"New Project","idCompany":1}
```

When updating an existing project, the JSON structure is as follows:

```
{"idProject":7,"projectName":"Existing Project with
ID=7","idCompany":1}
```

You will also notice that we once again have the same block of code replicated in each method, as we did in the `CompanyHandler` class:

```
if (sessionUser == null) {
    return getJsonErrorMsg("User is not logged on");
}
```

Every method in each of the remaining handlers will also require the same check; a user *must* be in session to perform the action. This is precisely why we will simplify our code by introducing the concept of Spring request handler interceptors.

The Spring HandlerInterceptor interface

Spring's request handling mapping mechanism includes the ability to intercept requests by using handler interceptors. These interceptors are used to apply some type of functionality to the requests as in our example of checking whether a user is in session. The interceptors must implement the `HandlerInterceptor` interface from the `org.springframework.web.servlet` package where it is possible to apply the functionality in the following three ways:

- Before the handler method is executed by implementing the `preHandle` method
- After the handler method is executed by implementing the `postHandle` method
- After the complete request has finished execution by implementing the `afterCompletion` method

The `HandlerInterceptorAdapter` abstract class, along with the predefined empty implementations for each method, is normally used to implement custom handlers. Our `UserInSessionInterceptor` class is defined as follows:

```
package com.gieman.tttracker.web;

import com.gieman.tttracker.domain.User;
import static com.gieman.tttracker.web.SecurityHelper.getSessionUser;
import javax.servlet.http.HttpServletRequest;
import javax.servlet.http.HttpServletResponse;
import org.slf4j.Logger;
import org.slf4j.LoggerFactory;
import org.springframework.web.servlet.handler.
HandlerInterceptorAdapter;

public class UserInSessionInterceptor extends
HandlerInterceptorAdapter {

    private final Logger logger = LoggerFactory.getLogger(this.
getClass());

    @Override
```

```
        public boolean preHandle(HttpServletRequest request,
HttpServletResponse response, Object handler)
            throws Exception {

        logger.info("calling preHandle with url=" + request.
getRequestURI());

        User sessionUser = getSessionUser(request);

        if (sessionUser == null) {
            String json = "{\"success\":false,\"msg\":\"A valid user
is not logged on!\"}";
            response.getOutputStream().write(json.getBytes());
            return false;
        } else {
            return true;
        }
    }
}
```

When intercepting a request with the UserInSessionInterceptor, the code in the preHandle method checks if there is a user in session. If a sessionUser is found, the handler returns true to indicate that normal processing should continue. Normal processing may result in additional handler interceptors being called, if configured, before finally reaching the mapped handler method.

If a sessionUser is not found, a simple JSON string is immediately sent to the response output stream. The preHandle method then returns false to indicate that the interceptor has already dealt with the response and no further processing is required.

By applying the UserInSessionInterceptor to each request that requires the user session test, we can remove the following code from each handler method:

```
if (sessionUser == null) {
    return getJsonErrorMsg("User is not logged on");
}
```

How do we apply the interceptor to the appropriate handler methods? This is done when we customize the Spring MVC configuration.

The Spring MVC configuration

The Spring MVC framework can be configured with XML files or Java configuration classes. We will configure our application using Spring MVC configuration classes, the first being the `WebAppConfig` class:

```
package com.gieman.tttracker.web;

import org.springframework.context.annotation.ComponentScan;
import org.springframework.context.annotation.Configuration;
import org.springframework.web.servlet.config.annotation.EnableWebMvc;
import org.springframework.web.servlet.config.annotation.
InterceptorRegistry;
import org.springframework.web.servlet.config.annotation.
WebMvcConfigurerAdapter;

@EnableWebMvc
@Configuration
@ComponentScan("com.gieman.tttracker.web")
public class WebAppConfig extends WebMvcConfigurerAdapter {

    @Override
    public void addInterceptors(InterceptorRegistry registry) {
        registry.addInterceptor(new UserInSessionInterceptor())
                .addPathPatterns(new String[]{
                    "/**"
                }).excludePathPatterns("/security/**");
    }
}
```

The `WebAppConfig` class extends `WebMvcConfigurerAdapter`, which is a convenient base class that provides empty implementations for each of the `WebMvcConfigurer` interface methods. We override the `addInterceptors` method to register our `UserInSessionInterceptor` and define the handler mappings that will be used to apply the interceptor. The path pattern `/**` will intercept *all* the mappings from which we *exclude* the `/security/**` mappings. The security mappings should *not* include a user session check because the user has not yet been authenticated and will not be in session.

The @ComponentScan("com.gieman.tttracker.web") annotation will trigger a scan for @Controller annotated classes in the com.gieman.tttracker. web package. Our handler classes will then be identified and loaded by Spring. The @EnableWebMvc annotation identifies this class as a Spring web MVC configuration class. This annotation results in Spring loading the required WebMvcConfigurationSupport configuration properties. The remaining @ Configuration annotation identifies the class as a candidate for component scanning during Spring application startup. The WebAppConfig class is then automatically loaded for use in the Spring MVC container.

The WebAppConfig class configures the MVC environment; it is the WebApp class that configures the servlet container:

```
package com.gieman.tttracker.web;

import org.springframework.web.servlet.support.
AbstractAnnotationConfigDispatcherServletInitializer;

public class WebApp extends
AbstractAnnotationConfigDispatcherServletInitializer {

    @Override
    protected String[] getServletMappings() {
        return new String[]{
            "/ttt/*"
        };
    }

    @Override
    protected Class<?>[] getRootConfigClasses() {
        return new Class<?>[0];
    }

    @Override
    protected Class<?>[] getServletConfigClasses() {
        return new Class<?>[]{WebAppConfig.class};
    }
}
```

The `AbstractAnnotationConfigDispatcherServletInitializer` class was introduced in Spring 3.2 as a base class for `WebApplicationInitializer` implementations. These implementations register a `DispatcherServlet` configured with annotated classes as defined in the `WebAppConfig` class (note how this class is returned in the `getServletConfigClasses` method).

The final configuration item of interest is the `getServletMappings` method, which maps incoming requests to the `WebAppConfig` set of handlers that are discovered via the `@ComponentScan` annotation. Every URL in our application that starts with `/ttt/` will be directed to an appropriate request handler for processing. Some example URLs submitted from an Ext JS 4 client could include the following:

- `/ttt/company/findAll.json` will map to the `CompanyHandler.findAll` method
- `/ttt/project/find.json?idProject=5` will map to the `ProjectHandler.find` method

Note that the `/ttt/` prefix in the URL defines the *entry point* to our Spring MVC components. URLs that do not start with `/ttt/` will *not* be handled by the Spring MVC container.

We will now implement one more handler to introduce data binding in Spring controllers.

Defining the TaskLogHandler class

The `TaskLogHandler` class processes the task log actions and is mapped to the `/taskLog/` URL pattern:

```
package com.gieman.tttracker.web;

import com.gieman.tttracker.domain.*;
import com.gieman.tttracker.service.TaskLogService;
import com.gieman.tttracker.vo.Result;
import static com.gieman.tttracker.web.SecurityHelper.getSessionUser;
import java.text.ParseException;
import java.text.SimpleDateFormat;

import java.util.Date;
import java.util.List;
import javax.json.JsonObject;
import javax.servlet.http.HttpServletRequest;
import org.springframework.beans.factory.annotation.Autowired;
import org.springframework.beans.propertyeditors.CustomDateEditor;
```

```java
import org.springframework.stereotype.Controller;
import org.springframework.web.bind.WebDataBinder;
import org.springframework.web.bind.annotation.InitBinder;
import org.springframework.web.bind.annotation.RequestMapping;
import org.springframework.web.bind.annotation.RequestMethod;
import org.springframework.web.bind.annotation.ResponseBody;
import org.springframework.web.bind.annotation.RequestParam;

@Controller
@RequestMapping("/taskLog")
public class TaskLogHandler extends AbstractHandler {

    static final SimpleDateFormat DATE_FORMAT_yyyyMMdd = new
SimpleDateFormat("yyyyMMdd");

    @Autowired
    protected TaskLogService taskLogService;
    @InitBinder
    public void initBinder(WebDataBinder binder) {

        binder.registerCustomEditor(Date.class, new
CustomDateEditor(DATE_FORMAT_yyyyMMdd, true));

    }

    @RequestMapping(value="/find", method = RequestMethod.GET,
produces = {"application/json"})
    @ResponseBody
    public String find(
            @RequestParam(value = "idTaskLog", required = true)
Integer idTaskLog,
            HttpServletRequest request) {

        User sessionUser = getSessionUser(request);

        Result<TaskLog> ar = taskLogService.find(idTaskLog,
sessionUser.getUsername());

        if (ar.isSuccess()) {
            return getJsonSuccessData(ar.getData());
        } else {
            return getJsonErrorMsg(ar.getMsg());
        }
    }
```

```java
    @RequestMapping(value = "/store", method = RequestMethod.POST,
produces = {"application/json"})
    @ResponseBody
    public String store(
            @RequestParam(value = "data", required = true) String
jsonData,
            HttpServletRequest request) throws ParseException {

        User sessionUser = getSessionUser(request);

        JsonObject jsonObj = parseJsonObject(jsonData);

        String dateVal = jsonObj.getString("taskLogDate");

        Result<TaskLog> ar = taskLogService.store(
                getIntegerValue(jsonObj.get("idTaskLog")),
                getIntegerValue(jsonObj.get("idTask")),
                jsonObj.getString("username"),
                jsonObj.getString("taskDescription"),
                DATE_FORMAT_yyyyMMdd.parse(dateVal),
                jsonObj.getInt("taskMinutes"),
                sessionUser.getUsername());

        if (ar.isSuccess()) {
            return getJsonSuccessData(ar.getData());
        } else {
            return getJsonErrorMsg(ar.getMsg());
        }
    }

    @RequestMapping(value = "/remove", method = RequestMethod.POST,
produces = {"application/json"})
    @ResponseBody
    public String remove(
            @RequestParam(value = "data", required = true) String
jsonData,
            HttpServletRequest request) {

        User sessionUser = getSessionUser(request);

        JsonObject jsonObj = parseJsonObject(jsonData);

        Result<TaskLog> ar = taskLogService.remove(
                getIntegerValue(jsonObj.get("idTaskLog")),
                sessionUser.getUsername());
```

```
            if (ar.isSuccess()) {
                return getJsonSuccessMsg(ar.getMsg());
            } else {
                return getJsonErrorMsg(ar.getMsg());
            }
        }


    @RequestMapping(value = "/findByUser", method = RequestMethod.GET,
produces = {"application/json"})
    @ResponseBody
    public String findByUser(
            @RequestParam(value = "username", required = true) String
username,
            @RequestParam(value = "startDate", required = true) Date
startDate,
            @RequestParam(value = "endDate", required = true) Date
endDate,
            HttpServletRequest request) {

        User sessionUser = getSessionUser(request);

        Result<List<TaskLog>> ar = taskLogService.findByUser(
                username,
                startDate,
                endDate,
                sessionUser.getUsername());

        if (ar.isSuccess()) {
            return getJsonSuccessData(ar.getData());
        } else {
            return getJsonErrorMsg(ar.getMsg());
        }
    }
}
```

The `TaskLogHandler` class will, hence, be mapped to the following URLs:

- `/taskLog/find` will map to the `find` method using a GET request
- `/taskLog/store` will map to the `store` method using a POST request
- `/taskLog/findByUser` will map to the `findByUser` method using a GET request
- `/taskLog/remove` will map to the `remove` method using a POST request

We have also introduced a new annotation: the `@InitBinder` annotation.

The @InitBinder annotation

The `@InitBinder` annotation is used to mark a method as "data binding aware". The method initializes the `WebDataBinder` object with editors that are used to transform String parameters into their Java equivalent. The most common need for this transformation is in the case of dates.

A date can be represented in many different ways. All of the following dates are equivalent:

- 06-Dec-2013
- 6 Dec 2013
- 06-12-2013 (UK date, short form)
- 12-06-2013 (U.S. date, short form)
- 06-Dez-2013 (German date)
- December 6, 2013

Sending date representations via HTTP requests can be confusing to say the least! We all understand what most of these dates represent, but how can we convert these dates into a `java.util.Date` object? This is where the `@InitBinder` method is used. The code to specify the required date format involves registering a `CustomDateEditor` constructor for the `Date` class:

```
binder.registerCustomEditor(Date.class, new
CustomDateEditor(DATE_FORMAT_yyyyMMdd, true));
```

This will allow Spring to use the `DATE_FORMAT_yyyyMMdd` instance to parse the dates sent by clients in the `yyyyMMdd` format. The following URL will now be transformed correctly for the arguments required in the `findByUser` method:

```
/taskLog/findByUser?username=bjones&startDate=20130719&endDa
te=20130812
```

The `true` argument in the `CustomDateEditor` constructor ensures that empty dates are given the value `null`.

More on Spring MVC

Our handler methods and Spring MVC implementations use only a small portion of the Spring MVC framework. There will be scenarios that the real-world applications encounter that have not been covered in this chapter. These include requirements such as the following:

- URI template patterns to access portions of a URL through path variables. They are especially useful to simplify RESTful processing and allow the handler methods to access the variables in URL patterns. The company `find` method could then be mapped to a URL such as `/company/find/5/`, where 5 represents the `idCompany` value. This is achieved through the use of the `@PathVariable` annotations and mappings in the form of `/company/find/{idCompany}`.

- Using the `@SessionAttrribute` annotation to store data in the HTTP session between requests.

- Mapping cookie values with the `@CookieValue` annotation to allow a method parameter to be bound to the value of an HTTP cookie.

- Mapping request header attributes with the `@RequestHeader` annotation to allow a method parameter to be bound to a request header.

- Asynchronous request processing to allow the main servlet container thread to be released and allowed to process other requests.

- Integrating Spring MVC with Spring Security (highly recommended for enterprise applications).

- Parsing multipart requests to allow the users to upload files from HTML forms.

The testing of the handler classes using the Spring MVC Test framework should also be considered for enterprise Spring MVC applications. For more information, see the comprehensive guide at `http://docs.spring.io/spring/docs/3.2.x/spring-framework-reference/html/testing.html#spring-mvc-test-framework`. The framework provides JUnit support for testing the client- and server-side Spring MVC applications.

There is much more to the Spring MVC framework than can ever be covered in a single chapter. We recommend users find out more about Spring MVC capabilities from the excellent online resource at `http://docs.spring.io/spring/docs/3.2.x/spring-framework-reference/html/mvc.html`.

Exercises

Implement the `UserHandler` and `TaskHandler` classes, mapping the requests to the following methods:

- `/task/find` will map to the `TaskHandler.find` method using a `GET` request
- `/task/store` will map to the `TaskHandler.store` method using a `POST` request

- `/task/findAll` will map to the `TaskHandler.findAll` method using a GET request
- `/task/remove` will map to the `TaskHandler.remove` method using a POST request
- `/user/find` will map to the `UserHandler.find` method using a GET request
- `/user/store` will map to the `UserHandler.store` method using a POST request
- `/user/findAll` will map to the `UserHandler.findAll` method using a GET request
- `/user/remove` will map to the `UserHandler.remove` method using a POST request

Summary

Our Java web interface is now complete—we have created a fully functional request handling layer that is optimized for Ext JS 4 clients. The HTTP client-accessible URLs are mapped to the request-handling classes through the `@RequestMapping` annotations at the class and method levels. Each handler method interacts with the service layer through well-defined interfaces and processes the `Result` data transfer objects before returning JSON data in the HTTP response. We have configured the Spring Web MVC container with Java configuration classes and implemented a Spring interceptor to check whether a user has been authenticated.

In *Chapter 8, Running 3T on GlassFish*, we will complete our Spring configuration and deploy the 3T application on the GlassFish 4 server. Each layer in our application stack will then be ready to play its part in serving the Ext JS 4 client requests.

8
Running 3T on GlassFish

In this chapter we will deploy our 3T application on the GlassFish 4 server. A successful deployment will require several new configuration files as well as updates to existing files. You will already be familiar with some of these files from the testing configuration defined in *Chapter 5, Testing the DAO Layer with Spring and JUnit*, but a few new files specific to GlassFish will be introduced.

We will also be configuring the GlassFish server to run independent of the NetBeans IDE. Enterprise environments will usually have many GlassFish server instances running on different hosts. Understanding basic GlassFish configuration is an important skill and we will cover connection pool configuration in detail.

At the end of this chapter you will be able to see dynamic HTTP responses based on the URLs you have mapped so carefully in *Chapter 7, The Web Request Handling Layer*.

Configuring the 3T web application

The web application configuration requires several new files that will need to be added to the WEB-INF directory, as shown in the following screenshot. Create these files now:

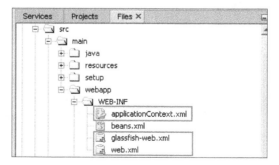

Note that the beans.xml file was created by NetBeans but is not required for our configuration. Let's now look at each of these files in detail.

The Spring applicationContext.xml file

The applicationContext.xml file configures the Spring container and is very similar to the testingContext.xml file we created in *Chapter 5, Testing the DAO Layer with Spring and JUnit*. The contents of the file are as follows:

```xml
<?xml version="1.0" encoding="UTF-8"?>
<beans xmlns="http://www.springframework.org/schema/beans"
  xmlns:xsi="http://www.w3.org/2001/XMLSchema-instance"
  xmlns:p="http://www.springframework.org/schema/p"
  xmlns:context="http://www.springframework.org/schema/context"
  xmlns:tx="http://www.springframework.org/schema/tx"
  xsi:schemaLocation="
      http://www.springframework.org/schema/beans
      http://www.springframework.org/schema/beans/spring-beans-3.2.xsd
  http://www.springframework.org/schema/context
  http://www.springframework.org/schema/context/spring-context-3.2.xsd
  http://www.springframework.org/schema/tx
  http://www.springframework.org/schema/tx/spring-tx-3.2.xsd">
    <bean id="loadTimeWeaver"
class="org.springframework.instrument.classloading.glassfish.
GlassFishLoadTimeWeaver" />
    <bean id="entityManagerFactory"
        p:persistenceUnitName="tttPU"
class="org.springframework.orm.jpa.
LocalContainerEntityManagerFactoryBean"
    />

    <!-- Transaction manager for JTA  -->
    <tx:jta-transaction-manager />
    <!-- enable the configuration of transactional behavior based on
annotations -->
    <tx:annotation-driven />

    <!-- checks for @Autowired beans -->
    <context:annotation-config/>

    <!-- Scan for Repository/Service annotations -->
    <context:component-scan base-package="com.gieman.tttracker.dao"/>
    <context:component-scan base-package="com.gieman.tttracker.
service"/>
</beans>
```

This file is used by Spring to initialize and configure the JPA `EntityManagerFactory` and `TransactionManager` DAO and Service layer objects. Comparing the `applicationContext.xml` file with the `testingContext.xml` file identifies the key differences between a simple Java container and a Java EE container provided by an enterprise application server:

- The data source is retrieved via **JNDI (Java Naming and Directory Interface)** from the GlassFish application server and is not created or managed by Spring in the `applicationContext.xml` file. The JNDI configuration setting in the `persistence.xml` file is defined later in this chapter.

- The load time weaver is specific to GlassFish.

- The transaction manager is **JTA**-based (**Java Transaction API**) and is provided by the GlassFish server. It is not created or managed by Spring. The `<tx:jta-transaction-manager />` and `<tx:annotation-driven />` definitions are all that is required to configure transactional behavior within the Spring container.

 You should be familiar with the remaining configuration properties. Note that component scanning is performed against both the `dao` and `service` packages to ensure the auto-wiring of Spring beans in these classes.

When the `applicationContext.xml` file is loaded by the Spring container, the MVC configuration classes defined in *Chapter 7, The Web Request Handling Layer*, are automatically discovered by classpath scanning and are loaded to configure the web application components.

The web.xml file

The `web.xml` web application deployment descriptor file represents the configuration of a Java web application. It is used to configure the servlet container and map URLs to each configured servlet. Each Java web application must have a `web.xml` in the `WEB-INF` directory of the web application root.

The 3T web application requires the following `web.xml` definition:

```
<?xml version="1.0" encoding="UTF-8"?>
<web-app version="3.0" xmlns="http://java.sun.com/xml/ns/
javaee" xmlns:xsi="http://www.w3.org/2001/XMLSchema-instance"
xsi:schemaLocation="http://java.sun.com/xml/ns/javaee http://java.sun.
com/xml/ns/javaee/web-app_3_0.xsd">
```

```
<context-param>
    <param-name>contextConfigLocation</param-name>
    <param-value>/WEB-INF/applicationContext.xml</param-value>
</context-param>
<listener>
    <listener-class>
        org.springframework.web.context.ContextLoaderListener
    </listener-class>
</listener>
<session-config>
    <session-timeout>30</session-timeout>
    <cookie-config>
        <name>JSESSIONID_3T</name>
    </cookie-config>
</session-config>
<welcome-file-list>
    <welcome-file>index.html</welcome-file>
</welcome-file-list>
</web-app>
```

Some key points are as follows:

- The `context-param` element defining the `contextConfigLocation` value is optional if the Spring configuration file is named `applicationContext.xml` (this is the expected default filename if not supplied). However, we always include this property for completeness. It defines the location of the main Spring configuration file.

- The listener with class `org.springframework.web.context.ContextLoaderListener` is used by Spring to initialize loading of the application context. It is the entry point to boot the Spring container and attempts to load the `contextConfigLocation` file. An exception is thrown if the file cannot be resolved or is invalid.

- The `session-config` properties define the session timeout (30 minutes of inactivity) and the session cookie name.

- The `welcome-file-list` identifies the file that will be served by GlassFish, if not specified explicitly in the URL.

The glassfish-web.xml file

The `glassfish-web.xml` file configures GlassFish with additional web application properties specific to the GlassFish server:

```xml
<?xml version="1.0" encoding="UTF-8"?>
<!DOCTYPE glassfish-web-app PUBLIC "-//GlassFish.org//DTD GlassFish
    Application Server 3.1 Servlet 3.0//EN"
    "http://glassfish.org/dtds/glassfish-web-app_3_0-1.dtd">
<glassfish-web-app>
<context-root>/</context-root>
</glassfish-web-app>
```

The `context-root` property identifies the web application's server path for deployment. We will deploy the 3T application to the context root of the server. This means that 3T request handlers can be accessed directly from the root of the web application as in the following example:

`/ttt/company/findAll.json`

Changing the `context-root` property to `/mylocation`, for example, will require a URL of the following format:

`/mylocation/ttt/company/findAll.json`

Configuring the Maven pom.xml file

You may have changed various `pom.xml` settings when experimenting with dependencies and plugins in the previous chapters. It is important to now revisit this file and confirm that the properties are correct for building and deploying the project. You should have the following basic `pom.xml` configuration:

```xml
<?xml version="1.0" encoding="UTF-8"?>
<project xmlns="http://maven.apache.org/POM/4.0.0" xmlns:xsi="http://
www.w3.org/2001/XMLSchema-instance" xsi:schemaLocation="http://maven.
apache.org/POM/4.0.0 http://maven.apache.org/xsd/maven-4.0.0.xsd">
    <modelVersion>4.0.0</modelVersion>

    <groupId>com.gieman</groupId>
    <artifactId>task-time-tracker</artifactId>
```

```xml
<version>1.0</version>
<packaging>war</packaging>
<name>task-time-tracker</name>
<properties>
    <endorsed.dir>
        ${project.build.directory}/endorsed
    </endorsed.dir>
    <project.build.sourceEncoding>
        UTF-8
    </project.build.sourceEncoding>
    <spring.version>3.2.4.RELEASE</spring.version>
    <logback.version>1.0.13</logback.version>
</properties>
<dependencies>
    <dependency>
        <groupId>org.eclipse.persistence</groupId>
        <artifactId>javax.persistence</artifactId>
        <version>2.1.0-SNAPSHOT</version>
        <scope>provided</scope>
    </dependency>
    <dependency>
        <groupId>org.eclipse.persistence</groupId>
        <artifactId>eclipselink</artifactId>
        <version>2.5.0-SNAPSHOT</version>
        <scope>provided</scope>
    </dependency>
    <dependency>
        <groupId>org.eclipse.persistence</groupId>
        <artifactId>
            org.eclipse.persistence.jpa.modelgen.processor
        </artifactId>
        <version>2.5.0-SNAPSHOT</version>
        <scope>provided</scope>
    </dependency>
    <dependency>
        <groupId>javax</groupId>
        <artifactId>javaee-web-api</artifactId>
        <version>7.0</version>
        <scope>provided</scope>
    </dependency>
    <dependency>
        <groupId>ch.qos.logback</groupId>
        <artifactId>logback-classic</artifactId>
```

```xml
            <version>${logback.version}</version>
</dependency>
<dependency>
        <groupId>junit</groupId>
        <artifactId>junit</artifactId>
        <version>4.11</version>
        <scope>test</scope>
</dependency>
<dependency>
        <groupId>mysql</groupId>
        <artifactId>mysql-connector-java</artifactId>
        <version>5.1.26</version>
        <scope>provided</scope>
</dependency>
<dependency>
        <groupId>org.springframework</groupId>
        <artifactId>spring-context</artifactId>
        <version>${spring.version}</version>
</dependency>
<dependency>
        <groupId>org.springframework</groupId>
        <artifactId>spring-context-support</artifactId>
        <version>${spring.version}</version>
</dependency>
<dependency>
        <groupId>org.springframework</groupId>
        <artifactId>spring-tx</artifactId>
        <version>${spring.version}</version>
</dependency>
<dependency>
        <groupId>org.springframework</groupId>
        <artifactId>spring-jdbc</artifactId>
        <version>${spring.version}</version>
</dependency>
<dependency>
        <groupId>org.springframework</groupId>
        <artifactId>spring-orm</artifactId>
        <version>${spring.version}</version>
</dependency>
<dependency>
        <groupId>org.springframework</groupId>
        <artifactId>spring-instrument</artifactId>
```

```xml
            <version>${spring.version}</version>
        </dependency>
        <dependency>
            <groupId>org.springframework</groupId>
            <artifactId>spring-webmvc</artifactId>
            <version>${spring.version}</version>
        </dependency>
        <dependency>
            <groupId>org.springframework</groupId>
            <artifactId>spring-test</artifactId>
            <version>${spring.version}</version>
            <scope>test</scope>
        </dependency>

    </dependencies>

    <build>
        <plugins>
            <plugin>
                <groupId>org.apache.maven.plugins</groupId>
                <artifactId>maven-compiler-plugin</artifactId>
                <version>3.1</version>
                <configuration>
                    <source>1.7</source>
                    <target>1.7</target>
                    <compilerArguments>
                        <endorseddirs>
                            ${endorsed.dir}
                        </endorseddirs>
                    </compilerArguments>
                </configuration>
            </plugin>
            <plugin>
                <groupId>org.apache.maven.plugins</groupId>
                <artifactId>maven-war-plugin</artifactId>
                <version>2.3</version>
                <configuration>
                  <warName>${project.build.finalName}</warName>
                  <failOnMissingWebXml>false</failOnMissingWebXml>
                </configuration>
            </plugin>
            <plugin>
```

```xml
                    <groupId>org.apache.maven.plugins</groupId>
                    <artifactId>maven-dependency-plugin</artifactId>
                    <version>2.6</version>
                    <executions>
                        <execution>
                            <id>copy-endorsed</id>
                            <phase>validate</phase>
                            <goals>
                                <goal>copy</goal>
                            </goals>
                            <configuration>
                                <outputDirectory>
                                    ${endorsed.dir}
                                </outputDirectory>
                                <silent>true</silent>
                                <artifactItems>
                                    <artifactItem>
                                        <groupId>javax</groupId>
                                        <artifactId>
                                            javaee-endorsed-api
                                        </artifactId>
                                        <version>7.0</version>
                                        <type>jar</type>
                                    </artifactItem>
                                </artifactItems>
                            </configuration>
                        </execution>
                        <execution>
                            <id>copy-all-dependencies</id>
                            <phase>compile</phase>
                            <goals>
                                <goal>copy-dependencies</goal>
                            </goals>
                            <configuration>
                                <outputDirectory>
                                    ${project.build.directory}/lib
                                </outputDirectory>
                                <includeScope>compile</includeScope>
                            </configuration>
                        </execution>
                    </executions>
                </plugin>
                <plugin>
```

```
                    <groupId>org.apache.maven.plugins</groupId>
                    <artifactId>maven-surefire-plugin</artifactId>
                    <version>2.14.1</version>
                    <configuration>
                        <skipTests>true</skipTests>
                        <includes>
                            <include>**/dao/*Test.java</include>
                            <include>**/service/*Test.java</include>
                        </includes>
                        <argLine>
-javaagent:target/lib/spring-instrument-${spring.version}.jar
                        </argLine>
                    </configuration>
                </plugin>

        </plugins>
    </build>
    <repositories>
        <repository>
          <url>
            http://download.eclipse.org/rt/eclipselink/maven.repo/
          </url>
          <id>eclipselink</id>
          <layout>default</layout>
          <name>
            Repository for library EclipseLink (JPA 2.1)
          </name>
        </repository>
    </repositories>
</project>
```

Several of these dependencies were added during the reverse engineering process, as was the `<repository>` definition for EclipseLink. There are only a few changes required:

- **Add the MySQL connector**: The most recent version should be used for the `mysql-connector-java` dependency. The MySQL connector is not provided by GlassFish and will be copied to the application server in a section later in this chapter. The scope is set to `provided` so as not to include this JAR when building the WAR file.

- **Turn off the Surefire testing plugin**: Your deployments will be much faster if you turn off testing during the build process. Change the `maven-surefire-plugin` entry `skipTests` to `true`. This will skip the testing phase when building and deploying the project locally.

Building enterprise applications is usually performed on a dedicated build server that executes test cases and reports on the success or failure of the build process. Disabling the test phase should only be done on developer machines to speed the build and deployment process. Developers will not appreciate waiting for 30 minutes to execute the testing suite every time they change a class. The testing phase should never be disabled for execution on the build server.

Adding eclipselink.target-server to the persistence.xml file

The `persistence.xml` file requires the inclusion of the `eclipselink.target-server` property to fully enable transactional behavior. The `persistence.xml` file located at `src/main/resources/META-INF` should look like the following:

```xml
<?xml version="1.0" encoding="UTF-8"?>
<persistence version="2.1"
  xmlns="http://xmlns.jcp.org/xml/ns/persistence"
  xmlns:xsi="http://www.w3.org/2001/XMLSchema-instance"
  xsi:schemaLocation="http://xmlns.jcp.org/xml/ns/persistence
  http://xmlns.jcp.org/xml/ns/persistence/persistence_2_1.xsd">

  <persistence-unit name="tttPU" transaction-type="JTA">
    <provider>
        org.eclipse.persistence.jpa.PersistenceProvider
    </provider>
    <jta-data-source>jdbc/tasktimetracker</jta-data-source>
    <exclude-unlisted-classes>false</exclude-unlisted-classes>
    <properties>
        <property name="eclipselink.target-server"
            value="SunAS9"/>
        <property name="eclipselink.logging.level"
            value="INFO"/>
    </properties>
  </persistence-unit>
</persistence>
```

Without this addition, transactions will not be available in your application. The `eclipselink.logging.level` may also be changed to increase or decrease logging output as desired.

Adding the logback.xml file to your resources directory

The `logback.xml` file should be added to `src/main/resources/` in order to enable logging into your application. The contents of this file will be the same as the testing `logback.xml` file as follows:

```xml
<?xml version="1.0" encoding="UTF-8"?>
<configuration scan="true" scanPeriod="30 seconds" >
    <contextName>TaskTimeTracker</contextName>
    <appender name="STDOUT"
        class="ch.qos.logback.core.ConsoleAppender">
        <encoder>
          <pattern>
          %d{HH:mm:ss.SSS} [%thread] %-5level %logger{5} - %msg%n
          </pattern>
        </encoder>
    </appender>
    <logger name="com.gieman.tttracker"
        level="DEBUG" additivity="false">
        <appender-ref ref="STDOUT" />
    </logger>
    <logger name="com.gieman.tttracker.dao"
        level="DEBUG" additivity="false">
        <appender-ref ref="STDOUT" />
    </logger>
    <logger name="com.gieman.tttracker.domain"
        level="DEBUG" additivity="false">
        <appender-ref ref="STDOUT" />
    </logger>
    <logger name="com.gieman.tttracker.service"
        level="DEBUG" additivity="false">
        <appender-ref ref="STDOUT" />
    </logger>
    <logger name="com.gieman.tttracker.web"
        level="DEBUG" additivity="false">
        <appender-ref ref="STDOUT" />
    </logger>
    <root level="INFO">
        <appender-ref ref="STDOUT" />
    </root>
</configuration>
```

Configuring the GlassFish server

The GlassFish 4 server bundled with NetBeans is automatically configured the first time you run the project. This means any required resources are set up dynamically based on the current state of the project. All such properties are copied to the `glassfish-resources.xml` file in the `setup` directory, as shown in the following screenshot:

The `glassfish-resources.xml` file was modified during the database reverse engineering process to include the database connection pool and JDBC resources required by JPA. As a result, the contents of this file define the required GlassFish connection pool details.

It is important to understand that this file is used by NetBeans to dynamically configure the GlassFish server assigned to the project. In a real-world situation, the GlassFish server is configured by administrators and deploying a web application is done either from the command line or through the GlassFish administration console. You will not be deploying your application through NetBeans in a normal enterprise environment and it is hence very useful to have a fundamental understanding of how GlassFish is configured from first principals. This section is dedicated to configuring the GlassFish server connection pool for use with 3T. Although this is not strictly required to run 3T on NetBeans, we strongly recommend you take the time to configure your GlassFish server fully via the following steps.

This will ensure you understand what is required to configure a GlassFish server on a different physical server for running the 3T application.

1. The first step in configuring your GlassFish server is to perform a **Clean and Build**:

2. When the build is complete, navigate to `target/lib` as shown in the following screenshot to view the JAR files required by your project:

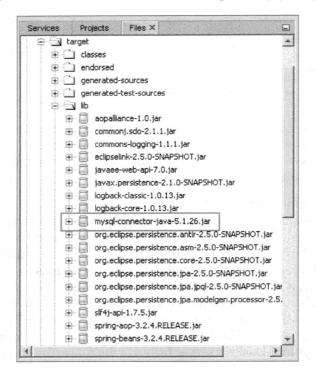

3. Open a file explorer window (Windows Explorer or OS X Finder) to navigate to this directory and copy the `mysql-connector-java-5.1.26.jar` file to your GlassFish domain `libs` directory, as shown in the following screenshot:

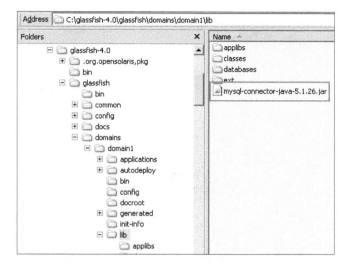

Renaming the setup directory

The `setup` directory, located at `src/main/`, contains the `glassfish-resources.xml` file and should be renamed to ensure NetBeans does not dynamically configure GlassFish with these properties. We suggest renaming the directory to `setup-original`.

Starting the GlassFish server in NetBeans

Navigate to the **Services** tab; by right-clicking on the **GlassFish Server 4.0** node, select **Start** as shown in the following screenshot:

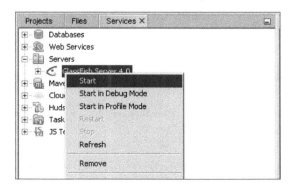

You should see server output at the bottom of the NetBeans IDE and the GlassFish Server 4.0 node reload. You can now right-click on the **GlassFish Server 4.0** node and select **View Domain Admin Console**:

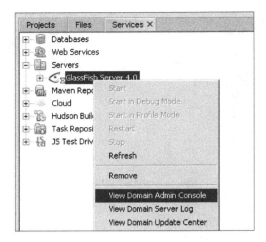

This will start your default browser and load the **Domain Admin Console**.

Configuring the JDBC connection pool

This section will use the GlassFish admin console to configure the JDBC connection pool and JDBC resource required by the 3T application.

1. Open the **Resources** node and navigate to the **JDBC Connection Pools** tab:

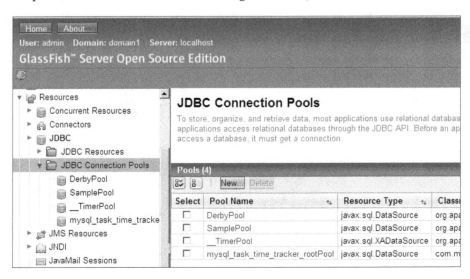

You may see a connection pool named `mysql_task_time_tracker_ rootPool` or something similar, as shown in the preceding screenshot. This was created by NetBeans during a previous run using the properties specified in the `glassfish-resources.xml` file. The remaining section may be skipped if you wish to continue using this connection pool. We recommend you delete this entry and continue to follow these steps to understand how to configure a GlassFish connection pool.

2. Click on the **New** button and enter the following details before clicking on the **Next** button:

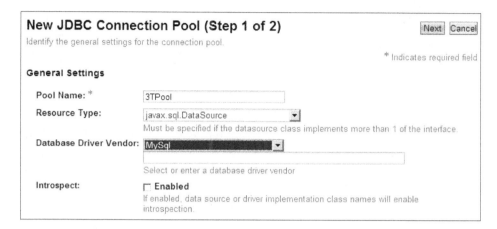

3. The next screen looks daunting but only a few entries are required. Scroll all the way down until you can view the **Additional Properties** section:

4. There are many properties here! Thankfully only a few are required unless you are familiar with MySQL database administration. You may safely delete all the listed properties to keep the configuration simple, and then enter the following properties that correspond to the original `glassfish-resources.xml` file:

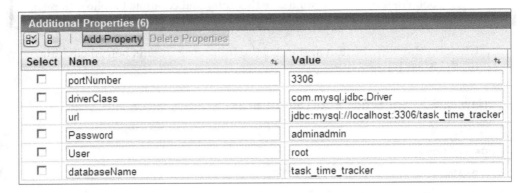

5. The basic fields that are required are **URL**, **User**, and **Password**. Saving these settings will return you to the **JDBC Connection Pools** screen:

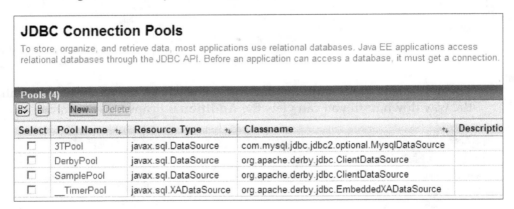

6. Click on the **3TPool** name to open the settings again and click on the **Ping** button to test the connection. You should now see the following result:

Configuring the JDBC resource

The final step is to create a **JDBC Resource**. Click on this node to display the configured resources:

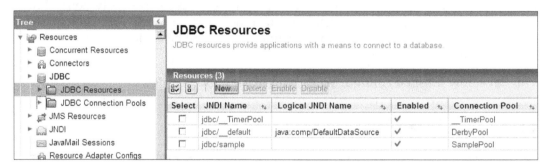

Click on the **New...** button and enter the following details:

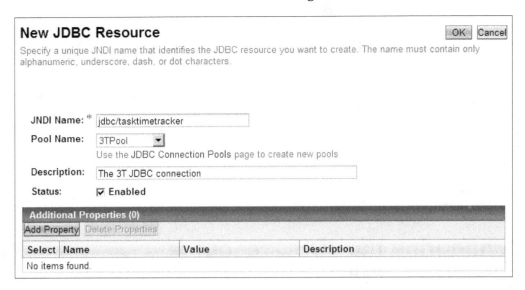

The **JNDI Name** must be the same as the `<jta-data-source>` property defined in the `persistence.xml` file and is hence set to `jdbc/tasktimetracker`. Click on the **OK** button to save the resource configuration. The refreshed node should now show the newly created resource.

You have now finished configuring the GlassFish JDBC settings.

Running 3T

Now we recommend you stop GlassFish and restart NetBeans to ensure all changes made previously are up-to-date in the IDE. The final step is to run the 3T application:

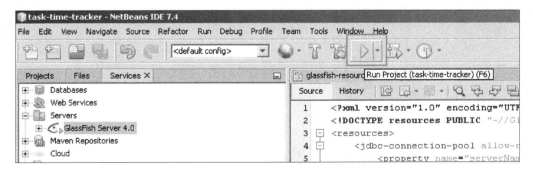

This should result in considerable output culminating in deployment of the 3T application to the GlassFish server:

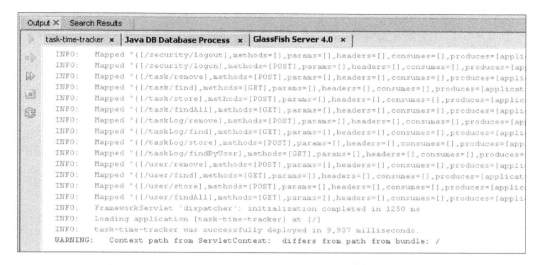

Note that the final **WARNING** in the **GlassFish Server 4.0** output can be ignored; this is a known issue when deploying an application to the root context from within NetBeans.

The final action by NetBeans will be to open your default browser to the welcome page displayed in *Chapter 1, Preparing Your Development Environment*. You should note that the URL in the browser will now be:

```
http://localhost:8080/
```

Instead of the original:

```
http://localhost:8080/task-time-tracker
```

This is due to the `<context-root>/</context-root>` property in `glassfish-web.xml`, which defines the root of the web application path. The 3T web application is now deployed to the context root and no prefix is required to reach the deployed 3T application.

You can now try to load a mapped URL such as `/ttt/company/findAll.json`. Enter this in the browser as shown and hit the *Enter* key. You should see the following result:

This message is coming from the `UserInSessionInterceptor` we implemented in the last chapter. The session check fails as we are not currently logged on, returning the preceding JSON message to the browser. The `logger.info` message in the class should also be visible in the GlassFish output:

```
xt path from ServletContext:  differs from path from bundle: /
.962 [http-listener-1(4)] INFO  c.g.t.w.UserInSessionInterceptor - calling preHandle with url=/ttt/company/findAll
```

You can now try a logon action with parameters as shown in the following screenshot:

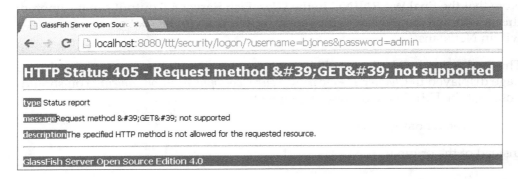

This result may surprise you. The request URL is mapped to the `SecurityHandler.logon` method, which is defined with `method = RequestMethod.POST` in the `@RequestMapping` annotation. This restricts access to this method to `POST` requests only, while the URL-encoded parameters submitted by the browser is a `GET` request. The GlassFish 405 HTTP status message is the result. In *Chapter 10, Logging On and Maintaining Users*, we will be implementing the logon process using the appropriate `POST` request.

You should note that all handler URLs will be accessed by AJAX calls from the Ext JS 4 application, which will be developed in subsequent chapters. You will never see these URLs in the browser as shown previously.

Managing GlassFish without NetBeans

Starting and stopping GlassFish in NetBeans is easy and convenient. However, in enterprise environments the stop/start process will be managed by scripts wrapping the `asadmin` utility. A full description of the utility can be found in the *GlassFish User Administration Guide* at `https://glassfish.java.net/docs/4.0/ administration-guide.pdf`.

The `asadmin` utility is used to perform administrative tasks for the GlassFish server from the command line or from a script. You can use this utility instead of the GlassFish administration console interface we used earlier in this chapter. Almost every action that can be performed in the administration console has an equivalent command that can be executed with `asadmin`.

The `asadmin` utility is found in the `{as-install}`/bin directory. Commands should be run from within this directory if the full path to `asadmin` is not provided. To start the domain, you can execute the following command:

```
asadmin start-domain domain1
```

The `domain1` argument represents the name of the domain to start. Executing this command from the Windows command prompt will result in the following output:

Stopping a running GlassFish domain is just as simple. Use the following command:

```
asadmin stop-domain domain1
```

This will result in the following output:

We will continue to start and stop GlassFish within NetBeans but will revisit `asadmin` in *Chapter 13, Moving Your Application to Production*.

Summary

This chapter has focused on the steps required to configure the 3T web application for deployment to the GlassFish 4 server. The Spring configuration files were defined and the `web.xml` file configured to load the Spring container on startup. You were guided through the GlassFish connection pool configuration process and the 3T web application was deployed to the context root of the GlassFish 4 server.

This is a pivotal point in our enterprise application development process. We have now fully covered the realm of the Java developer, building a functional backend system that will serve dynamic requests for any JSON client. *Chapter 9, Getting Started with Ext JS 4*, will introduce the powerful Ext JS 4 framework and begin our frontend development journey.

Getting Started with Ext JS 4

9

Ext JS 4 is, by far, the most sophisticated JavaScript library available and provides an amazing set of widgets for almost all practical design concerns. It does everything we could possibly want in order to develop complex, cross-browser compatible applications that require a high degree of user interaction. In this chapter, we will:

- Learn about core Ext JS 4 MVC concepts
- Explore practical project design and development conventions
- Install the Ext JS 4 development framework and introduce Sencha Cmd
- Generate an Ext JS 4 application skeleton for the 3T application

Ext JS has come a long way since starting out as an extension to the **Yahoo User Interface (YUI)** library. Each new version has been a significant improvement on the previous one and Ext JS 4 is no exception. Those new to Ext JS will appreciate the elegant framework design and consistent API, while those transitioning from Ext JS 3 will appreciate the improvements in many areas, including the introduction of the MVC design pattern. Regardless of your background, this chapter will help you be productive with Ext JS 4.

It should be noted that Ext JS 4 is not the only JavaScript MVC framework available today. `Angular.js` and `Backbone.js`, for example, are both very capable development frameworks, with MVC features similar to Ext JS 4. They do not, however, have the extensive documentation, build tools, and commercial support that make Ext JS 4 so appropriate for enterprise application development.

The importance of application design

Technology aside, a thoughtful and consistent application design is critical when developing enterprise applications. The quality of the application's architecture will determine the maintainability, scalability, and overall cost of the application during the project lifecycle. The benefits of a well-designed application include the following:

- The application will be easier to understand. New team members will quickly come up to speed if there is a consistent way of doing things.

- The application will be easier to maintain. Enhancements and new functionalities will be far simpler to implement if you have consistent application design guidelines.

- Code consistency. A well-designed application will have well-documented naming conventions, directory structures, and coding standards.

- The application will be multideveloper friendly. On large projects, many people will be involved and a consistent design strategy will ensure that everyone is on the same page.

Less-tangible benefits are often overlooked when you start a new project and excitedly work on the first prototype for the proof-of-concept presentation. The ability to refactor and scale a project from simple beginnings is often a key factor in enterprise application development. Regardless of how small the project may seem in the initial phases, you can be certain that business users will want to change workflows and layouts as soon as they become familiar with the application. New functionality will be requested and old functionality will be deprecated. Components will be moved and redesigned as the application evolves over time. A consistent and well-thought-out application design will make these project lifecycle processes less daunting. Thankfully, the Ext JS 4 application architecture itself encourages a formal and well-structured application design.

Ext JS 4 MVC concepts

When the MVC design pattern was introduced for the first time in Ext JS 4, it completely revolutionized the Ext JS framework. Although MVC was well known as a design pattern, this was the first time a sophisticated JavaScript framework had implemented the strategy. There are several key benefits as follows:

- The MVC design pattern organizes code into logical realms or component types, which makes the code easier to understand

- MVC modularity can simplify component testing and refactoring as each object has a well-defined purpose

- The MVC design pattern architecture encourages cleaner code, clearly separating data access, presentation, and business logic

These were a huge advantage over the previous Ext JS 3 where the only true MVC component was the **V (View)**. It was left to the Ext JS 3 developer to architect the **M (Model)** and **C (Controller)** as best they could, which often led to confusing and inconsistent code. Let's now look at how Ext JS 4 defines the MVC design pattern.

Model

An Ext JS 4 model is a collection of properties that represent a domain entity. It may not come as a surprise that our 3T application will require a `Company`, `Project`, `Task`, `User`, and `TaskLog` model definition, just like they are represented in our Java domain layer. The main difference with our Java domain objects is that the Ext JS 4 model equivalent will be persistence aware. Thanks to the Ext JS 4 `data` package, each model instance will know how to persist and manage its state.

View

The Ext JS 4 view represents a logical visual component block and may itself include panels, toolbars, grids, forms, trees, and charts. An Ext JS 4 view always resides in its own file and should be as *dumb* as possible. This means that there should be no JavaScript business logic in the view; its purpose is to present data and provide interactive ability for the user.

Controller

The Ext JS 4 controller can be loosely described as the glue that binds together your application logic. Controllers are central in handling event processing and cross-view interactions and define the application workflows. The vast majority of JavaScript business logic code will reside in controllers.

Ext JS 4 flexibility

Although we have a clear definition of the different MVC components, there is considerable implementation flexibility in the Ext JS 4 framework itself. We do not need to use controllers or models; in fact, we could easily build a fully working Ext JS 4 application using the same strategies followed in Ext JS 3. This would be a mistake, however, and should be avoided at all costs. The benefits of leveraging the MVC architecture for enterprise application development are significant, including, but not limited to, a simpler and more robust code base.

Ext JS 4 design conventions and concepts

The Sencha Ext JS 4 team has done an enormous amount of work in defining conventions, which you should consider following, for building enterprise applications. These include a standard directory structure, naming conventions, and detailed design best practices. We strongly urge you to browse the many tutorials and guides on the *Sencha Ext JS 4 Docs* website at `http://docs.sencha.com/extjs/4.2.2` to become familiar with their application design recommendations.

This book will adhere to the common design strategies outlined by the Ext JS 4 team, with minor differences noted and explained upon being introduced in their relevant sections. It is beyond the scope of the book to cover basic Ext JS 4 concepts and you may need to refer to the *Sencha Ext JS 4 Docs* to fine-tune your understanding.

Practical conventions

A well-structured Ext JS 4 project with consistent naming conventions will be a joy to work with. Enterprise applications with hundreds of files should be structured in a way that is easy to learn and maintain. It should be a rare occurrence when you ask a colleague, "Where is the file that displays the editing toolbar for the xyz widget?".

Project structure

The Ext JS 4 directory structure, comprising a top-level app and subdirectories named `controller`, `model`, `store`, and `view`, should always be used. This is the default directory structure for any Ext JS 4 application and allows out-of-the-box integration with the Sencha Cmd build tools.

Large projects have many hundreds of JavaScript files, so it is important to have a consistent project structure. Practical namespacing, especially in the `view` directory, can simplify a project structure and make it easier to find components. In *Chapter 10, Logging On and Maintaining Users*, *Chapter 11, Building the Task Log User Interface*, and *Chapter 12, 3T Administration Made Easy*, for example, we will be creating a `view` structure containing the files displayed in the following screenshot (on the left-hand side):

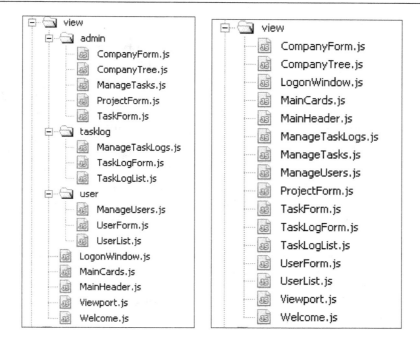

The preceding screenshot displays all views (on its right-hand side) in the same directory. Which is the better way? That depends on the nature of the project and the number of files. Enterprise projects are usually namespaced at a modular level with many subdirectories logically grouping related components. Smaller projects can just as easily have a flat structure where all files are found in the same directory. Whichever structure you choose, be consistent! It should be easy for any new developer to find a component without searching through a large number of files and directories.

Naming conventions

We recommend defining a consistent naming convention that is easy to understand and follow. It should be easy to locate files, both on the filesystem and in the IDE you are using.

Naming stores and models

Each model should be named as the singular of the entity it represents (for example, `Company`, `Project`, `Task`, `TaskLog`, and `User`). Each store should be named in a similar singular manner. We have seen `Store` added as a postfix to store names in Ext JS 3 (for example, `ProjectStore`), but this is not recommended for Ext JS 4. Controllers automatically create a `get` function for each store by adding `Store` to the store name. Naming a store `ProjectStore` will result in a function named `getProjectStoreStore` in each controller that the store is referenced. For this reason, we recommend that you use store names without the `Store` postfix.

The store name in its singular form is often replaced with the plural version. For example, a Project store is often named `Projects`. Once again, consistency is the key. If you decide to use the plural form, use it for each store name. In our application, this would result in `Companies`, `Projects`, `Tasks`, `TaskLogs`, and `Users` stores. This tends to sometimes cause confusion in spelling; we have seen both Companies and Companys used for the plural version of Company. When English is not your first language, it may be difficult to know the correct plural name for entities, such as territories, countries, companies, currencies, and statuses. For this reason, we prefer using the singular version when naming stores.

Naming views

Consider the following situation, in which we have been researching panels on the Sencha Docs website:

There are four different **Panel** files open (`Ext.grid.Panel`, `Ext.tab.Panel`, `Ext.form.Panel`, and `Ext.panel.Panel`). It is frustrating to try and locate the `Ext.grid.Panel` file in this situation; in the worst case, you will need to click on four different tab items. In a large project, there may be many panel containers worthy of the name `Panel`. We recommend giving each file a unique name, regardless of how it is namespaced. Unlike models and stores, where the same filename is used for the model and store namespaces, we do not recommend using the same filename between view classes. For example, the files `app.view.user.List` and `app.view.tasklog.List` cannot be easily differentiated in an IDE tab bar without examining the file content. It is far easier to make these filenames unique, even though they may exist in different namespaces.

The use of postfixing class types is another issue worthy of discussion. Ext JS 3 used typed postfixing on class names. This resulted in `GridPanel`, `FormPanel`, `TabPanel`, and `Panel` filenames. They were all panels. It was easy to identify what the class was by examining the filename. Ext JS 4 took a namespaced approach and dropped the descriptive name. The preceding examples became `Ext.grid.Panel`, `Ext.tab.Panel`, `Ext.form.Panel`, and `Ext.panel.Panel`. Each file is named `Panel`, which is not very helpful without knowledge of the directory it resides in.

Whatever naming convention you implement, it is important to be consistent. We will use the following naming conventions:

- All namespacing folder names will be lowercase.
- Any class that is used to represent a list of items will have the class name postfixed with `List`. The implementation of `List` is not important; we do not care if the listing is created using a grid, simple template, or data view.
- Any class that is a form will be postfixed with `Form`.
- Any class that is a tree will be postfixed with `Tree`.
- Any class that is a window will be postfixed with `Window`.
- Any component that manages the positioning and layout of a set of related components will be prefixed with `Manage`. Such a class will usually contain toolbars, lists, forms, and tab panels arranged in an appropriate layout.

You may wish to introduce other conventions appropriate for your development environment. This is fine; the important point is to be consistent and ensure that everyone understands and adheres to your conventions.

Naming controllers

We recommend that all controller class names be postfixed with `Controller`. This makes them easy to identify in any IDE. The controller responsible for user maintenance, for example, would hence be named `UserController`.

Naming xtypes

We recommend using the lowercase class name as `xtype` for each class. This is another very good reason to ensure that the filename for each view class is unique. The `UserList` xtype is `userlist`, the `UserForm` xtype is `userform`, and the `ManageUsers` xtype is `manageusers`. There can be no confusion.

The Ext JS 4 development environment

There are two core components required for Ext JS 4 development as follows:

- **The Sencha Cmd Tool**: This is a cross-platform, Java-based, command-line tool that provides many options to help manage the lifecycle of your applications
- **Ext JS 4 SDK (Software Development Kit)**: This contains all source files, examples, resources, and minified scripts required for application development

We will now examine and install each of these components.

Installing Sencha Cmd

The Sencha Cmd Tool can be downloaded from `http://www.sencha.com/products/sencha-cmd/download`. The file is approximately 46 MB and needs to be unzipped before running the setup process.

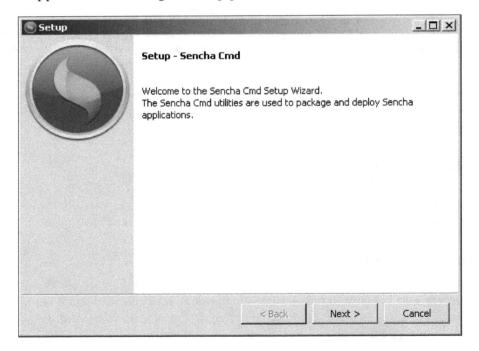

Click on **Next** to view the **License Agreement** section. You will need to accept the agreement before clicking on the **Next** button:

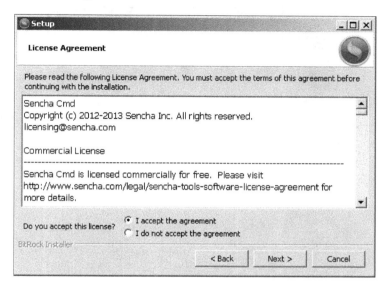

The screen shown in the following screenshot prompts for an **Installation Directory**. We recommend that you install the Sencha Cmd Tool on a directory that is easily accessible (/Users/Shared/ for Mac users and C:\ for Windows users):

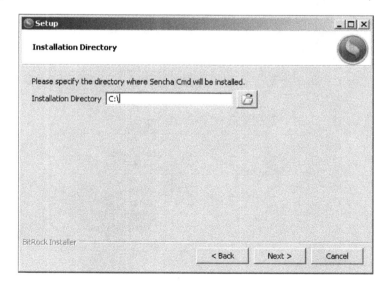

Click on **Next** to continue. This will show a prompt indicating that setup is now ready to begin installing Sencha Cmd on your computer. Click on **Next** again to continue the installation. The final prompt will confirm the installation of Sencha Cmd:

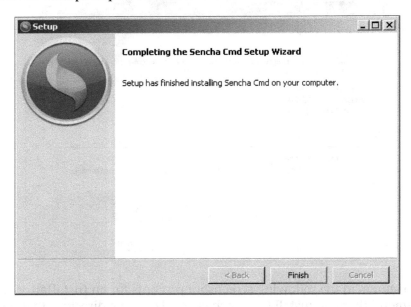

You can now view the installed files as shown in the following screenshot:

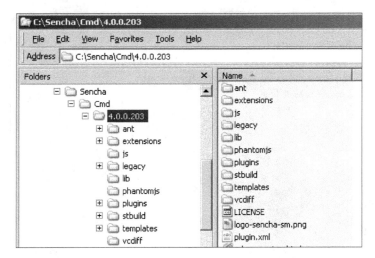

To confirm the installation, open a command prompt (Windows) or terminal (Mac), type sencha, and press the *Enter* key. This will confirm that Sencha Cmd has been added to your system path and should result in output similar to that shown in the following screenshot:

```
Command Prompt
C:\>sencha
Sencha Cmd v4.0.0.203
Sencha Cmd provides several categories of commands and some global switches. In
most cases, the first step is to generate an application based on a Sencha SDK
such as Ext JS or Sencha Touch:

    sencha -sdk /path/to/sdk generate app MyApp /path/to/myapp

Sencha Cmd supports Ext JS 4.1.1a and higher and Sencha Touch 2.1 and higher.

To get help on commands use the help command:

    sencha help generate app

For more information on using Sencha Cmd, consult the guides found here:

http://docs.sencha.com/ext-js/4-2/#!/guide/command
http://docs.sencha.com/ext-js/4-1/#!/guide/command

http://docs.sencha.com/touch/2-2/#!/guide/command
http://docs.sencha.com/touch/2-1/#!/guide/command

Options
    * --background, -b - Runs the web server in a background thread
    * --cwd, -cw - Sets the directory from which commands should execute
    * --debug, -d - Sets log level to higher verbosity
    * --nologo, -n - Suppress the initial Sencha Cmd version display
    * --plain, -pl - enables plain logging output (no highlighting)
    * --quiet, -q - Sets log level to warnings and errors only
    * --sdk-path, -s - The location of the SDK to use for non-app commands
    * --time, -ti - Display the execution time after executing all commands
Categories
    * app - Perform various application build processes
```

Note that any currently open console/terminal windows will need to be closed and reopened to ensure that the installation path changes are reloaded. The final step is to check whether or not there are any upgrades available by typing:

```
sencha upgrade --check
```

This command should display an appropriate message as shown in the following screenshot:

```
Command Prompt
C:\>sencha upgrade --check
Sencha Cmd v4.0.0.203
[INF] Determining the latest version of Sencha Cmd
[INF] The latest version of Sencha Cmd is 4.0.0.203
[INF] Sencha Cmd 4.0.0.203 is this version.

C:\>
```

It is possible to upgrade versions of Sencha Cmd by omitting the `--check` argument. For a full list of Sencha command-line options, refer to `http://docs.sencha.com/extjs/4.2.2/#!/guide/command`. This page also contains many helpful troubleshooting tips and explanations. In addition, you may also use the command-line help by executing `sencha help`. Executing the `sencha help` command will display detailed help options:

```
Command Prompt                                                    _ □ ×
Sencha Cmd v4.0.0.203
Sencha Cmd provides several categories of commands and some global switches
most cases, the first step is to generate an application based on a Sencha
such as Ext JS or Sencha Touch:

    sencha -sdk /path/to/sdk generate app MyApp /path/to/myapp

Sencha Cmd supports Ext JS 4.1.1a and higher and Sencha Touch 2.1 and highe

To get help on commands use the help command:

    sencha help generate app

For more information on using Sencha Cmd, consult the guides found here:

http://docs.sencha.com/ext-js/4-2/#!/guide/command
http://docs.sencha.com/ext-js/4-1/#!/guide/command

http://docs.sencha.com/touch/2-2/#!/guide/command
http://docs.sencha.com/touch/2-1/#!/guide/command

Options
  * --background, -b - Runs the web server in a background thread
  * --cwd, -cw - Sets the directory from which commands should execute
```

Installing Ext JS 4 SDK

The SDK can be downloaded from `http://www.sencha.com/products/extjs`. The previous step will have created a Sencha directory in the following location:

- `C:\Sencha` for Windows users
- `/Users/Shared/Sencha` for Mac users

After downloading the SDK, you should create an ext-xxx directory within this Sencha directory where xxx represents the version of the Ext JS 4 framework. You can then unzip the SDK into this directory resulting in the structure shown in the following screenshot:

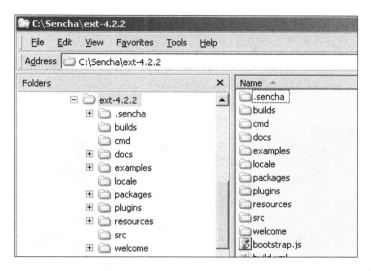

You are now ready to initialize the Ext JS 4 3T application skeleton.

Generating the 3T Ext JS 4 application skeleton

The format of the skeleton generation command is:

```
sencha -sdk /path/to/sdk generate app MyApp /path/to/MyApp
```

Running this command will copy all required SDK files to the /path/to/MyApp directory and create a skeleton of the resources ready for development. You must use full paths for both the SDK and MyApp directories.

It is important to remember that the 3T application is a Maven project and that the web content root is the webapp directory located within the Maven directory structure. The project folder that was created in *Chapter 1, Preparing Your Development Environment,* and the webapp directory (on Windows) can be found at C:\projects\task-time-tracker\src\main\webapp.

On Mac, it can be found at /Users/{username}/projects/task-time-tracker/src/main/webapp.

The 3T application skeleton can now be generated by executing the following command (for Windows platforms):

```
sencha -sdk C:\Sencha\ext-4.2.2 generate app TTT C:\projects\
    task-time-tracker\src\main\webapp
```

Note that this command must be on a single line. The `TTT` argument represents the application name and will be used to generate the application namespace. We could have used `TaskTimeTracker`, but the abbreviated form is easier to write!

Executing the command from the terminal should produce considerable output, ending with some red errors:

```
 Command Prompt                                                          _|□|x|
[INF]
[INF] before-upgrade:
[INF]
[INF] generate-app-impl:
[ERR] Cannot merge to c:\projects\task-time-tracker\src\main\webapp\index.html - no base version
[ERR] Manual merge required:

        c:\projects\task-time-tracker\src\main\webapp\index.html
        c:\projects\task-time-tracker\src\main\webapp\index.html.$old

[INF]
[INF] generate-starter-app:
[INF]     [mkdir] Created dir: c:\projects\task-time-tracker\src\main\webapp\resources
[INF]     [mkdir] Created dir: c:\projects\task-time-tracker\src\main\webapp\overrides
[INF]     [mkdir] Created dir: c:\projects\task-time-tracker\src\main\webapp\sass\src
[INF]     [mkdir] Created dir: c:\projects\task-time-tracker\src\main\webapp\sass\var
[INF]     [mkdir] Created dir: c:\projects\task-time-tracker\src\main\webapp\sass\etc
[INF] [x-property-file] Updating property file: c:\projects\task-time-tracker\src\main\webapp\.se
[INF]
[INF] after-upgrade:
[INF]
[INF] -after-generate-app:
[INF] [x-property-file] Updating property file: c:\projects\task-time-tracker\src\main\webapp\.se
[ERR] Upgrade encountered 1 merge conflicts. Please resolve all merge conflicts then run 'sencha
        at org.apache.tools.ant.taskdefs.Exit.execute(Exit.java:164)
        at org.apache.tools.ant.UnknownElement.execute(UnknownElement.java:291)
        at sun.reflect.GeneratedMethodAccessor24.invoke(Unknown Source)
        at sun.reflect.DelegatingMethodAccessorImpl.invoke(Unknown Source)
        at java.lang.reflect.Method.invoke(Unknown Source)
        at org.apache.tools.ant.dispatch.DispatchUtils.execute(DispatchUtils.java:106)
        at org.apache.tools.ant.Task.perform(Task.java:348)
        at org.apache.tools.ant.taskdefs.Sequential.execute(Sequential.java:68)
        at net.sf.antcontrib.logic.IfTask.execute(IfTask.java:197)
        at sun.reflect.NativeMethodAccessorImpl.invoke0(Native Method)
```

Don't be too concerned with the **[ERR]** warnings; Sencha Cmd has identified the presence of the `index.html` file and replaced it with the Sencha Cmd version. The original file was copied to `index.html.$old`. We don't need the backup file (it was created during the NetBeans project creation process); it can safely be deleted.

Opening the NetBeans IDE will now display many new files and directories within the webapp directory of the 3T project:

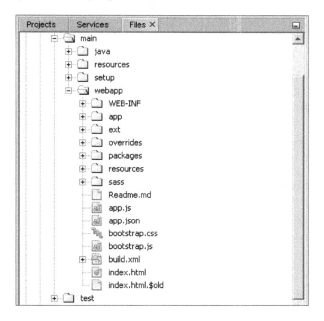

You can now run the project to view the output in the browser:

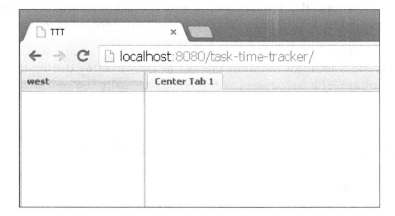

This output is the default Ext JS 4 application content in the index.html page, created by the generate app command when building the project skeleton. Let's now look at the key files that have been generated.

The index.html file

The `index.html` file consists of the following listings:

```html
<!DOCTYPE HTML>
<html>
<head>
  <meta charset="UTF-8">
  <title>TTT</title>
  <!-- <x-compile> -->
    <!-- <x-bootstrap> -->
      <link rel="stylesheet" href="bootstrap.css">
      <script src="ext/ext-dev.js"></script>
      <script src="bootstrap.js"></script>
    <!-- </x-bootstrap> -->
    <script src="app.js"></script>
  <!-- </x-compile> -->
</head>
<body></body>
</html>
```

Note the `x-compile` and `x-bootstrap` tags within the page content. These are used by the Sencha Cmd Tool and allow the compiler to identify the scripts at the root of your application (the default file is always `app.js`). The compiler also ignores the bootstrap part of the framework that is used only during development. When generating a production application, all of the required files are pulled in during the build process. This will be covered in detail in *Chapter 13, Moving Your Application to Production*.

You should note that the `ext-dev.js` file is the only Ext JS 4 framework resource required. This file is used for dynamic JavaScript class loading during the development phase. The framework will then dynamically retrieve any JavaScript resources required by the application.

The app.js and Application.js files

The `app.js` file is the entry point of the application. The contents of the file, including generated comments, looks as follows:

```
/*
    This file is generated and updated by Sencha Cmd. You can edit
this file as needed for your application, but these edits will have to
be merged by Sencha Cmd when upgrading.
*/
```

```
Ext.application({
  name: 'TTT',
  extend: 'TTT.Application',
  autoCreateViewport: true
});
```

The Ext.application extends the TTT.Application class, which is defined in the app/Application.js file as follows:

```
Ext.define('TTT.Application', {
  name: 'TTT',
  extend: 'Ext.app.Application',
  views: [
    // TODO: add views here
  ],
  controllers: [
    // TODO: add controllers here
  ],
  stores: [
    // TODO: add stores here
  ]
});
```

It is the Application.js file that will contain our 3T application-specific code.

 You should note that this is a different setup to that described in earlier Ext JS 4 tutorials where the app.js file contains application-specific properties (views, controllers, stores, and application functions). The approach outlined previously keeps all application-specific code within the app directory.

Our first change to the autogenerated Application.js file is to add the launch function:

```
Ext.define('TTT.Application', {
  name: 'TTT',
  extend: 'Ext.app.Application',
  views: [
    // TODO: add views here
  ],
  controllers: [
    // TODO: add controllers here
  ],
  stores: [
    // TODO: add stores here
```

```
    ],
    launch: function() {
        Ext.create('TTT.view.Viewport');
    }
});
```

We can now remove `autoCreateViewport:true` from the `app.js` file as the logic for creating the viewport is now in the `launch` function. The `launch` function itself will be enhanced in the next chapter to implement the user logon, so there is plenty of code to come! The updated `app.js` file is as follows:

```
Ext.application({
    name: 'TTT',
    extend: 'TTT.Application'
});
```

The bootstrap.js and bootstrap.css files

The `bootstrap.js` and `bootstrap.css` files were generated by Sencha Cmd and should not be edited. They are used internally to initialize and configure the development environment.

The app/Viewport.js and app/view/Main.js files

An Ext JS 4 viewport is a container that resizes itself to use the entire browser window. The `Viewport.js` definition is as follows:

```
Ext.define('TTT.view.Viewport', {
    extend: 'Ext.container.Viewport',
    requires:[
        'Ext.layout.container.Fit',
        'TTT.view.Main'
    ],
    layout: {
        type: 'fit'
    },
    items: [{
        xtype: 'app-main'
    }]
});
```

There is only one view added to the `items` array; the `TTT.view.Main`, function, which has an `xtype` function called `app-main`:

```
Ext.define('TTT.view.Main', {
    extend: 'Ext.container.Container',
    requires:[
        'Ext.tab.Panel',
        'Ext.layout.container.Border'
    ],
    xtype: 'app-main',
    layout: {
        type: 'border'
    },
    items: [{
        region: 'west',
        xtype: 'panel',
        title: 'west',
        width: 150
    },{
        region: 'center',
        xtype: 'tabpanel',
        items:[{
            title: 'Center Tab 1'
        }]
    }]
});
```

The preceding file defines the border layout and textual content of the two regions that are displayed in the browser.

> Not confident with Ext JS views, xtypes, viewports, border layouts, or panels? We recommend browsing and reviewing the basic Ext JS 4 component concepts at `http://docs.sencha.com/extjs/4.2.2/#!/guide/components.`

The app/controller/Main.js file

The final generated file we will examine is the `Main.js` controller:

```
Ext.define('TTT.controller.Main', {
    extend: 'Ext.app.Controller'
});
```

There is no functionality in this class as there is nothing yet to control.

Creating components using Sencha Cmd

It is possible to use Sencha Cmd to generate skeleton components. The most useful of these commands are those used to generate basic models.

Generating model skeletons

A model skeleton can be generated very easily using the Sencha Cmd Tool. The syntax is as follows:

```
sencha generate model ModelName
  [field1:fieldType,field2:fieldType...]
```

This command must be executed in the application root (the directory in which the app.js file is found). Note that there must not be any spaces in the comma-separated field listing. The company model skeleton can be generated by executing the following command:

```
sencha generate model Company idCompany:int,companyName:string
```

The final string for the companyName field is not strictly required as the default property type is string, if not specified. The output from this command looks as shown in the following screenshot:

The generated `Company.js` file is written into the `app/model` directory and has the following content:

```
Ext.define('TTT.model.Company', {
    extend: 'Ext.data.Model',
    fields: [
        { name: 'idCompany', type: 'int' },
        { name: 'companyName', type: 'string'}
    ]
});
```

This is a very simple model and has two fields as expected. We can also generate more complex models using different data types:

```
sencha generate model TaskLog
    idTaskLog:int,taskDescription:string,taskLogDate:
    date,taskMinutes:int,hours:float,username:string,
    userFullName:string,idTask:int,taskName:string,
    idProject:int,projectName:string,idCompany:int,
    companyName:string
```

The preceding command will generate the `TaskLog` model with fields of types `int`, `string`, `date`, and `float`.

```
Ext.define('TTT.model.TaskLog', {
    extend: 'Ext.data.Model',
    fields: [
        { name: 'idTaskLog', type: 'int' },
        { name: 'taskDescription', type: 'string' },
        { name: 'taskLogDate', type: 'date' },
        { name: 'taskMinutes', type: 'int' },
        { name: 'hours', type: 'float' },
        { name: 'username', type: 'string' },
        { name: 'userFullName', type: 'string' },
        { name: 'idTask', type: 'int' },
        { name: 'taskName', type: 'string' },
        { name: 'idProject', type: 'int' },
        { name: 'projectName', type: 'string' },
        { name: 'idCompany', type: 'int' },
        { name: 'companyName', type: 'string' }
    ]
});
```

The model skeletons for the three remaining entities can be created by executing the following commands:

```
sencha generate model Project idProject:int,projectName:
  string, idCompany:int,companyName:string
```

```
sencha generate model Task
  idTask:int,taskName:string,idProject:int,projectName:string,
  idCompany:int,companyName:string
```

```
sencha generate model User
  username:string,firstName:string,lastName:string,
  fullName:string,email:string,password:string,adminRole:string
```

Note that each of these models matches the JSON structure generated by the `addJson` (`JsonObjectBuilder`) method in the equivalent Java domain classes. You should now have the files shown in the following screenshot in the `app/model` directory:

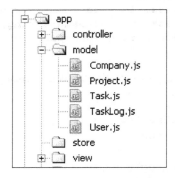

Although we have used the Sencha Cmd Tool to generate these model skeletons, it would have been just as easy to create the appropriate files and definitions in the NetBeans IDE.

Generating views and controllers using Sencha Cmd

It is also possible to generate basic view and controller skeletons, but the contents of these files are very limited. The following command will create a view named `ManageUsers`:

```
sencha generate view ManageUsers
```

The `ManageUsers.js` file will be written to the `app/view` directory and have the following contents:

```
Ext.define("TTT.view.ManageUsers", {
    extend: 'Ext.Component',
    html: 'Hello, World!!'
});
```

In a similar manner, you could create a controller skeleton for `UserController`:

```
sencha generate controller UserController
```

The `UserController.js` file would be written to the `app/controller` directory and have the following contents:

```
Ext.define('TTT.controller.UserController', {
    extend: 'Ext.app.Controller'
});
```

We believe it is simpler to create views and controllers in the NetBeans IDE and will not be using Sencha Cmd for this purpose.

Summary

This chapter has configured the Ext JS 4 development environment and introduced practical design conventions and concepts. We have installed Sencha Cmd and generated the 3T application skeleton, examining the core generated files to understand the recommended application structure. Our model entities have been generated using Sencha Cmd and are ready for enhancement in the following chapters. The scene has been set for building our 3T application frontend.

In *Chapter 10, Logging On and Maintaining Users*, we will develop the Ext JS 4 components required to log on to the 3T application and maintain users. Our creative journey through **User Interface (UI)** design is just starting!

10
Logging On and Maintaining Users

The most creative part of the enterprise application lifecycle revolves around the user interface design. Your goal as an enterprise application developer is to create a user interface that is intuitive, consistent, and easy to use. User interface design requires a thorough understanding of the tools you have available. Thankfully, Ext JS 4 has a comprehensive range of widgets that cover the core functionality required for any enterprise application. If you have not already visited the examples page, then take some time now to become familiar with the full range of Ext JS 4 components at `http://docs.sencha.com/extjs/4.2.2/#!/example`.

This chapter will focus on building the logon and user administration interfaces. We will develop a set of view components and wire them together with controllers to perform the following:

- Log on to the application
- Display the main application viewport
- Provide a user maintenance interface

The user maintenance interface will introduce model persistence and validation properties that are used for CRUD operations. We have quite a bit to do, so let's start by examining the application layouts and workflow.

Layouts, screens, and workflows

The application starts by displaying the logon window. Without a successful logon you will be unable to reach the main application viewport. The logon window has a very simple design as shown in the following screenshot:

A successful logon will be displayed on the welcome screen as shown in the following screenshot:

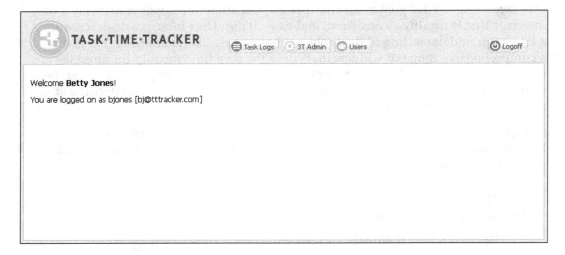

The welcome screen has a number of buttons in the header dependent on your permissions. A normal user will only see the **Task Logs** button and the **Logoff** button. An admin user will see the additional **3T Admin** and **Users** buttons. We will leave the **3T Admin** and **Task Log** modules for the subsequent chapters.

The user administration interface is based on the most common design pattern in modern enterprise applications. This layout displays a list of users in the left-hand side panel and the user details in the right-hand side panel:

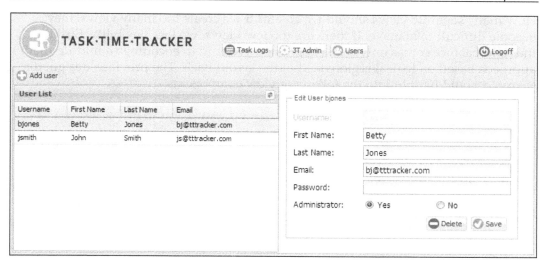

Each of these screen designs has icons and a logo that are not part of the Ext JS framework. The code in the following sections will define the appropriate styles but you will need to include the required resources to achieve the same look and feel. The full source code including resources can be downloaded from this book's website.

Defining view components

One of the hardest decisions to make when implementing wireframes and UI mockups is how to split up the view. Consider our user maintenance screen as shown in the following screenshot:

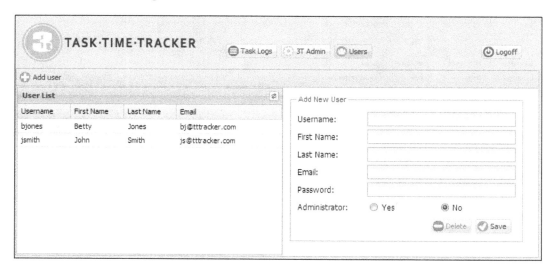

How many separate views should we create? If we create too many views, they become difficult to manage. If there are too few views, we lose flexibility. Striking the right balance comes only with experience. We tend to encourage a middle-road approach based on logical regions within the layout itself. The previous design, for example, could be split into the following view components:

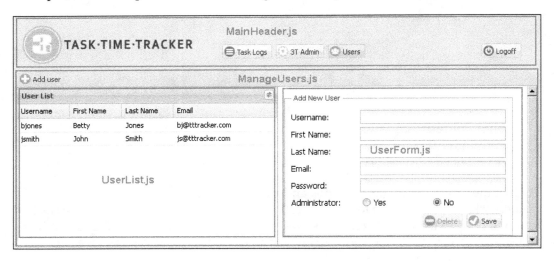

This is the structure we will be implementing. However, we could easily implement the following design:

The second version would use a single view to encapsulate the user grid, form, and toolbar. The resulting `ManageUsers.js` file would be approximately 200 lines long; not a large file by any stretch of the imagination. From a functional perspective there would be no difference between the two designs. However, the first approach gives us more flexibility. We can easily rearrange the views on the page or refactor the interface without much effort (for example, moving `UserForm` to a pop-up window and allowing the user list to fill the entire width of the screen). This would not be as easy with the second design version.

When in doubt, you should err on the side of simplicity. Complex views with many hundreds or even thousands of lines of code should be avoided at all costs. Think of your views as discrete objects with specific purposes and keep them simple.

Building our views

Now that we have some practical guidelines to building views, it is time to create our application interface. A user must be able to log on successfully to work with the application, so let's start with the logon window.

Defining the Logon window

The **Task Time Tracker Logon** window is the first thing a user will see, which is shown in the following screenshot:

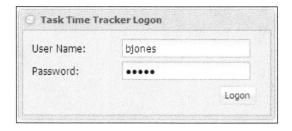

The logon window definition follows the given code:

```
Ext.define('TTT.view.LogonWindow', {
    extend: 'Ext.window.Window',
    xtype: 'logonwindow',
    closable: false,
    iconCls: 'logo-small',
    width: 300,
```

```
        bodyPadding: 10,
        title: 'Task Time Tracker Logon',
        requires: ['Ext.form.field.Text'],
        initComponent: function() {
            var me = this;
            Ext.applyIf(me, {
                items: [{
                    xtype: 'textfield',
                    fieldLabel: 'User Name',
                    name: 'username',
                    allowBlank: false,
                    validateOnBlur: true,
                    emptyText: 'Enter a Username'
                }, {
                    xtype: 'textfield',
                    name: 'password',
                    fieldLabel: 'Password',
                    inputType: 'password',
                    validateOnBlur: true,
                    allowBlank: false
                }, {
                    xtype: 'toolbar',
                    ui: 'footer',
                    layout: {
                        pack: 'end',
                        type: 'hbox'
                    },
                    items: [{
                        xtype: 'button',
                        text: 'Logon'
                    }]
                }]
            });
            me.callParent(arguments);
        }
    });
```

This window definition extends the Ext.window.Window and adds the two text fields and logon button. The LogonWindow class is namespaced to view and will hence reside in the app/view directory. The defined xtype property is the lowercase version of the class name and will be used in the controller to reference the LogonWindow instance.

An `xtype` property is a symbolic name (alias or shortcut) for a class. The xtype property is a powerful concept in Ext JS that allows components to be configured, but not rendered, until the owning container deems it necessary. A full explanation of components' lazy initialization by `xtype` can be found here `http://docs.sencha.com/extjs/4.2.2/#!/guide/components`.

The MVC design pattern encourages Ext JS 4 developers to implement business logic in the controller layer, leaving the views as dumb objects. The only meta logic we are applying in this window is the `allowBlank:false` property combined with `validateOnBlur:true`. This will give the user a visual clue if moving off the field without entering text.

Using the initComponent() function

The `initComponent` function is a template function that is invoked by the constructor during object creation. The template design pattern allows subclasses to define specific behavior without changing the semantics of the base class processing algorithm. A detailed explanation of this pattern can be found here: `http://en.wikipedia.org/wiki/Template_method_design_pattern`. Ext JS uses the template design pattern to allow developers to specify logic during certain well-defined phases in the component's lifecycle. The `initComponent` function is probably the most used but there are many other template hooks that can be implemented. A full list of component template functions can be found here: `http://docs.sencha.com/extjs/4.2.2/#!/guide/components`.

The `initComponent` function is used to initialize data, set up configurations, and attach event handlers to the component. The recommended usage pattern for this function (or any template function) includes:

- Reference the current scope as a local closured variable using `var me = this`. Use the `me` reference everywhere in the function when referring to the object instance. This will help with correct JavaScript closure for complex objects by ensuring `me` and `this` refer to the correct object scope.

- Use `Ext.applyIf` to add class-specific properties to the configuration. Note that we are not using `Ext.apply`, which will override properties that are already defined; only new properties that do not exist in `me` will be copied. This ensures that xtype-based configuration properties take precedence.

- Complete the `initComponent` function by calling the parent function with the supplied arguments using `me.callParent(arguments)`.

These three points outline some advanced concepts that may be a bit beyond the intermediate reader. Don't despair if some of this doesn't make sense yet; follow the design pattern and things will become clearer with experience!

Defining the viewport

The `Viewport` view uses a `vbox` layout to split the view into two regions, the header and the main content areas, as shown in the following screenshot:

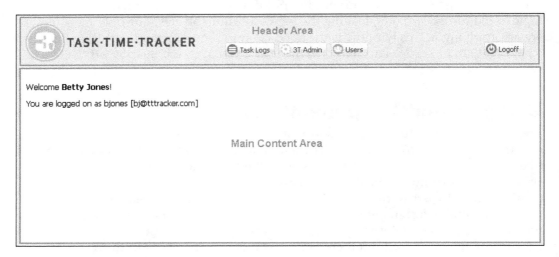

We could have used a `border` layout to achieve the same visual result but the `vbox` layout is a lighter weight component. Only use the `border` layout if your application needs additional functionality such as expandable/collapsible regions or resizable split views.

The `Viewport` definition is as follows:

```
Ext.define('TTT.view.Viewport', {
    extend: 'Ext.container.Viewport',
    cls: 'x-border-layout-ct',
    requires: ['TTT.view.MainHeader', 'TTT.view.MainCards',
      'Ext.layout.container.VBox'],
    padding: 5,
    layout: {
        type: 'vbox',
        align: 'stretch'
    },
    items: [{
        xtype: 'mainheader',
```

```
            height: 80
        }, {
            xtype: 'maincards',
            flex: 1
        }]
    });
```

There are two views that now need to be defined: one for the main header, the second for the main region card layout.

The MainHeader.js view

The `MainHeader` defines and positions the 3T logo and buttons as shown in the following code:

```
Ext.define('TTT.view.MainHeader', {
    extend: 'Ext.container.Container',
    xtype: 'mainheader',
    requires: ['Ext.toolbar.Toolbar'],
    layout: {
        align: 'stretch',
        type: 'hbox'
    },
    initComponent: function() {
        var me = this;
        Ext.applyIf(me, {
            items: [{
                xtype: 'container',
                cls: 'logo',
                width: 300
            }, {
                xtype: 'toolbar',
                flex: 1,
                ui: 'footer',
                layout: {
                    pack: 'end',
                    padding: '20 20 0 0',
                    type: 'hbox'
                },
                items: [{
                    xtype: 'button',
                    itemId: 'taskLogsBtn',
                    iconCls: 'tasklog',
                    text: 'Task Logs'
                }, {
```

```
                        xtype: 'button',
                        itemId: 'taskAdminBtn',
                        iconCls: 'admin',
                        hidden: !TTT.getApplication().isAdmin(),
                        text: '3T Admin'
                  }, {
                        xtype: 'button',
                        itemId: 'userAdminBtn',
                        hidden: !TTT.getApplication().isAdmin(),
                        iconCls: 'users',
                        text: 'Users'
                  }, '->',
                  {
                        xtype: 'button',
                        itemId: 'logoffBtn',
                        iconCls: 'logoff',
                        text: 'Logoff'
                  }]
            }]
        });
        me.callParent(arguments);
    }
});
```

Each button defines an `itemId` property to help uniquely identify the button
when using selectors in the controller. The two administrative buttons use the
`hidden` property to hide the button if the user is not an administrator. The `TTT.`
`getApplication().isAdmin()` function has not been defined as yet but this
will be added to the `Application.js` function in the section ahead.

The MainCards.js file

The `MainCards` component is a card layout container that holds all the components
that will be rendered in the main content area as shown in the following code:

```
Ext.define('TTT.view.MainCards', {
    extend: 'Ext.container.Container',
    xtype: 'maincards',
    requires: ['Ext.layout.container.Card', 'TTT.view.Welcome',
      'TTT.view.user.ManageUsers'],
    layout: 'card',
    initComponent: function() {
        var me = this;
        Ext.applyIf(me, {
```

```
            items: [{
                xtype: 'welcome',
                itemId: 'welcomCard'
            }, {
                xtype: 'manageusers',
                itemId: 'manageUsersCard'
            }]
        });
        me.callParent(arguments);
    }
});
```

We will be adding items to the MainCards as we build our functionality. For this chapter we will focus on the Welcome and ManageUsers components.

Defining the Welcome panel

The Welcome panel uses an XTemplate to render a simple welcome message based on the logged-on user. The user data is retrieved from the application using the TTT.getApplication().getUser() function that will be added to the Application.js function after a successful logon.

```
Ext.define('TTT.view.Welcome', {
    extend: 'Ext.panel.Panel',
    xtype: 'welcome',
    requires: ['Ext.XTemplate'],
    initComponent: function() {
        var me = this;
        var tpl = new Ext.XTemplate('<tpl for=".">', '<p>Welcome
          <b>{fullName}</b>!</p>', '<p>You are logged on as
            {username} [{email}]</p>', '</tpl>');
        var welcomeHtml =
          tpl.apply(TTT.getApplication().getUser());
        Ext.applyIf(me, {
            items: [{
                xtype: 'container',
                padding: 10,
                html: welcomeHtml
            }]
        });
        me.callParent(arguments);
    }
});
```

Defining the user management components

The user management interface consists of three view files as shown in the
following screenshot:

In addition to the views we will also need to define a user store that manages the
data displayed in the user listing.

The ManageUsers.js file

The ManageUsers file is a simple hbox layout that displays the UserList and
UserForm. The toolbar contains the single **Add User** button. This file has a very
simple definition, which is as follows:

```
Ext.define('TTT.view.user.ManageUsers', {
    extend: 'Ext.panel.Panel',
    xtype: 'manageusers',
    requires: ['Ext.toolbar.Toolbar', 'TTT.view.user.UserList',
      'TTT.view.user.UserForm'],
    layout: {
        type: 'hbox',
        align: 'stretch'
    },
    initComponent: function() {
        var me = this;
        Ext.applyIf(me, {
            dockedItems: [{
                xtype: 'toolbar',
                dock: 'top',
                items: [{
                    xtype: 'button',
                    itemId: 'addUserBtn',
```

```
                                  iconCls: 'addnew',
                                  text: 'Add user'
                          }]
                  }],
                  items: [{
                          xtype: 'userlist',
                          width: 400,
                          margin: 1
                  }, {
                          xtype: 'userform',
                          flex: 1
                  }]
          });
          me.callParent(arguments);
      }
});
```

The UserForm.js file

This UserForm.js file displays the user details as shown in the following code:

```
Ext.define('TTT.view.user.UserForm', {
    extend: 'Ext.form.Panel',
    xtype: 'userform',
    requires: ['Ext.form.FieldSet', 'Ext.form.field.Radio',
      'Ext.form.RadioGroup', 'Ext.toolbar.Toolbar'],
    layout: {
        type: 'anchor'
    },
    bodyPadding: 10,
    border: false,
    autoScroll: true,
    initComponent: function() {
        var me = this;
        Ext.applyIf(me, {
            items: [{
                xtype: 'fieldset',
                padding: 10,
                width: 350,
                fieldDefaults: {
                    anchor: '100%'
                },
                title: 'User',
                items: [{
```

```
            xtype: 'textfield',
            name: 'username',
            fieldLabel: 'Username'
        }, {
            xtype: 'textfield',
            name: 'firstName',
            fieldLabel: 'First Name'
        }, {
            xtype: 'textfield',
            name: 'lastName',
            fieldLabel: 'Last Name'
        }, {
            xtype: 'textfield',
            name: 'email',
            fieldLabel: 'Email'
        }, {
            xtype: 'textfield',
            name: 'password',
            inputType: 'password',
            fieldLabel: 'Password'
        }, {
            xtype: 'radiogroup',
            fieldLabel: 'Administrator',
            items: [{
                boxLabel: 'Yes',
                name: 'adminRole',
                inputValue: 'Y'
            }, {
                boxLabel: 'No',
                name: 'adminRole',
                inputValue: 'N'
            }]
        }, {
            xtype: 'toolbar',
            ui: 'footer',
            layout: {
                pack: 'end',
                type: 'hbox'
            },
            items: [{
                xtype: 'button',
                itemId: 'deleteBtn',
                iconCls: 'delete',
                text: 'Delete'
```

```
            }, {
                xtype: 'button',
                itemId: 'saveBtn',
                iconCls: 'save',
                text: 'Save'
            }]
        }]
    }]
});
        me.callParent(arguments);
    }
});
```

Each button has an `itemId` property defined to allow us to uniquely identify them in the controller. Each field name in the form exactly matches the field name in the `User` model defined in the previous chapter. This will allow us to easily load a user model instance into the form.

The UserList.js file

The `UserList` file is a grid panel with the following definition:

```
Ext.define('TTT.view.user.UserList', {
    extend: 'Ext.grid.Panel',
    xtype: 'userlist',
    store: 'User',
    title: 'User List',
    viewConfig: {
        markDirty: false,
        stripeRows: false
    },
    initComponent: function() {
        var me = this;
        Ext.applyIf(me, {
            tools: [{
                type: 'refresh',
                tooltip: 'Refresh user list'
            }],
            columns: [{
                xtype: 'gridcolumn',
                dataIndex: 'username',
                flex: 1,
                text: 'Username'
            }, {
```

```
                       xtype: 'gridcolumn',
                       dataIndex: 'firstName',
                       flex: 1,
                       text: 'First Name'
                 }, {
                       xtype: 'gridcolumn',
                       flex: 1,
                       dataIndex: 'lastName',
                       text: 'Last Name'
                 }, {
                       xtype: 'gridcolumn',
                       flex: 2,
                       dataIndex: 'email',
                       text: 'Email'
                 }]
          });
          me.callParent(arguments);
      }
});
```

The grid columns use the `flex` config property to define the relative width of each column. The `email` column will hence be twice the width of the other columns.

The `markDirty:false` in the `viewConfig` is used to remove the dirty cell indicator when a cell value is modified. Without this property the grid would render changed cell values as shown, even after the record has been successfully saved:

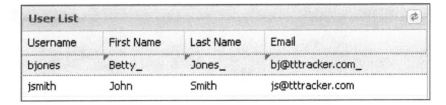

The `User` store is yet to be defined, so let's add it now.

The User store

The `User` store loads users from the `ttt/user/findAll.json` URL. which is mapped to the `UserHandler.findAll` method. Readers should recall that the `ttt/` prefix URL corresponds to the servlet mapping specified in the `com.gieman.tttracker.web.WebApp.getServletMappings()` method in *Chapter 7, The Web Request Handling Layer*. Each user record in the JSON array will result in the creation of a `TTT.model.User` model instance. The store definition is explained in the following code:

```
Ext.define('TTT.store.User', {
    extend: 'Ext.data.Store',
    requires: ['TTT.model.User'],
    model: 'TTT.model.User',
    proxy: {
        type: 'ajax',
        url: 'ttt/user/findAll.json',
        reader: {
            type: 'json',
            root: 'data'
        }
    }
});
```

The `User` model was defined in the previous chapter and currently looks like the following:

```
Ext.define('TTT.model.User', {
    extend: 'Ext.data.Model',

    fields: [
        { name: 'username', type: 'string' },
        { name: 'firstName', type: 'string' },
        { name: 'lastName', type: 'string' },
        { name: 'fullName', type: 'string' },
        { name: 'email', type: 'string' },
        { name: 'password', type: 'string' },
        { name: 'adminRole', type: 'string' }
    ]
});
```

Ext JS 4 models are a key part of the MVC framework and we will now spend some time learning about these important objects.

Models and persistence

Ext JS 4 models are similar to JPA entities in that they define data fields that represent columns in the underlying database tables. Each model instance represents a row in the table. The primary key field is defined using the idProperty of the model, which must match one of the field names. The User model can now be updated as shown:

```
Ext.define('TTT.model.User', {
    extend: 'Ext.data.Model',

    fields: [
        { name: 'username', type: 'string' },
        { name: 'firstName', type: 'string' },
        { name: 'lastName', type: 'string' },
        { name: 'fullName', type: 'string' },
        { name: 'email', type: 'string' },
        { name: 'password', type: 'string' },
        { name: 'adminRole', type: 'string' }
    ],
    idProperty: 'username'
});
```

Defining the proxy

Each model can be made persistent aware by configuring an appropriate proxy. All loading and saving of data is then handled by the proxy when the load, save, or destroy method on the model is called. There are several different types of proxies but the most widely used is the Ext.data.ajax.Proxy (alternate name Ext.data. AjaxProxy). The AjaxProxy uses AJAX requests to read and write data from the server. Requests are sent as GET or POST methods depending on the operation.

A second useful proxy is Ajax.data.RestProxy. The RestProxy is a specialization of the AjaxProxy that maps the four CRUD actions to the appropriate RESTful HTTP methods (GET, POST, PUT, and DELETE). The RestProxy would be used when connecting to RESTful web services. Our application will use AjaxProxy.

The `User` model definition including proxy follows:

```
Ext.define('TTT.model.User', {
    extend: 'Ext.data.Model',

    fields: [
        { name: 'username', type: 'string' },
        { name: 'firstName', type: 'string' },
        { name: 'lastName', type: 'string' },
        { name: 'fullName', type: 'string', persist:false },
        { name: 'email', type: 'string' },
        { name: 'password', type: 'string' },
        { name: 'adminRole', type: 'string' }
    ],
    idProperty: 'username',
    proxy: {
        type: 'ajax',
        idParam:'username',
        api:{
            create:'ttt/user/store.json',
            read:'ttt/user/find.json',
            update:'ttt/user/store.json',
            destroy:'ttt/user/remove.json'
        },
        reader: {
            type: 'json',
            root: 'data'
        },
        writer: {
            type: 'json',
            allowSingle:true,
            encode:true,
            root:'data',
            writeAllFields: true
        }
    }
});
```

The proxy is defined as type `ajax` and specifies the primary key field in the model with the `idParam` property. The `idParam` is used when generating the URL for the `read` operation. For example, if trying to load the user record with username `bjones`, the proxy would generate a URL as follows:

`ttt/user/find.json?username=bjones`

If the `idParam` property was omitted, the URL generated would be as follows:

`ttt/user/find.json?id=bjones`

The `api` properties define the URLs to call on CRUD action methods. Each URL maps to an appropriate handler method in `UserHandler`. Note that the `update` and `create` URLs are the same as both actions are handled by the `UserHandler.store` method.

It is important to note that the `AjaxProxy` read operation uses a `GET` request while all other operations use `POST` requests. This is different from the `RestProxy` method, which uses a different request method for each operation.

Comparing AJAX and REST proxies

Our request handling layer has been designed to consume AJAX requests in a format submitted by Ext JS 4 clients. Each handler that processes an update action is configured with `RequestMethod.POST` and expects a `data` parameter that holds the JSON object applicable to the action.

We could have implemented the request handling layer as a RESTful API where each method is mapped to an appropriate request method type (GET, POST, PUT, or DELETE). Implementing a delete action would then encode the `id` of the item in the URL of a DELETE submitted request. Deleting the `bjones` user, for example, could be achieved by submitting a DELETE request method URL as follows:

`user/bjones`

The `UserHandler.remove` method could then be defined as:

```
@RequestMapping(value = "/user/{username}",
method=RequestMethod.DELETE)
@ResponseBody
public String remove(final @PathVariable String username, final
  HttpServletRequest request) {
// code continues…
```

The `@PathVariable` extracts the `username` (in our sample URL this is `bjones`) from the URL, which is then used in the call to the `userService.remove` method. The `@RequestMapping method` of `RequestMethod.DELETE` ensures the method is only executed when a DELETE request matching the URL path of `/user/{username}` is submitted.

The RESTful API is a specific style of using HTTP that encodes the item you want to retrieve or manipulate in the URL itself (via its ID) and encodes what action you want to perform on it in the HTTP method used (GET for retrieving, POST for changing, PUT for creating, DELETE for deleting). The Rest proxy in Ext JS is a specialization of the AjaxProxy that simply maps the four CRUD actions to their RESTful HTTP equivalent method.

There is no significant difference in implementing either the AJAX or REST alternative in Ext JS 4. Configuring the proxy with type:'ajax' or type:'rest' is all that is required. The request handling layer, however, would need to be implemented in a very different way to process the @PathVariable parameters. We prefer the AJAX implementation for the following reasons:

- REST has traditionally been used for server-to-server communication, most notably in web services, and not for browser-server interactions.

- The URLs for CRUD AJAX requests are unique and become self-documenting.

- The 3T application is not a web service and is based on HTML 5.

- The HTML 5 specification no longer supports PUT and DELETE as HTTP methods for form elements (see http://www.w3.org/TR/2010/WD-html5-diff-20101019/#changes-2010-06-24).

- REST is not a flexible solution and is usually based around atomic actions (one item processed per request). AJAX and Ext JS combine to allow more complex interactions with bulk updating possible (many updates in a single request are possible for all create, update, and destroy URLs. This will be explained later in the *Defining the writer* section).

- PUT and DELETE requests are often considered a security risk (in addition to OPTIONS, TRACE, and CONNECT methods) and are often disabled in enterprise web application environments. Applications that specifically require these methods (for example, web services) usually expose these URLs to a limited number of trusted users under secure conditions (usually with SSL certificates).

There is no definitive or compelling reason to use AJAX over REST or vice versa. In fact the online discussions around when to use REST over AJAX are quite extensive, and often very confusing. We have chosen what we believe to be is the simplest and most flexible implementation by using AJAX without the need for REST.

Defining the reader

The `reader` with type `json` instantiates a `Ext.data.reader.Json` instance to decode the server's response to an operation. It reads the JSON `data` node (identified by the `root` property of the reader) and populates the field values in the model. Executing a read operation for the `User` model using `ttt/user/find.json?username=bjones` will return:

```
{
    success: true,
    data: {
        "username": "bjones",
        "firstName": "Betty",
        "lastName": "Jones",
        "fullName": "Betty Jones",
        "email": "bj@tttracker.com",
        "adminRole": "Y"
    }
}
```

The reader will then parse the JSON file and set the corresponding field values on the model.

Defining the writer

The `writer` with type `json` instantiates an `Ext.data.writer.Json` instance to encode any request sent to the server in the JSON format. The `encode:true` property combines with the `root` property to define the HTTP request parameter that holds the JSON data. This combination ensures that a single request parameter with name `data` will hold the JSON representation of the model. For example, saving the previous `bjones` user record will result in a request being submitted with one parameter named `data` holding the following string:

```
{
    "username": "bjones",
    "firstName": "Betty",
    "lastName": "Jones",
    "email": "bj@tttracker.com",
    "password": "thepassword",
    "adminRole": "Y"
}
```

It should be noted that this representation is formatted for readability; the actual data will be a string of characters on one line. This representation is then parsed into a JsonObject in the UserHandler.store method:

```
JsonObject jsonObj = parseJsonObject(jsonData);
```

The appropriate jsonObject values are then extracted as required.

The writeAllFields property will ensure that all fields in the model are sent in the request, not just the modified fields. Our handler methods require all model fields to be present. However, note that we have added the persist:false property to the fullName field. This field is not required as it is not a persistent field in the User domain object.

The final writer property that needs explanation is allowSingle:true. This is the default value and ensures a single record is sent without a wrapping array. If your application performs bulk updates (multiple records are sent in the same single request) then you will need to set this property to false. This would result in single records being sent within an array, as shown in the following code:

```
[{
    "username": "bjones",
    "firstName": "Betty",
    "lastName": "Jones",
    "email": "bj@tttracker.com",
    "password": "thepassword",
    "adminRole": "Y"
}]
```

The 3T application does not implement bulk updates and always expects a single JSON record to be sent in each request.

Defining validations

Each model has built-in support for validating field data. The core validation functions include checks for presence, length, inclusion, exclusion, format (using regular expressions), and email. A model instance can be validated by calling the validate function, which returns an Ext.data.Errors object. The errors object can then be tested to see if there are any validation errors.

The `User` model validations are as follows:

```
validations: [
  {type: 'presence',  field: 'username'},
  {type: 'length', field: 'username', min: 4},
  {type: 'presence',  field: 'firstName'},
  {type: 'length', field: 'firstName', min: 2},
  {type: 'presence',  field: 'lastName'},
  {type: 'length', field: 'lastName', min: 2},
  {type: 'presence',  field: 'email'},
  {type: 'email',  field: 'email'},
  {type: 'presence',  field: 'password'},
  {type: 'length', field: 'password', min: 6},
  {type: 'inclusion', field: 'adminRole', list:['Y','N']}
]
```

The `presence` validation ensures that a value is present for the field. The `length` validation checks for field size. Our validations require a minimum `password` size of six characters and a minimum `username` of four characters. First and last names have a minimum size of two characters. The `inclusion` validation tests to ensure the field value is one of the entries in the defined list. As a result, our `adminRole` value must be either a `Y` or `N`. The `email` validation ensures the e-mail field has a valid e-mail format.

The final code listing for our `User` model can now be defined as:

```
Ext.define('TTT.model.User', {
    extend: 'Ext.data.Model',

    fields: [
        { name: 'username', type: 'string' },
        { name: 'firstName', type: 'string' },
        { name: 'lastName', type: 'string' },
        { name: 'fullName', type: 'string', persist:false },
        { name: 'email', type: 'string' },
        { name: 'password', type: 'string' },
        { name: 'adminRole', type: 'string' }
    ],
    idProperty: 'username',
    proxy: {
        type: 'ajax',
        idParam:'username',
        api:{
```

```
            create:'ttt/user/store.json',
            read:'ttt/user/find.json',
            update:'ttt/user/store.json',
            destroy:'ttt/user/remove.json'
        },
        reader: {
            type: 'json',
            root: 'data'
        },
        writer: {
            type: 'json',
            allowSingle:true,
            encode:true,
            root:'data',
            writeAllFields: true
        }
    },
    validations: [
        {type: 'presence',  field: 'username'},
        {type: 'length', field: 'username', min: 4},
        {type: 'presence',  field: 'firstName'},
        {type: 'length', field: 'firstName', min: 2},
        {type: 'presence',  field: 'lastName'},
        {type: 'length', field: 'lastName', min: 2},
        {type: 'presence',  field: 'email'},
        {type: 'email',  field: 'email'},
        {type: 'presence',  field: 'password'},
        {type: 'length', field: 'password', min: 6},
        {type: 'inclusion', field: 'adminRole', list:['Y','N']}
    ]
});
```

Controlling the Logon and Viewport actions

We are now ready to define the `MainController` that will be used to process the core application actions. These include logging on, logging off, and clicking on the header buttons to display the different management panels in the main content area.

The MainController.js file

The `MainController.js` definition is as the following code:

```
Ext.define('TTT.controller.MainController', {
    extend: 'Ext.app.Controller',
    requires: ['Ext.window.MessageBox'],
    views: ['TTT.view.MainHeader', 'TTT.view.MainCards',
        'TTT.view.LogonWindow'],
    refs: [{
        ref: 'mainCards',
        selector: 'maincards'
    }, {
        ref: 'usernameField',
        selector: 'logonwindow textfield[name=username]'
    }, {
        ref: 'passwordField',
        selector: 'logonwindow textfield[name=password]'
    }],
    init: function(application) {
        this.control({
            'mainheader button': {
                click: this.doHeaderButtonClick
            },
            'logonwindow button': {
                click: this.doLogon
            }
        });
    },
    doHeaderButtonClick: function(button, e, options) {
        var me = this;
        if (button.itemId === 'userAdminBtn') {
            me.getMainCards().getLayout()
                .setActiveItem('manageUsersCard');
        } else if (button.itemId === 'taskAdminBtn') {
            me.getMainCards().getLayout()
                .setActiveItem('manageTasksCard');
        } else if (button.itemId === 'taskLogsBtn') {
            me.getMainCards().getLayout()
                .setActiveItem('taskLogCard');
        } else if (button.itemId === 'logoffBtn') {
            me.doLogoff();
        }
    },
```

```
    doLogon: function() {
        var me = this;
        if (me.getUsernameField().validate() &&
            me.getPasswordField().validate()) {
            Ext.Ajax.request({
                url: 'ttt/security/logon.json',
                params: {
                    username: me.getUsernameField().getValue(),
                    password: me.getPasswordField().getValue()
                },
                success: function(response) {
                    var obj =
                        Ext.JSON.decode(response.responseText);
                    if (obj.success) {

                        TTT.getApplication().doAfterLogon
                            (obj.data);
                    } else {
                        Ext.Msg.alert('Invalid Logon', 'Please
                            enter a valid username and password');
                    }
                }
            });
        } else {
            Ext.Msg.alert('Invalid Logon', 'Please enter a valid
                username and password');
        }
    },
    doLogoff: function() {
        Ext.Msg.confirm('Confirm Logout', 'Are you sure you want
            to log out of 3T?', function(button) {
            if (button === 'yes') {
                Ext.Ajax.request({
                    url: 'ttt/security/logout.json',
                    success: function() {
                        window.location.reload();
                    }
                });
            }
        });
    }
});
```

The `MainController` is responsible for managing three views as defined in the views configuration array: `MainHeader`, `MainCards`, and `LogonWindow`. Each `ref` defines a component that is needed by the controller to perform an action. The `ref` value is used during initialization of the controller to automatically create a `getter` function that can be used to access the component. In our `MainController` the ref value `mainCards` will result in a `getMainCards` function being created. This function is used in the `doHeaderButtonClick` function to access the `MainCards` component.

> The name of a function should identify the core purpose of the code it defines. We will prefix all functions that perform actions with `do`. In our example, it should be clear to any developer what the purpose of the `doHeaderButtonClick` function is.

The `MainController.init()` function calls the `control()` function to configure event handling in the views. The `control()` function is a convenient method to assign a set of event listeners in one action. The `mainheader` button selector configures the `click` event on all button objects in the `MainHeader`. Whenever a button in the header is clicked the `doHeaderButtonClick` function is called. This function will then determine which button has been clicked by examining the `itemId` of the `button` argument. The appropriate card in the `MainCards` is then activated.

> Note we have added code to display the `manageTasksCard` and `taskLogCard` even though they are not currently available. These user interfaces will be developed in the following chapters.

The `logonwindow` button selector configures the `click` event on the **Logon** button of the `LogonWindow`. The `doLogon` function is called when the button is clicked to trigger the logon process. This function validates the `username` and `password` fields and, if both are valid, submits an AJAX request to authenticate the user. A successful logon will then call the `TTT.getApplication().doAfterLogon()` function passing the user JSON data as the argument.

The `doLogoff` function is triggered when the user clicks on the **Logout** button in the header. A prompt is presented to the user and if confirmed the `logout` action is processed. This will clear the session in the backend before reloading the browser window and presenting the user with the `LogonWindow` once again.

Controlling our user views

The glue that links the three user views together is the `UserController`. It is here that we place all logic for managing user maintenance. You have seen that each view defined earlier is dumb in that there is only presentation logic defined. Actions, validations, and selections are all handled within the `UserController` and are explained in the following code:

```
Ext.define('TTT.controller.UserController', {
    extend: 'Ext.app.Controller',
    views: ['user.ManageUsers'],
    refs: [{
        ref: 'userList',
        selector: 'manageusers userlist'
    }, {
        ref: 'userForm',
        selector: 'manageusers userform'
    }, {
        ref: 'addUserButton',
        selector: 'manageusers #addUserBtn'
    }, {
        ref: 'saveUserButton',
        selector: 'manageusers userform #saveBtn'
    }, {
        ref: 'deleteUserButton',
        selector: 'manageusers userform #deleteBtn'
    }, {
        ref: 'userFormFieldset',
        selector: 'manageusers userform fieldset'
    }, {
        ref: 'usernameField',
        selector: 'manageusers userform textfield[name=username]'
    }],
    init: function(application) {
        this.control({
            'manageusers #addUserBtn': {
                click: this.doAddUser
            },
            'userlist': {
                itemclick: this.doSelectUser,
                viewready: this.doInitStore
            },
```

```
            'manageusers userform #saveBtn': {
                click: this.doSaveUser
            },
            'manageusers userform #deleteBtn': {
                click: this.doDeleteUser
            },
            'manageusers userform': {
                afterrender: this.doAddUser
            },
            'userlist header tool[type="refresh"]': {
                click: this.doRefreshUserList
            }
        });
    },
    doInitStore: function() {
        this.getUserList().getStore().load();
    },
    doAddUser: function() {
        var me = this;
        me.getUserFormFieldset().setTitle('Add New User');
        me.getUsernameField().enable();
        var newUserRec = Ext.create('TTT.model.User', {
            adminRole: 'N'
        });
        me.getUserForm().loadRecord(newUserRec);
        me.getDeleteUserButton().disable();
    },
    doSelectUser: function(grid, record) {
        var me = this;
        me.getUserForm().loadRecord(record);
        me.getUserFormFieldset().setTitle('Edit User ' +
          record.get('username'));
        me.getUsernameField().disable();
        me.getDeleteUserButton().enable();
    },
    doSaveUser: function() {
        var me = this;
        var rec = me.getUserForm().getRecord();
        if (rec !== null) {
            me.getUserForm().updateRecord();
            var errs = rec.validate();
            if (errs.isValid()) {
                rec.save({
                    success: function(record, operation) {
```

```
                if (typeof record.store === 'undefined') {
                    // the record is not yet in a store
                    me.getUserList().
                        getStore().add(record);
                }
                me.getUserFormFieldset().setTitle('Edit
                    User ' + record.get('username'));
                me.getUsernameField().disable();
                me.getDeleteUserButton().enable();
            },
            failure: function(rec, operation) {
                Ext.Msg.alert('Save Failure',
                    operation.request.scope.
                        reader.jsonData.msg);
            }
        });
    } else {
        me.getUserForm().getForm().markInvalid(errs);
        Ext.Msg.alert('Invalid Fields', 'Please fix the
            invalid entries!');
    }
}
},
doDeleteUser: function() {
    var me = this;
    var rec = me.getUserForm().getRecord();
    Ext.Msg.confirm('Confirm Delete User', 'Are you sure you
        want to delete user ' + rec.get('fullName') + '?',
        function(btn) {
            if (btn === 'yes') {
                rec.destroy({
                    failure: function(rec, operation) {
                        Ext.Msg.alert('Delete Failure',
                            operation.request.scope.
                                reader.jsonData.msg);
                    }
                });
                me.doAddUser();
            }
        });
},
doRefreshUserList: function() {
    this.getUserList().getStore().load();
}
});
```

The `UserController` is defined with a single view to manage users as shown in the following code:

```
views: [
  'user.ManageUsers'
]
```

This allows us to define a set of references using the component query language starting with the `manageusers` root selector. We can hence reference the save button on the `UserForm` by the selector:

```
'manageusers userform #saveBtn'
```

The `#saveBtn` refers to the component with `itemId saveBtn` on the `userform` within the `manageusers` component.

 Only define references that are used by the controller to process business logic. Do not create a reference for components that are never accessed within your code. Keep your code simple and clean!

The `init` function defines the listeners that should be processed in the interface. Each button click is matched to an appropriate `handler` function. The user list `itemclick` event is handled by the `doSelectUser` function. The `viewready` event on the `userlist` triggers the initial load of the grid's store. Each listener event is handled by a single function with a clear purpose. Let's now examine the core functions in detail.

The doAddUser function

The `doAddUser` function is called when the **Add User** button is clicked. We set the title on the form `fieldset` to display **Add New User** and then enable the `username` field as shown in the following code:

```
me.getUserFormFieldset().setTitle('Add New User');
me.getUsernameField().enable();
```

We only enable the `username` field when adding a new user; the `username` field is not editable for existing users as it represents the primary key. We then create a new User model and load the record into the user form:

```
var newUserRec = Ext.create('TTT.model.User', {
    adminRole: 'N'
});
me.getUserForm().loadRecord(newUserRec);
```

At this stage the user form would look like the following screenshot:

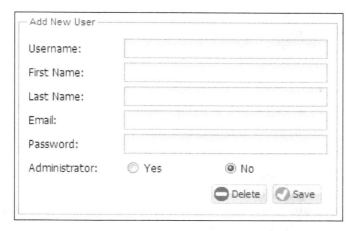

The **Delete** button serves no useful purpose for adding a new user and hence we disable it as shown in the following code:

```
me.getDeleteUserButton().disable();
```

This gives us the following **Add New User** interface as shown in the following screenshot:

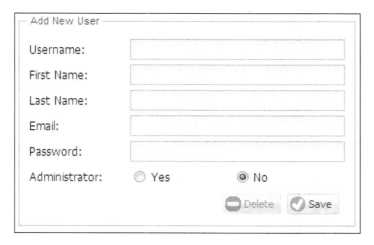

We could just as easily have hidden the delete button instead of disabling it; your approach will depend on your client specifications.

The form is now ready for entering a new user.

The doSelectUser function

The `doSelectUser` function handles the `itemclick` event on the `userlist` grid panel. The arguments to this function are the grid itself and the selected record. This makes loading the form with the selected user record a simple task:

```
var me = this;
me.getUserForm().loadRecord(record);
me.getUserFormFieldset().setTitle('Edit User ' + record.data.
username);
me.getUsernameField().disable();
me.getDeleteUserButton().enable();
```

The `fieldset` title is changed to reflect the user being edited and the `username` field is disabled. We also ensure the **Delete** button is enabled as we require the option to delete an existing record. Clicking on the **Betty Jones** record in the user list would then display the following screenshot:

 Readers will note that the **Password** field is empty. This means that saving a user record via the form will require a password to be set. The backend handler method and service layer also require a valid password when saving a user. In the real world this would not be the case; you do not want an administrator changing the password every time they save user details! A **Change Password** form, perhaps in a pop-up window, would normally trigger a separate AJAX request to change the user's password.

It is now time to code the **Save** button action.

The doSaveUser function

The `doSaveUser` function processes the saving of a user record. In most applications the `save` function will contain the most code as validations and user feedback are important steps in the process.

The first step is to retrieve the user record instance that was loaded in the form as shown in the following code:

```
var rec = me.getUserForm().getRecord();
```

If valid, the record is updated with the values entered in the form text fields as shown in the following code:

```
me.getUserForm().updateRecord();
```

At this stage the user record will be in sync with the fields entered in the form. This means all fields in the form will have been copied to the model instance. We can now validate the user record as given in the following code:

```
var errs = rec.validate();
```

If there are no validation errors, the record is saved using the `save()` function on the record itself. There are two possible callbacks depending on the returned JSON response. A successful save will trigger the success handler as shown in the following code:

```
success: function(record, operation) {
    if (typeof record.store === 'undefined') {
        // the record is not yet in a store
        me.getUserList().getStore().add(record);
        // select the user in the grid
        me.getUserList().getSelectionModel().select(record,true);
    }
    me.getUserFormFieldset().setTitle('Edit User ' +
      record.data.username);
    me.getUsernameField().disable();
    me.getDeleteUserButton().enable();
}
```

The `success` callback will check if the record exists in the store. If not, the record is added to the `User` store and selected in the user list. The **Delete** button will then be enabled and the `fieldset` title set appropriately.

The `failure` action will simply inform the user of the cause as shown in the following code:

```
failure: function(rec, operation) {
    Ext.Msg.alert('Save Failure',
        operation.request.scope.reader.jsonData.msg);
}
```

If there are errors encountered during validation, we mark the invalid fields and display a generic error message as shown in the following code:

```
me.getUserForm().getForm().markInvalid(errs);
Ext.Msg.alert('Invalid Fields', 'Please fix the invalid
    entries!');
```

Trying to save a user record without a valid e-mail or password would then display a message as follows:

The doDeleteUser function

The final handler processes the delete action. The `doDeleteUser` function prompts the user for confirmation before triggering the `destroy` function on the record if required:

```
Ext.Msg.confirm('Confirm Delete User', 'Are you sure you want to
    delete user ' + rec.data.fullName + '?', function(btn) {
    if (btn === 'yes') {
rec.destroy({
        failure: function(rec, operation) {
    Ext.Msg.alert('Delete Failure',
        operation.request.scope.reader.jsonData.msg);
        }
```

```
        });
    me.doAddUser();
        }
    });
```

The `User` store will automatically remove the successfully destroyed user model from the store itself. Any failure will inform the user of the reason. Attempting to delete the record for **John Smith** will result in the message shown in the following code:

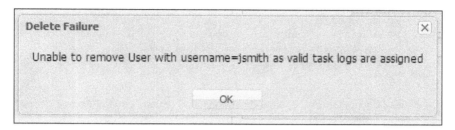

Where is this message coming from? It is generated in the service layer `UserServiceImpl.remove` method that was coded when implementing the business logic for the delete action. What about trying to delete the currently logged-on user? This will result in the following message:

Once again this is coming from the service layer business logic.

Let's log on!

It is now time to enable our controllers and test the functionality. Update the `Application.js` file as displayed in the following code:

```
Ext.define('TTT.Application', {
    name: 'TTT',
    extend: 'Ext.app.Application',
    requires: ['TTT.view.Viewport', 'TTT.view.LogonWindow'],
    models: ['User'],
```

```
        controllers: ['MainController', 'UserController'],
        stores: ['User'],
        init: function(application){
            TTT.URL_PREFIX = 'ttt/';
            Ext.Ajax.on('beforerequest', function(conn, options,
              eOpts){
                options.url = TTT.URL_PREFIX + options.url;
            });
        },
        launch: function() {
            var me = this;
            TTT.console = function(output) {
                if (typeof console !== 'undefined') {
                    console.info(output);
                }
            };
            me.logonWindow = Ext.create('TTT.view.LogonWindow');
            me.logonWindow.show();
        },
        doAfterLogon: function(userObj) {
            TTT.console(userObj);
            var me = this;
            me.getUser = function() {
                return userObj;
            };
            me.isAdmin = function() {
                return userObj.adminRole === 'Y';
            };
            Ext.create('TTT.view.Viewport');
            me.logonWindow.hide();
        }
    });
```

The `Application.js` represents the entire application and defines all components bundled in the application (models, stores, and controllers). Note that views are not listed here as they are managed by the controllers directly.

We have defined a `requires` array containing the `TTT.view.LogonWindow` and `TTT.view.Viewport` classes. Although this is strictly not essential, as these definitions also reside in the appropriate controllers, it is considered best practice to always include `requires` entries for all `Ext.create()` function calls in the class. We create both the `TTT.view.LogonWindow` and `TTT.view.Viewport` using `Ext.create()`, so have included these in the `requires` list.

Our `controllers` array contains the `MainController` and `UserController` as expected. We have also added the `User` model as this is the only model we currently need. Likewise the `User` store has been added to the `stores` array.

The `init` function is a template method that is called when the application boots. We have added code to the `Ext.Ajax` `beforerequest` event to prefix all URLs with the servlet path configured in the `com.gieman.tttracker.web.WebApp.` `getServletMappings()` method; this is shown in the following code:

```
protected String[] getServletMappings() {
  return new String[]{
    "/ttt/*"
  };
}
```

The `ttt/` prefix is added to each `Ext.Ajax` request URL to ensure the correct mapping to the request handling layer. Without this `beforerequest` event code each URL would need to be prefixed with `ttt` as we have already coded in the `User` model `api`, the `User` store URL, and the `Ajax.request` URLs for logon actions in the `MainController`. We can now omit the `ttt/` prefix in all URLs that access servlet resources. The `User` model `api` can now be changed to the following code:

```
api:{
  create: 'user/store.json',
  read: 'user/find.json',
  update: 'user/store.json',
  destroy: 'user/remove.json'
}
```

In a similar way we can now remove the `ttt/` prefix from the `User` store and `MainController.doLogon/Logoff` URLs.

> This technique of using the `beforerequest` event to prefix all Ajax URLs may only be used for simple projects that consume resources from a single mapped servlet. If multiple mappings are used, a different strategy would need to be implemented.

The `launch` function is another template method called when the page is ready and all JavaScript has been loaded. The `TTT.console` function defines a lightweight logger that sends the output to the browser console, if available. It is not a replacement for the `Ext.log()` function but is simpler to use. We encourage you to use the `TTT.console` function liberally to analyze your code and debug processing.

The final step in the `launch` function creates and assigns the `LogonWindow` instance to the application scoped variable `logonWindow`. This will display the logon window when the application is loaded.

The `doAfterLogon` function is used to postprocess the successful logon and initialises the application environment. The `doAfterLogon` argument is the JSON data object returned after a successful logon and has the following structure:

```
{
     "username": "bjones",
     "firstName": "Betty",
     "lastName": "Jones",
     "fullName": "Betty Jones",
     "email": "bj@tttracker.com",
     "adminRole": "Y"
}
```

This function will create two helper functions that can be called by any component to retrieve user details and to test if the user is an administrator. An example of calling these functions in code has already been shown in the `MainHeader.js`. The `TTT` namespace is used to access the application functions via `TTT.getApplication().isAdmin()` and `TTT.getApplication().getUser()`.

The final step in the `doAfterLogon` process is to create the application viewport and hide the logon window. We will be calling the `doAfterLogon` function, strangely enough, after we have successfully logged on!

Run the application and test the logon screen with username `bjones` and password `admin`. You should see the interface with all header buttons enabled, as **Betty Jones** is an admin user:

Test the logon screen with username `jsmith` and password `admin`. You should see the interface without the admin buttons, as **John Smith** is a normal user:

Try clicking on the **Logoff** button. You should be prompted with a confirmation window as shown:

Selecting the **Yes** option will trigger the `MainController.doLogoff` function to log out the user and reload the browser to display the `LogonWindow` again.

Let's maintain users

Log on as the **bjones** user and click on the **Users** button. The following screen will be displayed:

Enter the letter A in all fields and click the **Save** button. The **Invalid Fields** message will then be displayed:

Enter valid entries (remembering the validation rules!) and click the **Save** button. The new user record should then be added to the user list:

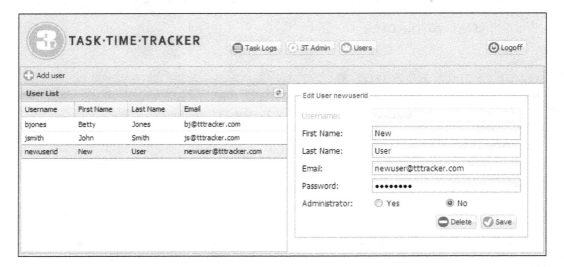

You can now try to delete and update users to test the different functions you have written. There is a lot of activity hidden from view when you are performing such tests. You can open the JavaScript console appropriate for your browser (Safari Web Inspector, Firefox Firebug, Chrome Developer Tools, or the generic Fiddler `http://fiddler2.com/get-fiddler`) to inspect the requests being sent. Try logging on again as `bjones`, clicking on the **Users** button, adding a new user, and then deleting this new user. You will see the following requests being sent to the server:

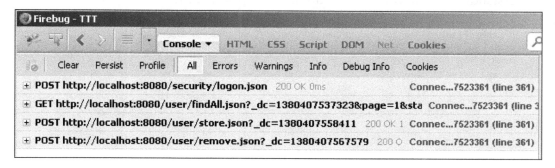

Liberal use of `TTT.console()` in your functions will also help in debugging properties and application state. Adding the statement `TTT.console(userObj);` to the first line of the `Application.js doAfterLogon(userObj)` function will output the following to the console after a successful logon:

Take your time to test and experiment with the different functions you have written. We have covered a lot of concepts in this chapter!

Summary

This chapter has introduced Ext JS 4 view and controller concepts, building the logon window, and user maintenance interfaces. We have also introduced key model concepts including persistence and validations. The pieces of the puzzle have finally fallen into place, with our frontend actions interacting with backend business logic. *Chapter 11, Building the Task Log User Interface*, will continue to enhance our understanding of Ext JS 4 components as we implement the Task Log user interface.

11
Building the Task Log User Interface

The task log user interface allows users to keep track of the time spent on different tasks. This interface allows task log searching and data entry. A user will be able to:

- Search for task logs within a specified time period
- Sort the list of task log entries
- Edit existing task logs
- Add new task log entries
- View the total time spent on tasks within a time period

The interface we will be building looks like the following screenshot:

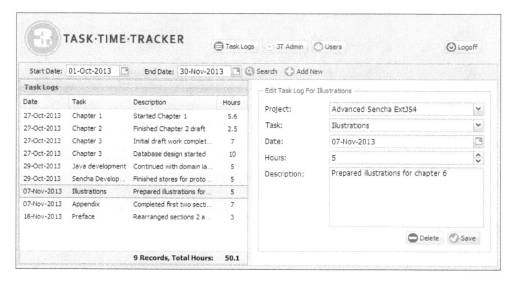

The **Start Date** and **End Date** fields are prefilled with the current month's start and end dates. Clicking on the **Search** button will trigger a search and fill the **Task Logs** grid with matching records. Clicking on a record from the list will open the item in the **Edit Task Log For {task name}** form. Clicking on the **Add New** button in the toolbar will clear the task log form fields and set the title to **Add Task Log**. Let's now look at these actions in detail.

Task log workflows and layouts

Searching for task logs will require a valid start and end date. An appropriate message will be displayed if either field is missing after clicking on the **Search** button:

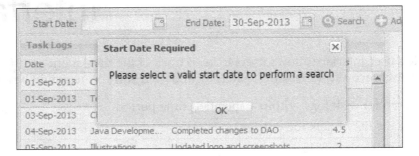

Selecting a task log item from the list will open the record in the **Edit Task Log For Testing** form. The **Project** dropdown in the task log form will display the company name in addition to the project name when the list is shown:

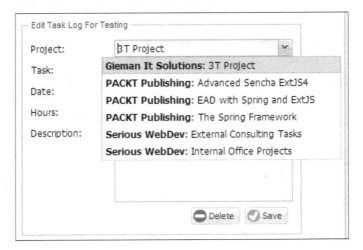

The selection of a **Project** from this list will filter the tasks displayed in the **Task** combobox:

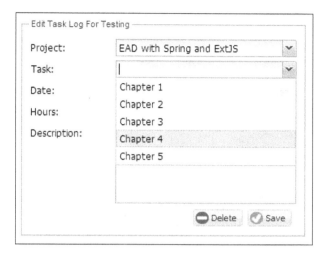

If a **Project** that has no assigned tasks is selected, the following message is displayed:

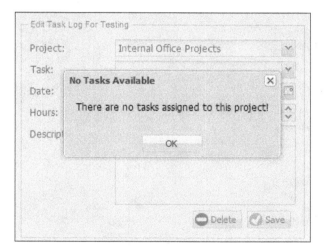

Adding a new task log will preserve the currently selected **Date** and **Project**, if present:

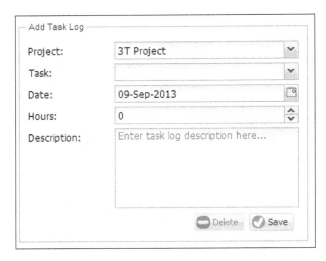

Deleting a task log will ask the user to confirm their action:

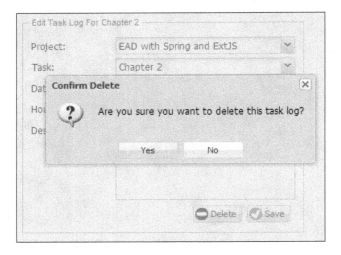

 This should be the standard practice for all deletions when developing enterprise projects; never delete a record without first confirming the action with the user!

Selecting **Yes** will delete the task log record and remove the record from the search results.

Building our task log views

The task log user interface contains a variety of different components including date pickers and combo boxes. We will implement the UI by dividing the screen into three views. The outermost `ManageTaskLogs` view will contain a toolbar and define a border layout to hold the `TaskLogList` and `TaskLogForm` views:

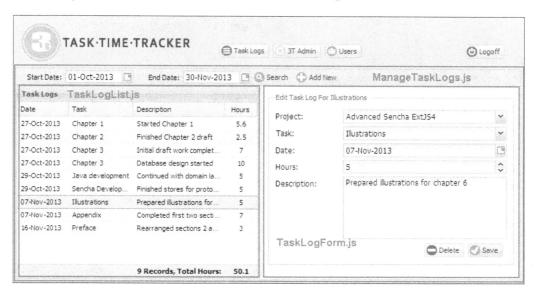

The ManageTaskLogs.js file

We have chosen the `border` layout for this view to allow resizing of the `TaskLogForm` view that is initially fixed to a width of 400px in the `east` region. The `ManageTaskLogs` definition is as follows:

```
Ext.define('TTT.view.tasklog.ManageTaskLogs', {
    extend: 'Ext.panel.Panel',
    xtype: 'managetasklogs',
    requires: ['Ext.toolbar.Toolbar', 'Ext.layout.container.Border',
'Ext.form.field.Date', 'TTT.view.tasklog.TaskLogList', 'TTT.view.
tasklog.TaskLogForm'],
    layout: {
        type: 'border'
    },
    initComponent: function() {
        var me = this;
        var now = new Date();
        Ext.applyIf(me, {
            dockedItems: [{
```

```
                    xtype: 'toolbar',
                    dock: 'top',
                    items: [{
                        xtype: 'datefield',
                        labelAlign: 'right',
                        name: 'startDate',
                        format: 'd-M-Y',
                        fieldLabel: 'Start Date',
                        value: Ext.Date.getFirstDateOfMonth(now),
                        width: 180,
                        labelWidth: 70
                    }, {
                        xtype: 'datefield',
                        labelAlign: 'right',
                        name: 'endDate',
                        format: 'd-M-Y',
                        fieldLabel: 'End Date',
                        value: Ext.Date.getLastDateOfMonth(now),
                        width: 180,
                        labelWidth: 70
                    }, {
                        xtype: 'button',
                        iconCls: 'search',
                        itemId: 'searchBtn',
                        text: 'Search'
                    }, {
                        xtype: 'button',
                        iconCls: 'addnew',
                        itemId: 'addTaskLogBtn',
                        text: 'Add New'
                    }]
                }],
                items: [{
                    xtype: 'taskloglist',
                    region: 'center',
                    margin: 1
                }, {
                    xtype: 'tasklogform',
                    region: 'east',
                    split: true,
                    width: 400
                }]
            });
            me.callParent(arguments);
        }
    });
```

This class is defined in the `view.tasklog` namespace. You will need to create the `view/tasklog` sub directory before adding the `ManageTaskLogs.js` file.

The `date` fields are initialized with the start and end dates of the current month using the `Ext.Date.getFirstDateOfMonth()` and `Ext.Date.getLastDateOfMonth()` functions. Manipulating the dates is a common task in Ext JS 4 development, and there are many helpful functions in the `Ext.Date` class that make such tasks easy.

The `TaskLogList` view has been placed in the `center` region of the `border` layout, while the `TaskLogForm` view has been given an initial fixed width of `400` in the `east` region. This will ensure that larger screen resolutions scale the task log list to give a balanced view. A screen width of 1200px would hence show the following layout:

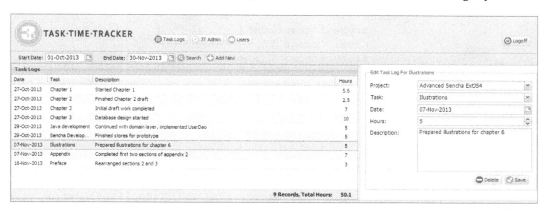

The `border` layout also allows resizing of the `TaskLogForm` view should the user wish to increase the width of the data entry fields.

The TaskLogForm.js file

The `TaskLogForm` view is used to display a task log record:

```
Ext.define('TTT.view.tasklog.TaskLogForm', {
    extend: 'Ext.form.Panel',
    xtype: 'tasklogform',
    requires: ['Ext.form.FieldSet', 'Ext.form.field.ComboBox', 'Ext.
form.field.Date', 'Ext.form.field.Number', 'Ext.form.field.TextArea',
'Ext.toolbar.Toolbar'],
    layout: {
        type: 'anchor'
    },
```

```
bodyPadding: 10,
border: false,
autoScroll: true,
initComponent: function() {
    var me = this;
    Ext.applyIf(me, {
        items: [{
            xtype: 'fieldset',
            hidden: true,
            padding: 10,
            fieldDefaults: {
                anchor: '100%'
            },
            title: 'Task Log Entry',
            items: [{
                xtype: 'combobox',
                name: 'project',
                fieldLabel: 'Project',
                queryMode: 'local',
                store: 'Project',
                valueField: 'idProject',
                listConfig: {
                    minWidth: 300
                },
                tpl: Ext.create('Ext.XTemplate', '<tpl for=".">',
'<div class="x-boundlist-item"><b>{companyName}</b>: {projectName}</
div>', '</tpl>'),
                displayTpl: Ext.create('Ext.XTemplate', '<tpl
for=".">', '{projectName}', '</tpl>')
            }, {
                xtype: 'combobox',
                name: 'idTask',
                fieldLabel: 'Task',
                displayField: 'taskName',
                queryMode: 'local',
                store: 'Task',
                valueField: 'idTask'
            }, {
                xtype: 'datefield',
                name: 'taskLogDate',
                format: 'd-M-Y',
                fieldLabel: 'Date'
            }, {
                xtype: 'numberfield',
                name: 'hours',
                minValue: 0,
                decimalPrecision: 2,
                itemId: 'taskHours',
                fieldLabel: 'Hours'
            }, {
```

```
                    xtype: 'textareafield',
                    height: 100,
                    name: 'taskDescription',
                    fieldLabel: 'Description',
                    emptyText: 'Enter task log description here...'
                }, {
                    xtype: 'toolbar',
                    ui: 'footer',
                    layout: {
                        pack: 'end',
                        type: 'hbox'
                    },
                    items: [{
                        xtype: 'button',
                        iconCls: 'delete',
                        itemId: 'deleteBtn',
                        disabled: true,
                        text: 'Delete'
                    }, {
                        xtype: 'button',
                        iconCls: 'save',
                        itemId: 'saveBtn',
                        text: 'Save'
                    }]
                }]
            }]
        });
        me.callParent(arguments);
    }
});
```

The **Project** combobox defines two different templates: one for rendering the list and one for rendering the selected item text. The `tpl` property combines the company name and project name for display in the dropdown:

When an item is selected, only the project name is shown as rendered by the `displayTpl` template.

The TaskLogList.js file

The TaskLogList view is defined as:

```
Ext.define('TTT.view.tasklog.TaskLogList', {
    extend: 'Ext.grid.Panel',
    xtype: 'taskloglist',
    viewConfig: {
        markDirty: false,
        emptyText: 'There are no task log records to display...'
    },
    title: 'Task Logs',
    store: 'TaskLog',
    requires: ['Ext.grid.feature.Summary', 'Ext.grid.column.Date',
'Ext.util.Point'],
    features: [{
        ftype: 'summary',
        dock: 'bottom'
    }],
    initComponent: function() {
        var me = this;
        Ext.applyIf(me, {
            columns: [{
                xtype: 'datecolumn',
                dataIndex: 'taskLogDate',
                format: 'd-M-Y',
                width: 80,
                text: 'Date'
            }, {
                xtype: 'gridcolumn',
                dataIndex: 'taskName',
                text: 'Task'
            }, {
                xtype: 'gridcolumn',
                dataIndex: 'taskDescription',
                flex: 1,
                text: 'Description',
                summaryType: 'count',
                summaryRenderer: function(value, summaryData,
dataIndex) {
                    return Ext.String.format('<div style="font-
weight:bold;text-align:right;">{0} Records, Total Hours:</div>',
value);
                }
            }, {
                xtype: 'gridcolumn',
                dataIndex: 'taskMinutes',
                width: 80,
                align: 'center',
                text: 'Hours',
```

```
                        summaryType: 'sum',
                        renderer: function(value, metaData, record) {
                            return record.get('hours');
                        },
                        summaryRenderer: function(value, summaryData,
    dataIndex) {
                            var valHours = value / 60;
                            return Ext.String.format('<b>{0}</b>', valHours);
                        }
                }]
            });
            me.callParent(arguments);
        }
    });
```

The `viewConfig` properties are used to create an instance of the `Ext.grid.View` class, which provides a grid-specific view functionality. We will be performing updates on a per record basis, not by using batch updates via the store. The `markDirty:false` property will ensure that the records saved successfully are not rendered with the dirty flag in the grid. If a task log search returns no records, the `emptyText` value will be displayed in the grid to give the user immediate feedback.

The `TaskLogList` view uses the `summary` feature to display a total row containing the **Records** count and **Total Hours** displayed in the search listing. The `summaryType` and `summaryRender` definitions are used to configure the `feature` displayed in the footer of the `taskDescription` and `taskMinutes` columns. The `summary` value may be one of `count`, `sum`, `min`, `max`, or `average`, of which we are using the `count` and `sum` values. More information about the `summary` feature can be found at `http://docs.sencha.com/extjs/4.2.2/#!/api/Ext.grid.feature.Summary`. The following screenshot displays the `summary` feature in use:

Task Logs			
Date	Task	Description	Hours
27-Oct-2013	Chapter 1	Started Chapter 1	5.6
27-Oct-2013	Chapter 2	Finished Chapter 2 draft	2.5
27-Oct-2013	Chapter 3	Initial draft work completed	7
27-Oct-2013	Chapter 3	Database design started	10
29-Oct-2013	Java development	Continued with domain layer, impleme...	5
29-Oct-2013	Sencha Develop...	Finished stores for prototype	5
07-Nov-2013	Illustrations	Prepared illustrations for chapter 6	6
07-Nov-2013	Appendix	Completed first two sections of appen...	7
16-Nov-2013	Preface	Rearranged sections 2 and 3	3
		9 Records, Total Hours:	**51.1**

There is also some code to note in the column representing the hours of work assigned to the task:

```
{
    xtype: 'gridcolumn',
    dataIndex: 'taskMinutes',
    width:80,
    align:'center',
    text: 'Hours',
    summaryType:'sum',
    renderer:function(value, metaData, record){
return record.get('hours');
    },
    summaryRenderer: function(value, summaryData, dataIndex) {
var valHours = value/60;
return Ext.String.format('<b>{0}</b>', valHours);
    }
}
```

The time worked per task log is stored in the database in minutes but displayed on the frontend as hours. The column is bound to the `taskMinutes` field in the model. The renderer displays the (calculated) `hours` field of the `TaskLog` model (this will be defined in the section that follows). The summary feature uses the `taskMinutes` field to calculate the total time as the feature requires a real (not converted) model field to act on. This total time in minutes is then converted in the `summaryRenderer` function to hours for display.

Defining our models

Our `Project`, `Task`, and `TaskLog` models were created with basic fields using Sencha Cmd in *Chapter 9, Getting Started with Ext JS 4*, but they lacked in persistence or validation logic. It is now time to add the required code.

The TaskLog Model

The `TaskLog` model is the most complicated model in our application. The complete `TaskLog` model with all required logic is as follows:

```
Ext.define('TTT.model.TaskLog', {
    extend: 'Ext.data.Model',
    fields: [
        { name: 'idTaskLog', type: 'int', useNull:true },
        { name: 'taskDescription', type: 'string' },
        { name: 'taskLogDate', type: 'date', dateFormat:'Ymd' },
```

```
        { name: 'taskMinutes', type: 'int' },
        { name: 'hours', type: 'float', persist:false,
convert:function(value, record){
            return record.get('taskMinutes') / 60;
        }},
        { name: 'username', type: 'string' },
        { name: 'userFullName', type: 'string', persist:false },
        { name: 'idTask', type: 'int', useNull:true },
        { name: 'taskName', type: 'string', persist:false },
        { name: 'idProject', type: 'int', persist:false },
        { name: 'projectName', type: 'string', persist:false },
        { name: 'idCompany', type: 'int', persist:false },
        { name: 'companyName', type: 'string', persist:false }
    ],
    idProperty: 'idTaskLog',
    proxy: {
        type: 'ajax',
        idParam:'idTaskLog',
        api:{
            create:'taskLog/store.json',
            read:'taskLog/find.json',
            update:'taskLog/store.json',
            destroy:'taskLog/remove.json'
        },
        reader: {
            type: 'json',
            root: 'data'
        },
        writer: {
            type: 'json',
            allowSingle:true,
            encode:true,
            root:'data',
            writeAllFields: true
        }
    },
    validations: [
        {type: 'presence',  field: 'taskDescription'},
        {type: 'length', field: 'taskDescription', min: 2},
        {type: 'presence',  field: 'username'},
        {type: 'presence',  field: 'taskLogDate'},
        {type: 'presence',  field: 'idTask'},
        {type: 'length', field: 'idTask', min: 1},
        {type: 'length', field: 'taskMinutes', min: 0}
    ]
});
```

This is the first time we have used the `useNull` property on a field. The `useNull` property is important when converting JSON data into an `int`, `float`, `Boolean`, or `String` type. When a value cannot be parsed by the reader, the following default values are set for the model field:

Field type	Default value with useNull:true	Default value with useNull:false
int	null	0
float	null	0
boolean	null	false
String	null	"" (empty string)
Date	null	null

If the value cannot be parsed by the reader, `null` will be assigned to the field value if the field is configured with `useNull:true`. Otherwise, a default value for that type will be used as displayed in the third column in the preceding table. Note that the `Date` fields are always set to `null` if the value cannot be parsed. In most circumstances, it is important to be able to discern whether a field is null after reading the record, and hence, we recommend setting the `useNull:true` property for all primary key fields.

This is also the first time that we have used the `dateFormat` property. This property defines the format of the date while encoding or decoding JSON `date` fields via the configured `writer` and `reader` classes. The `YYYYMMDD` format string represents an 8-digit number. For example, the date 18th August, 2013, is equivalent to 20130818. The other format strings are documented in the `Ext.Date` API at `http://docs.sencha.com/extjs/4.2.2/#!/api/Ext.Date`. It is strongly recommended that you always specify an explicit date format for any `date` field.

The use of the `convert` function for the `hours` field is also new. It converts a value provided by the `reader` class and stores it in the configured `name` field of the model. In our `TaskLog` model, the number of minutes is converted into a decimal value and stored in the `hours` field. It will be far more convenient for the 3T user to enter a value of 2.5 hours rather than 150 minutes.

Note that we have once again used the `persist:false` property to restrict the fields that are not required for persistence in our `TaskLogHandler` methods. Our validations for the `TaskLog` model should also be self-explanatory!

The Project model

The Project model defines our usual proxy and validation properties:

```
Ext.define('TTT.model.Project', {
    extend: 'Ext.data.Model',
    fields: [
        { name: 'idProject', type: 'int', useNull:true },
        { name: 'projectName', type: 'string' },
        { name: 'idCompany', type:'int', useNull:true },
        { name: 'companyName', type:'string', persist:false }
    ],
    idProperty: 'idProject',
    proxy: {
        type: 'ajax',
        idParam:'idProject',
        api:{
            create:'project/store.json',
            read:'project/find.json',
            update:'project/store.json',
            destroy:'project/remove.json'
        },
        reader: {
            type: 'json',
            root: 'data'
        },
        writer: {
            type: 'json',
            allowSingle:true,
            encode:true,
            root:'data',
            writeAllFields: true
        }
    },
    validations: [
        {type: 'presence',  field: 'projectName'},
        {type: 'length', field: 'projectName', min: 2},
        {type: 'presence',  field: 'idCompany'},
        {type: 'length', field: 'idCompany', min: 1}
    ]
});
```

There is no need to include the companyName field while persisting a record and hence the field includes the persist:false property.

The Task Model

The `Task` model also has a simple structure:

```
Ext.define('TTT.model.Task', {
    extend: 'Ext.data.Model',
    fields: [
        { name: 'idTask', type: 'int', useNull:true },
        { name: 'taskName', type: 'string' },
        { name: 'idProject', type: 'int', useNull:true },
        { name: 'projectName', type: 'string', persist:false },
        { name: 'idCompany', type: 'int', useNull:true, persist:false
    },
        { name: 'companyName', type: 'string', persist:false }

    ],
    idProperty: 'idTask',
    proxy: {
        type: 'ajax',
        idParam:'idTask',
        api:{
            create:'task/store.json',
            read:'task/find.json',
            update:'task/store.json',
            destroy:'task/remove.json'
        },
        reader: {
            type: 'json',
            root: 'data'
        },
        writer: {
            type: 'json',
            allowSingle:true,
            encode:true,
            root:'data',
            writeAllFields: true
        }
    },
    validations: [
        {type: 'presence',  field: 'taskName'},
        {type: 'length', field: 'taskName', min: 2},
        {type: 'presence',  field: 'idProject'},
        {type: 'length', field: 'idProject', min: 1}
    ]
});
```

Once again we have several fields that do not need to be persisted and are hence configured with the `persist:false` property. It is now time to define the stores required to build our task log user interface.

Defining our stores

The `TaskLogList` and `TaskLogForm` views require stores to function.
The `TaskLogList` view requires a `TaskLog` store, while the `TaskLogForm`
view requires a `Project` and a `Task` store. Let's define them now.

The TaskLog store

We define this store with a helper method to allow easy loading for the task
log searches. The definition is as follows:

```
Ext.define('TTT.store.TaskLog', {
    extend: 'Ext.data.Store',
    requires: ['TTT.model.TaskLog'],
    model: 'TTT.model.TaskLog',
    proxy: {
        type: 'ajax',
        url: 'taskLog/findByUser.json',
        reader: {
            type: 'json',
            root: 'data'
        }
    },
    doFindByUser: function(username, startDate, endDate) {
        this.load({
            params: {
                username: username,
                startDate: Ext.Date.format(startDate, 'Ymd'),
                endDate: Ext.Date.format(endDate, 'Ymd')
            }
        });
    }
});
```

Note that we are formatting the start and end dates in the `doFindByUser` method
using the `Ext.Date.format` function. This is to ensure that the dates sent to the
server are in the expected 8-digit yyyymmdd format.

The Project store

The `Project` store will be sorted to achieve the required company name grouping that is displayed in the **Project** combobox:

```
Ext.define('TTT.store.Project', {
    extend: 'Ext.data.Store',
    requires: ['TTT.model.Project'],
    model: 'TTT.model.Project',
    sorters: [{
        property: 'companyName',
        direction: 'ASC'
    }, {
        property: 'projectName',
        direction: 'ASC'
    }],
    proxy: {
        type: 'ajax',
        url: 'project/findAll.json',
        reader: {
            type: 'json',
            root: 'data'
        }
    }
});
```

Note that all the project records will be loaded by the `project/findAll.json` URL that is mapped to the `findAll` method in the `ProjectHandler` Java class. The `sorters` property configures the sorting routine that will be applied to the results after loading the store. The records will first be sorted by the `companyName` field in the ascending order after which the `projectName` field will be used to apply a secondary sort.

The Task store

The Task store has a very simple structure. The following definition should hold no surprises for you:

```
Ext.define('TTT.store.Task', {
    extend: 'Ext.data.Store',
    requires: ['TTT.model.Task'],
    model: 'TTT.model.Task',
    proxy: {
```

```
        type: 'ajax',
        url:'task/findAll.json',
        reader: {
            type: 'json',
            root: 'data'
        }
    }
});
```

All the task records will be loaded by the `task/findAll.json` URL that is mapped
to the `findAll` method in the `TaskHandler` Java class.

Controlling the TaskLog actions

The `TaskLogController` definition is the most complex controller definition
we have yet developed. The definition that follows excludes the `refs` and `init`
configuration. You can download the full source code from this book's website:

```
Ext.define('TTT.controller.TaskLogController', {
    extend: 'Ext.app.Controller',
    views: ['tasklog.ManageTaskLogs'],
    stores: ['TaskLog', 'Project', 'Task'],
    refs: omitted...
    init: omitted...
    doAfterActivate: function() {
        var me = this;
        me.getTaskStore().load();
        me.getProjectStore().load();
    },
    doSelectProject: function(combo, records) {
        var me = this;
        var rec = records[0];
        if (!Ext.isEmpty(rec)) {
            me.getTaskCombo().getStore().clearFilter();
            me.getTaskCombo().getStore().filter({
                property: 'idProject',
                value: rec.get('idProject'),
                exactMatch: true
            });
            me.getTaskCombo().setValue('');
            if (me.getTaskCombo().getStore().getCount() === 0) {
```

```
                    Ext.Msg.alert('No Tasks Available', 'There are no
tasks assigned to this project!');
                }
            }
        },
    doSelectTaskLog: function(grid, record) {
        var me = this;
        me.getTaskCombo().getStore().clearFilter();
        me.getTaskCombo().getStore().filter({
            property: 'idProject',
            value: record.get('idProject'),
            exactMatch: true
        });
        me.getProjectCombo().setValue(record.get('idProject'));
        me.getTaskLogForm().loadRecord(record);
        me.getTaskLogFormFieldset().show();
        me.getTaskLogFormFieldset().setTitle('Edit Task Log For ' +
record.get('taskName'));
        me.getTaskLogForm().getForm().clearInvalid();
        me.getDeleteTaskLogButton().enable();
    },
    doAddTaskLog: function() {
        var me = this;
        me.getTaskLogFormFieldset().show();
        me.getTaskLogFormFieldset().setTitle('Add Task Log');
        var taskLogDate = me.getTaskLogDateField().getValue();
        if (Ext.isEmpty(taskLogDate)) {
            taskLogDate = new Date();
        }
        var tl = Ext.create('TTT.model.TaskLog', {
            taskDescription: '',
            username: TTT.getApplication().getUser().username,
            taskLogDate: taskLogDate,
            taskMinutes: 0,
            idTask: null
        });
        me.getTaskLogForm().loadRecord(tl);
        me.getDeleteTaskLogButton().disable();
        var idProject = me.getProjectCombo().getValue();
        if (Ext.isEmpty(idProject)) {
            var firstRec = me.getProjectCombo().getStore().getAt(0);
            me.getProjectCombo().setValue(firstRec.get('idProject'),
true);
```

```
            me.getTaskCombo().getStore().clearFilter();
            me.getTaskCombo().getStore().filter({
                property: 'idProject',
                value: firstRec.get('idProject'),
                exactMatch: true
            });
            me.getTaskCombo().setValue('');
        }
    },
    doDeleteTaskLog: function() {
        var me = this;
        var rec = me.getTaskLogForm().getRecord();
        Ext.Msg.confirm('Confirm Delete', 'Are you sure you want to
delete this task log?', function(btn) {
            if (btn === 'yes') {
                rec.destroy({
                    failure: function(rec, operation) {
                        Ext.Msg.alert('Delete Failure', operation.
request.scope.reader.jsonData.msg);
                    }
                });
                me.doAddTaskLog();
            }
        });
    },
    doSaveTaskLog: function() {
        var me = this;
        var rec = me.getTaskLogForm().getRecord();
        if (!Ext.isEmpty(rec)) {
            me.getTaskLogForm().updateRecord();
            // update the minutes field of the record
            var hours = me.getTaskHoursField().getValue();
            rec.set('taskMinutes', hours * 60);
            var errs = rec.validate();
            if (errs.isValid() && me.getTaskLogForm().isValid()) {
                rec.save({
                    success: function(record, operation) {
                        if (typeof record.store === 'undefined') {
                            me.getTaskLogStore().add(record);
                        }
                        me.getTaskLogFormFieldset().setTitle('Edit
Task Log For ' + record.get('taskName'));
                        me.getDeleteTaskLogButton().enable();
                    },
```

```
                    failure: function(rec, operation) {
                         Ext.Msg.alert('Save Failure', operation.
request.scope.reader.jsonData.msg);
                    }
               });
          } else {
               me.getTaskLogForm().getForm().markInvalid(errs);
               Ext.Msg.alert('Invalid Fields', 'Please fix the
invalid entries!');
          }
     }
   },
   doSearch: function() {
        var me = this;
        var startDate = me.getStartDateField().getValue();
        if (Ext.isEmpty(startDate)) {
             Ext.Msg.alert('Start Date Required', 'Please select a
valid start date to perform a search');
             return;
        }
        var endDate = me.getEndDateField().getValue();
        if (Ext.isEmpty(endDate)) {
             Ext.Msg.alert('End Date Required', 'Please select a valid
end date to perform a search');
             return;
        }
        me.getTaskLogStore().doFindByUser(TTT.getApplication().
getUser().username, startDate, endDate);
        me.getTaskLogFormFieldset().hide();
   }
});
```

The `TaskLogController` section defines the three stores that are used by the views.
The `Project` and `Task` stores are loaded in the `doAfterActivate` function that is
triggered when the `ManageTaskLogs` panel is activated. This ensures that the **Task**
and **Project** comboboxes have valid data to operate on.

Each `ref` item defined in the controller is used in one or more functions to access the
underlying component and perform an appropriate action. The autogenerated set
method for each `ref` item makes referencing the components in our code easy.

> It is important to note that the `ref` item will always return a single object, so it cannot be used like the `Ext.ComponentQuery.query` function to retrieve a collection of components. To retrieve objects dynamically (without using refs) or to retrieve a collection of objects, the `ComponentQuery.query` function should be used. For more information, see `http://docs.sencha.com/extjs/4.2.2/#!/api/Ext.ComponentQuery`.

Each possible user action is handled by an appropriately named function. The function arguments will depend on the event source. The `click` event handler function for a `button` object will always pass a reference to the button itself as the first argument of the event handler. The grid `itemclick` event handling function will always receive a reference to the grid itself as the first argument followed by the record that was clicked on. You should examine the Sencha Ext JS 4 docs to become familiar with the event handling function arguments of common components.

Performing a search requires a valid start and end date. The `doSearch` function will validate the two `date` fields before allowing a search. Note the use of the `TTT.getApplication().getUser()` function to access the user who is currently logged in.

A successful search will list the task log records that match the search criteria. A user can then click on an item in the list to load the task log form. This is done in the `doSelectTaskLog` function.

Adding a new task log will create a new `TaskLog` model record and load the form. The record will have the currently logged in `username` property set. The currently selected **Project** in the project combo is retained if available; otherwise, the first item in the combo is selected.

Selecting a project will filter the task store to only display the tasks assigned to the project. This is achieved in the `doSelectProject` function:

```
me.getTaskCombo().getStore().filter({
property:'idProject',
value:rec.get('idProject'),
exactMatch:true
});
```

Note that we are defining an `exactMatch` on the `idProject` field. Without this property, partial matches would be returned (for example, filtering with an `idProject` value of 2 would match a task with an `idProject` value of 20; a trap for unwary developers!).

The `doSaveTaskLog` and `doDeleteTaskLog` functions perform the appropriate actions on the record that was loaded into the task log form. Just like in the previous chapter, the form is used to display and enter data but the data is never submitted. All the save data actions are triggered via the `model` instance.

Testing the task log interface

Before running the application and testing your new files, you need to add the `TaskLogController` as well as the new stores and models to your `Application.js` file:

```
controllers: [
  'MainController',
  'UserController',
  'TaskLogController'
],
models: [
  'User',
  'Project',
  'Task',
  'TaskLog'
],
stores: [
  'User',
  'Project',
  'Task',
  'TaskLog'
]
```

You also need to add the `ManageTaskLogs` view to the `MainCards` view's `items` array as shown:

```
Ext.define('TTT.view.MainCards', {
    extend: 'Ext.container.Container',
    xtype: 'maincards',
    requires: ['Ext.layout.container.Card', 'TTT.view.Welcome', 'TTT.
view.user.ManageUsers', 'TTT.view.tasklog.ManageTaskLogs'],
    layout: 'card',
```

```
initComponent: function() {
    var me = this;
    Ext.applyIf(me, {
        items: [{
            xtype: 'welcome',
            itemId: 'welcomCard'
        }, {
            xtype: 'manageusers',
            itemId: 'manageUsersCard'
        }, {
            xtype: 'managetasklogs',
            itemId: 'taskLogCard'
        }]
    });
    me.callParent(arguments);
    }
});
```

You can now run the application in the GlassFish server and test the **Task Logs** interface. Start by logging in as the jsmith user with the password admin and perform searches with different date ranges. The data should be displayed for when you loaded the 3T tables in MySQL:

Try performing searches that do not return any records. You should see the `emptyText` value defined in the `viewConfig` property of the `TaskLogList` view:

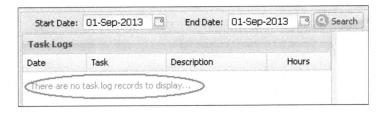

You can now try to add new records and edit the existing task logs to test the full range of the functionality. Can you make the following message pop up?

We will build the 3T administration interface in the next chapter to stop this from happening!

Summary

The task log user interface brought together multiple component interactions between the views, models, and stores. We introduced the `summary` feature for grids and filtered records in both the `Project` and `Task` stores. Searching for the `TaskLog` records required us to parse the dates into an appropriate format for backend processing, while our basic model skeletons were enhanced with persistence and validation properties. We have once again explored interesting Ext JS 4 territory and worked with a variety of components.

In *Chapter 12, 3T Administration Made Easy*, we will develop the 3T Administration interface and introduce the Ext JS 4 tree component. The `Ext.tree.Panel` is a very versatile component that is perfectly suited to displaying the Company-Project-Task relationship.

3T Administration Made Easy

12

The 3T administration interface allows a user to maintain company, project, and task relationships. As the relationship is hierarchical, we will be working with one of the most versatile components in Ext JS: Ext.tree.Panel.

The interface we will be building looks like the following screenshot:

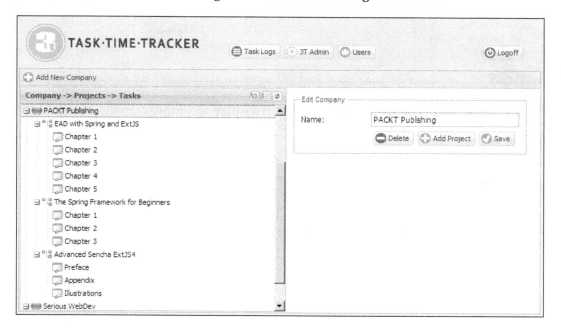

Selecting an item in the tree will display the appropriate record on the panel to the right, while the **Add New Company** button will allow the user to enter the name of a new company. Let's now examine these actions in detail.

Administration workflows and layouts

There are three different entities that may be edited (company, project, and task), with the preceding screenshot showing the company. Selecting a project in the tree will display the **Edit Project** form:

Selecting a task will display the **Edit Task** form:

Selecting the **Add New Company** button will display an empty company form:

Note that the **Delete** and **Add Project** buttons are disabled. When an action is not allowed, the appropriate button will be disabled in all the screens. In this situation, you cannot add a project to a company that has not yet been saved.

The tree tools will allow the user to expand, collapse, and refresh the tree:

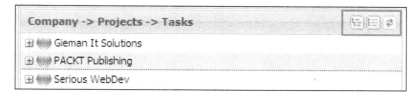

When the user first displays the administration interface, the **Add New Company** screen is shown. When any item is deleted, the **Please select an item from the tree...** message is displayed:

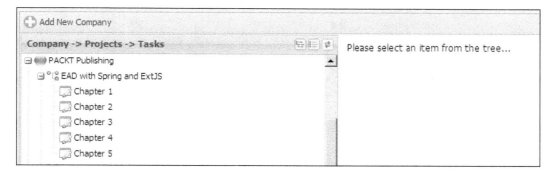

Now that we have defined the interfaces and their behavior, it is time to define our views.

Building the 3T administration interface

The 3T administration interface will require us to build the components displayed in the following screenshot. The `ProjectForm` and `TaskForm` views are not visible and will be displayed when required in a card layout:

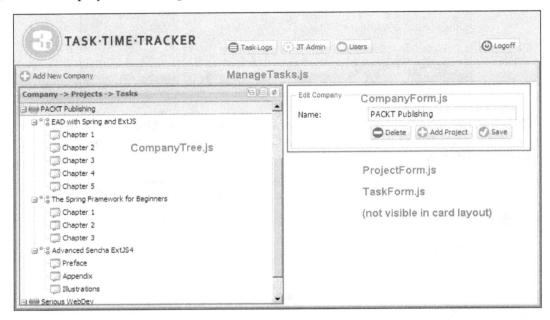

The `ManageTasks` view is an `hbox` layout that equally splits the left and right parts of the screen. The toolbar contains a single button to add a new company, while the region to the right is a card layout containing the `CompanyForm`, `ProjectForm`, and `TaskForm` views. Let's now look at each component in detail.

The ManageTasks.js file

The `ManageTasks` view defines the toolbar with the **Add New Company** button and splits the view into an `hbox` layout. The `companytree` panel and `container` defined with the card layout are configured by `xtype`. The card layout container contains the `CompanyForm`, `ProjectForm`, and `TaskForm`. The `ManageTasks` view is defined as follows:

```
Ext.define('TTT.view.admin.ManageTasks', {
    extend: 'Ext.panel.Panel',
    xtype: 'managetasks',
    requires: ['TTT.view.admin.CompanyTree',
        'TTT.view.admin.TaskForm', 'TTT.view.admin.ProjectForm',
        'TTT.view.admin.CompanyForm', 'Ext.toolbar.Toolbar',
```

```
                    'Ext.layout.container.Card'],
        layout: {
            type: 'hbox',
            align: 'stretch'
        },
        initComponent: function() {
            var me = this;
            Ext.applyIf(me, {
                dockedItems: [{
                    xtype: 'toolbar',
                    dock: 'top',
                    items: [{
                        xtype: 'button',
                        itemId: 'addCompanyBtn',
                        iconCls: 'addnew',
                        text: 'Add New Company'
                    }]
                }],
                items: [{
                    xtype: 'companytree',
                    flex: 1,
                    margin: 1
                }, {
                    xtype: 'container',
                    itemId: 'adminCards',
                    activeItem: 0,
                    flex: 1,
                    layout: {
                        type: 'card'
                    },
                    items: [{
                        xtype: 'container',
                        padding: 10,
                        html: 'Please select an item from the tree...'
                    }, {
                        xtype: 'companyform'
                    }, {
                        xtype: 'projectform'
                    }, {
                        xtype: 'taskform'
                    }]
                }]
            });
            me.callParent(arguments);
        }
    });
```

Note the use of a simple container as the first item of the card layout to display the
Please select an item from the tree... message.

The CompanyForm.js file

The `CompanyForm` view has a very simple interface that only has one data entry field:
`companyName`. This can be seen in the following lines of code:

```
Ext.define('TTT.view.admin.CompanyForm', {
    extend: 'Ext.form.Panel',
    xtype: 'companyform',
    requires: ['Ext.form.FieldSet', 'Ext.form.field.Text',
        'Ext.toolbar.Toolbar'],
    layout: {
        type: 'anchor'
    },
    bodyPadding: 10,
    border: false,
    autoScroll: true,
    initComponent: function() {
        var me = this;
        Ext.applyIf(me, {
            items: [{
                xtype: 'fieldset',
                hidden: false,
                padding: 10,
                width: 350,
                fieldDefaults: {
                    anchor: '100%'
                },
                title: 'Company Entry',
                items: [{
                    xtype: 'textfield',
                    name: 'companyName',
                    fieldLabel: 'Name',
                    emptyText: 'Enter company name...'
                }, {
                    xtype: 'toolbar',
                    ui: 'footer',
                    layout: {
                        pack: 'end',
                        type: 'hbox'
                    },
                    items: [{
                        xtype: 'button',
                        iconCls: 'delete',
                        itemId: 'deleteBtn',
                        disabled: true,
```

```
                            text: 'Delete'
                        }, {
                            xtype: 'button',
                            iconCls: 'addnew',
                            itemId: 'addProjectBtn',
                            disabled: true,
                            text: 'Add Project'
                        }, {
                            xtype: 'button',
                            iconCls: 'save',
                            itemId: 'saveBtn',
                            text: 'Save'
                        }]
                    }]
                }]
            });
            me.callParent(arguments);
        }
    });
```

Note the initial state of the **Delete** and **Add Project** buttons are disabled until a valid company is loaded.

The ProjectForm.js file

The layout and structure of the `ProjectForm` view is very similar to the company form we have just defined:

```
Ext.define('TTT.view.admin.ProjectForm', {
    extend: 'Ext.form.Panel',
    xtype: 'projectform',
    requires: ['Ext.form.FieldSet', 'Ext.form.field.Text',
        'Ext.toolbar.Toolbar'],
    layout: {
        type: 'anchor'
    },
    bodyPadding: 10,
    border: false,
    autoScroll: true,
    initComponent: function() {
        var me = this;
        Ext.applyIf(me, {
            items: [{
                xtype: 'fieldset',
                hidden: false,
```

```
                padding: 10,
                width: 350,
                fieldDefaults: {
                    anchor: '100%'
                },
                title: 'Project Entry',
                items: [{
                    xtype: 'textfield',
                    name: 'projectName',
                    fieldLabel: 'Project Name',
                    emptyText: 'Enter project name...'
                }, {
                    xtype: 'toolbar',
                    ui: 'footer',
                    layout: {
                        pack: 'end',
                        type: 'hbox'
                    },
                    items: [{
                        xtype: 'button',
                        iconCls: 'delete',
                        itemId: 'deleteBtn',
                        disabled: true,
                        text: 'Delete'
                    }, {
                        xtype: 'button',
                        iconCls: 'addnew',
                        itemId: 'addTaskBtn',
                        disabled: true,
                        text: 'Add Task'
                    }, {
                        xtype: 'button',
                        iconCls: 'save',
                        itemId: 'saveBtn',
                        text: 'Save'
                    }]
                }]
            }]
        });
        me.callParent(arguments);
    }
});
```

Once again the initial state of the **Delete** and **Add Task** buttons is disabled until a valid project is loaded.

The TaskForm.js file

The `TaskForm` view is again similar to the previous forms but will only need two buttons that are defined as follows:

```
Ext.define('TTT.view.admin.TaskForm', {
    extend: 'Ext.form.Panel',
    xtype: 'taskform',
    requires: ['Ext.form.FieldSet', 'Ext.form.field.Text',
        'Ext.toolbar.Toolbar'],
    layout: {
        type: 'anchor'
    },
    bodyPadding: 10,
    border: false,
    autoScroll: true,
    initComponent: function() {
        var me = this;
        Ext.applyIf(me, {
            items: [{
                xtype: 'fieldset',
                hidden: false,
                padding: 10,
                width: 350,
                fieldDefaults: {
                    anchor: '100%'
                },
                title: 'Task Entry',
                items: [{
                    xtype: 'textfield',
                    name: 'taskName',
                    fieldLabel: 'Name',
                    emptyText: 'Enter task name...'
                }, {
                    xtype: 'toolbar',
                    ui: 'footer',
                    layout: {
                        pack: 'end',
                        type: 'hbox'
                    },
                    items: [{
                        xtype: 'button',
                        iconCls: 'delete',
                        itemId: 'deleteBtn',
```

```
                            disabled: true,
                            text: 'Delete'
                    }, {
                            xtype: 'button',
                            iconCls: 'save',
                            itemId: 'saveBtn',
                            text: 'Save'
                    }]
                }]
            }]
        });
        me.callParent(arguments);
    }
});
```

Once again, the initial state of the **Delete** button is disabled until a valid task has been loaded.

The CompanyTree.js file

The final view is the `CompanyTree` view that represents the relationship between the company, project, and task.

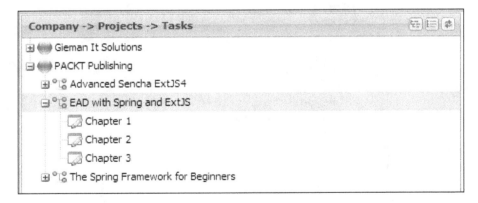

This view is defined as follows:

```
Ext.define('TTT.view.admin.CompanyTree', {
    extend: 'Ext.tree.Panel',
    xtype: 'companytree',
    title: 'Company -> Projects -> Tasks',
    requires: ['TTT.store.CompanyTree'],
    store: 'CompanyTree',
    lines: true,
```

```
        rootVisible: false,
        hideHeaders: true,
        viewConfig: {
            preserveScrollOnRefresh: true
        },
        initComponent: function() {
            var me = this;
            Ext.applyIf(me, {
                tools: [{
                    type: 'expand',
                    qtip: 'Expand All'
                }, {
                    type: 'collapse',
                    qtip: 'Collapse All'
                }, {
                    type: 'refresh',
                    qtip: 'Refresh Tree'
                }],
                columns: [{
                    xtype: 'treecolumn',
                    dataIndex: 'text',
                    flex: 1
                }]
            });
            me.callParent(arguments);
        }
    });
```

The `CompanyTree` view extends `Ext.tree.Panel` that requires a specialized `Ext.data.TreeStore` implementation which manages tree nodes and the relationship between items. The Ext JS 4 tree is a very flexible component and we recommend you become familiar with the core tree concepts at `http://docs.sencha.com/extjs/4.2.2/#!/guide/tree`.

Introducing the Ext.data.TreeStore class

The `Ext.data.TreeStore` class is the default store implementation used by `Ext.tree.Panel`. The `TreeStore` function provides many convenient functions for loading and managing hierarchical data. A `TreeStore` function may be defined with a model but this is not required. If a model is provided, it is decorated with the fields, methods, and properties of `Ext.data.NodeInterface` that are required for use in the tree. This additional functionality is applied to the prototype of the model to allow the tree to maintain the state and relationships between models.

If a model is not provided, one such model will be created by the store in a way that it implements the `Ext.data.NodeInterface` class. We recommend you browse the `NodeInterface` API documentation to see the full set of fields, methods, and properties available on nodes.

Our `CompanyTree` store definition for use in our tree is as follows:

```
Ext.define('TTT.store.CompanyTree', {
    extend: 'Ext.data.TreeStore',
    proxy: {
        type: 'ajax',
        url: 'company/tree.json'
    }
});
```

All the tree stores consume data that is in a hierarchical structure, either in JSON or XML format. We will generate JSON data in our request handling layer with the following structure:

```
{
    "success": true,
    "children": [
        {
            "id": "C_1",
            "text": "PACKT Publishing",
            "leaf": false,
            "expanded": true,
            "children": [
                {
                    "id": "P_1",
                    "text": "EAD with Spring and ExtJS",
                    "leaf": false,
                    "expanded": true,
                    "children": [
                        {
                            "id": "T_1",
                            "text": "Chapter 1",
                            "leaf": true
                        },
                        {
                            "id": "T_2",
                            "text": "Chapter 2",
```

```
                            "leaf": true
                        },
                        {
                            "id": "T_3",
                            "text": "Chapter 3",
                            "leaf": true
                        }
                    ]
                },
                {
                    "id": "P_2",
                    "text": "The Spring Framework for Beginners",
                    "leaf": false,
                    "expanded": true,
                    "children": [
                        {
                            "id": "T_4",
                            "text": "Chapter 1",
                            "leaf": true
                        },
                        {
                            "id": "T_5",
                            "text": "Chapter 2",
                            "leaf": true
                        },
                        {
                            "id": "T_6",
                            "text": "Chapter 3",
                            "leaf": true
                        }
                    ]
                }
            ]
        }
    ]
}
```

This structure defines the core properties used by any tree including id, children, text, leaf, and expanded.

The `children` property defines an array of nodes that exist at the same level and belong to the same parent. The top-level children in the structure belong to the root node and will be added to the root level of the tree. The tree panel property, `rootVisible:false`, will hide the root level from the view, displaying only the children. Enabling root-level visibility by setting the property to `rootVisible:true` will display the root node as defined in the `TreeStore` class. For example, adding the following definition to the tree store will result in the `Companies` node being displayed as shown in the following screenshot:

```
root: {
    text: 'Companies',
    expanded: true
}
```

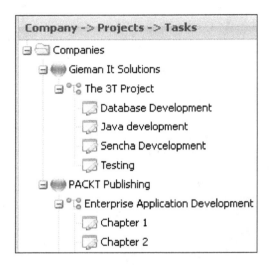

We wish to display each company at the top level of the tree and hence will be hiding the root node from the view.

The `id` property is used internally to uniquely identify each node. There can be no duplicates for this property within the tree structure, and we will hence prefix the `id` value with the type of node. A node representing a company will be prefixed with `C_`, a project node with `P_`, and a task node with `T_`. This `id` format will allow us to determine both the node type and the primary key of the node. If an ID is not provided, the store would generate one for us.

The ID can also be used to dynamically assign an `iconCls` class to the node. We do this through the use of the `append` listener of the store and define this later in the controller. Note that we could just as easily define the `iconCls` property in JSON itself:

```
{
    "success": true,
    "children": [
        {
            "id": "C_1",
            "iconCls": "company",
            "text": "PACKT Publishing",
            "leaf": false,
            "expanded": true,
            "children": [
                {
                    "id": "P_1",
                    "iconCls": "project",
                    "text": "EAD with Spring and ExtJS",
                    "leaf": false,
                    "expanded": true,
                    "children": [ etc…
```

However, we are now combining data with the presentation, and the Java method that generates JSON should not be concerned with how data is displayed.

The `text` field of the JSON tree is used to display the node's text. For simple trees, without multiple columns, this is the default field name if not explicitly set with a column definition (tree columns will be discussed later in this chapter).

The leaf property identifies whether this node can have children. All the task nodes have the `"leaf":true` setting. The `leaf` property defines whether the expand icon is shown next to the node.

The last property of interest is the `expanded` property that indicates whether the node should be displayed in an expanded state. This property must be set to `true` on each node that has children if we're loading an entire tree at once; otherwise, the proxy will attempt to load children for these nodes dynamically when they are expanded. Our JSON data will contain the entire tree, and hence we set the `expanded` property to `true` for each parent node.

Generating a JSON tree in the CompanyHandler class

It is now time to enhance the `CompanyHandler` class to generate the required JSON to load the tree store and display the company tree. We will create two new methods to implement this functionality.

The CompanyHandler.getTreeNodeId() method

The `CompanyHandler.getTreeNodeId()` helper method generates a unique ID based on the ID of the `EntityItem` class. It will be used to generate type-specific IDs for each node.

```
private String getTreeNodeId(EntityItem obj){
   String id = null;

   if(obj instanceof Company){
      id = "C_" + obj.getId();
   } else if(obj instanceof Project){
      id = "P_" + obj.getId();
   } else if(obj instanceof Task){
      id = "T_" + obj.getId();
   }
   return id;
}
```

The CompanyHandler.getCompanyTreeJson() method

The `CompanyHandler getCompanyTreeJson()` method is mapped to the `company/tree.json` URL and has the following definition:

```
@RequestMapping(value="/tree", method=RequestMethod.GET,
produces={"application/json"})
@ResponseBody
public String getCompanyTreeJson(HttpServletRequest request) {

   User sessionUser = getSessionUser(request);

   Result<List<Company>> ar =
      companyService.findAll(sessionUser.getUsername());
```

```java
if (ar.isSuccess()) {

  JsonObjectBuilder builder = Json.createObjectBuilder();
  builder.add("success", true);
  JsonArrayBuilder companyChildrenArrayBuilder =
    Json.createArrayBuilder();

  for(Company company : ar.getData()){

    List<Project> projects = company.getProjects();

    JsonArrayBuilder projectChildrenArrayBuilder =
      Json.createArrayBuilder();

    for(Project project : projects){

      List<Task> tasks = project.getTasks();

      JsonArrayBuilder taskChildrenArrayBuilder =
        Json.createArrayBuilder();

      for(Task task : tasks){

        taskChildrenArrayBuilder.add(
          Json.createObjectBuilder()
          .add("id", getTreeNodeId(task))
          .add("text", task.getTaskName())
          .add("leaf", true)
        );
      }

      projectChildrenArrayBuilder.add(
        Json.createObjectBuilder()
          .add("id", getTreeNodeId(project))
          .add("text", project.getProjectName())
          .add("leaf", tasks.isEmpty())
          .add("expanded", tasks.size() > 0)
          .add("children", taskChildrenArrayBuilder)
      );

    }

    companyChildrenArrayBuilder.add(
      Json.createObjectBuilder()
```

```
                .add("id", getTreeNodeId(company))
                .add("text", company.getCompanyName())
                .add("leaf", projects.isEmpty())
                .add("expanded", projects.size() > 0)
                .add("children", projectChildrenArrayBuilder)
        );
    }

    builder.add("children", companyChildrenArrayBuilder);

    return toJsonString(builder.build());

} else {

    return getJsonErrorMsg(ar.getMsg());

}
}
```

This method performs the following tasks:

- It creates a `JsonArrayBuilder` object with the name `companyChildrenArrayBuilder` to hold the set of company `JsonObjectBuilder` instances that will be created in the main `for` loop when iterating through the company list.

- It loops through each project assigned to each company, adding each project's `JsonObjectBuilder` tree node representation to the `projectChildrenArrayBuilder` `JsonArrayBuilder` instance. The `projectChildrenArrayBuilder` instance is then added as the `children` property of the owning company `JsonObjectBuilder` instance.

- It loops through each task assigned to each project, adding each task's `JsonObjectBuilder` tree node representation to the `taskChildrenArrayBuilder` `JsonArrayBuilder` instance. The `taskChildrenArrayBuilder` instance is then added as the `children` property of the owning project, the `JsonObjectBuilder` instance.

- It adds the `companyChildrenArrayBuilder` as the `children` property of the `builder` instance that will be used to build and return JSON from the method with `success` property `true`.

The `getCompanyTreeJson` method returns a hierarchical JSON structure that encapsulates the relationship between the company, project, and task in a format that can be consumed by the `CompanyTree` store.

Controlling the 3T administration

The TTT.controller.AdminController ties together the views and implements the many actions that are possible in this user interface. You must download the source code to see the complete definition of this controller as it is not reproduced completely within the following text.

The AdminController has references to the four stores required for processing actions. Each store is reloaded after an update or delete action to ensure the store is in sync with the database. For multiuser applications, this is an important point to consider; can view data be changed by a different user during the lifetime of a session? Unlike the task log interface, where data belongs to the user in the session, the 3T administration module may be actively used by different users at the same time.

> It is beyond the scope of this book to discuss strategies for data integrity in multiuser environments. This is usually achieved through the use of per record timestamps that indicate the last update time. Appropriate logic in the service layer would test the submitted record timestamp against the timestamp in the database and then process the action accordingly.

There is one store and model that is yet to be fully defined; we will do so now.

Defining the Company model and store

The Company model was first defined using Sencha Cmd in *Chapter 9, Getting Started with Ext JS 4*, but we now need to add the appropriate proxy and validations. The full definition is as follows:

```
Ext.define('TTT.model.Company', {
    extend: 'Ext.data.Model',
    fields: [
        { name: 'idCompany', type: 'int', useNull:true },
        { name: 'companyName', type: 'string'}
    ],
    idProperty: 'idCompany',
    proxy: {
        type: 'ajax',
        idParam:'idCompany',
        api:{
            create:'company/store.json',
            read:'company/find.json',
```

```
                update:'company/store.json',
                destroy:'company/remove.json'
            },
            reader: {
                type: 'json',
                root: 'data'
            },
            writer: {
                type: 'json',
                allowSingle:true,
                encode:true,
                root:'data',
                writeAllFields: true
            }
        },
        validations: [
            {type: 'presence',  field: 'companyName'},
            {type: 'length', field: 'companyName', min: 2}
        ]
    });
```

The Company store will load all the company records through the company/findAll.
json URL as follows:

```
Ext.define('TTT.store.Company', {
    extend: 'Ext.data.Store',
    requires: [
        'TTT.model.Company'
    ],
    model: 'TTT.model.Company',
    proxy: {
        type: 'ajax',
        url: 'company/findAll.json',
        reader: {
            type: 'json',
            root: 'data'
        }
    }
});
```

The Company model and store are our simplest definitions to date. We will now
examine the core actions in our AdminController.

The doAfterActivate function

The three stores that are required for 3T administration are loaded when the ManageTasks panel is activated. This will ensure that valid records are available in each store when selecting an item in the tree. The doAfterActivate function can be used for initializing the state of any components belonging to the AdminController. This is especially useful when configuring the drag-and-drop action at the end of this chapter.

Note that we are adding the **append** listener to the tree store view and assigning the doSetTreeIcon function. It is not possible to do this in the init function control config as the view is not yet configured and ready at this point in time. Assigning the doSetTreeIcon function to the listener after the activation ensures the component is fully configured. The doSetTreeIcon function dynamically assigns an iconCls class to each node depending on the node type.

The final step in the doAfterActivate function is to load the tree store to display the data in the tree.

The doSelectTreeItem function

The doSelectTreeItem function is called when a user selects an item in the tree. The node ID is retrieved and split to allow us to determine the type of node:

```
var recIdSplit = record.getId().split('_');
```

For each node, the primary key value is determined and used to retrieve the record from the appropriate store. The record is then loaded into the form, which is then set to be the active item in the admin card's layout.

The doSave functions

Each save function retrieves the record from the form and updates the record with the form values. The record is saved if the validation is successful and the form updated to reflect the changing button state. The store that owns the record is then reloaded to sync with the database.

The doDelete functions

Each delete function confirms the user action before calling the destroy method of the model. If successful, the active item in the admin card's layout is set to display the default message: **Please select an item from the tree**. If the deletion was not successful, an appropriate message is displayed to inform the user.

The doAdd functions

The **Add** buttons are on the form that is the parent for the Add action. You can only add a project to a company or add a task to a project. Each doAdd function retrieves the parent and creates an instance of the child before loading the appropriate form. Buttons on the child form are disabled as needed.

Testing the 3T administration interface

We now need to add our new components to our Application.js file:

```
models:[
   'Company',
   'Project',
   'Task',
   'User',
   'TaskLog'
],
controllers: [
   'MainController',
   'UserController',
   'AdminController',
   'TaskLogController'
],
stores: [
   'Company',
   'CompanyTree',
   'Project',
   'Task',
   'User',
   'TaskLog'
]
```

We also need to add the ManageTasks view to our MainCards:

```
Ext.define('TTT.view.MainCards', {
    extend: 'Ext.container.Container',
    xtype: 'maincards',
    requires: ['Ext.layout.container.Card', 'TTT.view.Welcome',
        'TTT.view.user.ManageUsers',
        'TTT.view.tasklog.ManageTaskLogs',
        'TTT.view.admin.ManageTasks'],
    layout: 'card',
    initComponent: function() {
        var me = this;
```

```
        Ext.applyIf(me, {
            items: [{
                xtype: 'welcome',
                itemId: 'welcomCard'
            }, {
                xtype: 'manageusers',
                itemId: 'manageUsersCard'
            }, {
                xtype: 'managetasklogs',
                itemId: 'taskLogCard'
            }, {
                xtype: 'managetasks',
                itemId: 'manageTasksCard'
            }]
        });
        me.callParent(arguments);
    }
});
```

You can now run the application in the GlassFish server and test the 3T administration interface by logging on as the `bjones` user (or any other user who has administrator permission).

Dynamically loading tree nodes

Enterprise applications usually have data sets that prohibit the loading of the full tree in a single JSON request. Large trees can be configured to load children on a per node basis by expanding levels on demand. A few minor changes to our code can allow us to implement this dynamic loading of node children.

When a node is expanded, the tree store proxy submits a request that contains a `node` parameter with the ID of the node being expanded. The URL submitted is that which is configured in the proxy. We will change our tree store proxy as follows:

```
proxy: {
  type: 'ajax',
  url: 'company/treenode.json'
}
```

Note that the URL of the proxy has been changed to `treenode`. This mapping, when implemented in `CompanyHandler`, will load one level at a time. The first request submitted by the proxy to load the top level of the tree will have the following format:

```
company/treenode.json?node=root
```

This will return the root node's list of companies:

```
{
    success: true,
    "children": [{
        "id": "C_2",
        "text": "Gieman It Solutions",
        "leaf": false
    }, {
        "id": "C_1",
        "text": "PACKT Publishing",
        "leaf": false
    }]
}
```

Note that there is no `children` array defined for each company, and the `leaf` property is set to `false`. The Ext JS tree will display an expander icon next to the node if there are no children defined and the node is not a leaf. Clicking on the expander icon will submit a request that has the `node` parameter set to the `id` value for the node being expanded. Expanding the `"PACKT Publishing"` node would hence submit a request to load the children via `company/treenode.json?node=C_1`.

The JSON response would consist of a `children` array that would be appended to the tree as children of the `PACKT Publishing` node. In our example, the response would include the projects assigned to the company:

```
{
    success: true,
    "children": [{
        "id": "P_3",
        "text": "Advanced Sencha ExtJS4 ",
        "leaf": false
    }, {
        "id": "P_1",
        "text": "EAD with Spring and ExtJS",
        "leaf": false
    }, {
        "id": "P_2",
        "text": "The Spring Framework for Beginners",
        "leaf": false
    }]
}
```

Once again each project would not define a `children` array, even if there are tasks assigned. Each project would be defined with `"leaf":false` to render an expander icon if there are tasks assigned. Expanding the `P_1` node would result in the proxy submitting a request to load the next level: `company/treenode.json?node=P_1`.

This would result in the following JSON being returned:

```
{
    success: true,
    "children": [{
        "id": "T_1",
        "text": "Chapter 1",
        "leaf": true
    }, {
        "id": "T_2",
        "text": "Chapter 2",
        "leaf": true
    }, {
        "id": "T_3",
        "text": "Chapter 3",
        "leaf": true
    }]
}
```

This time we define these nodes with `"leaf":true` to ensure the expander icon is not displayed and users are unable to attempt loading a fourth level of the tree.

The `CompanyHandler` method that is responsible for this logic can now be defined and mapped to the `company/treenode.json` URL:

```
@RequestMapping(value = "/treenode", method = RequestMethod.GET,
  produces = {"application/json"})
@ResponseBody
public String getCompanyTreeNode(
    @RequestParam(value = "node", required = true) String node,
    HttpServletRequest request) {

  User sessionUser = getSessionUser(request);

  logger.info(node);

  JsonObjectBuilder builder = Json.createObjectBuilder();
  builder.add("success", true);
```

```java
        JsonArrayBuilder childrenArrayBuilder =
          Json.createArrayBuilder();

    if(node.equals("root")){

      Result<List<Company>> ar =
        companyService.findAll(sessionUser.getUsername());
      if (ar.isSuccess()) {

        for(Company company : ar.getData()){
          childrenArrayBuilder.add(
            Json.createObjectBuilder()
              .add("id", getTreeNodeId(company))
              .add("text", company.getCompanyName())
              .add("leaf", company.getProjects().isEmpty())
          );
        }
      } else {

        return getJsonErrorMsg(ar.getMsg());
      }
    } else if (node.startsWith("C")){

      String[] idSplit = node.split("_");
      int idCompany = Integer.parseInt(idSplit[1]);
      Result<Company> ar = companyService.find(idCompany,
        sessionUser.getUsername());

      for(Project project : ar.getData().getProjects()){

        childrenArrayBuilder.add(
          Json.createObjectBuilder()
            .add("id", getTreeNodeId(project))
            .add("text", project.getProjectName())
            .add("leaf", project.getTasks().isEmpty())
        );
      }

    } else if (node.startsWith("P")){

      String[] idSplit = node.split("_");
      int idProject = Integer.parseInt(idSplit[1]);
      Result<Project> ar = projectService.find(idProject,
        sessionUser.getUsername());
```

```
    for(Task task : ar.getData().getTasks()){

        childrenArrayBuilder.add(
          Json.createObjectBuilder()
            .add("id", getTreeNodeId(task))
            .add("text", task.getTaskName())
            .add("leaf", true)
        );
    }
  }

  builder.add("children", childrenArrayBuilder);

  return toJsonString(builder.build());
}
```

The `getCompanyTreeNode` method determines the type of node being expanded and loads appropriate records from the service layer. The returned JSON is then consumed by the store and displayed in the tree.

We can now run the project in GlassFish and display the **3T Admin** interface. The first level of the tree is loaded as expected:

When the expander icon is clicked, the next level of the tree will be dynamically loaded:

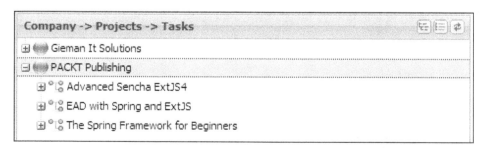

The third level can then be expanded to display the tasks:

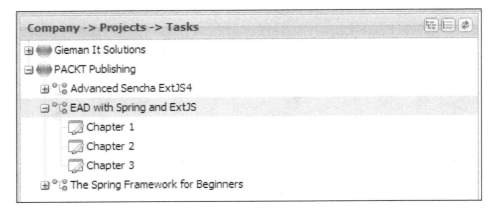

We will leave it to you to enhance the `AdminController` for use with dynamic trees. Reloading the tree after each successful save or delete would not be very user friendly; changing the logic to only reload the parent node would be a far better solution.

Displaying multiple tree columns

Ext JS 4 trees can be configured to display multiple columns for visualising advanced data structures. We will make a few minor changes to display the ID of each node in the tree. Simply adding a new column to the tree definition will achieve this purpose:

```
Ext.define('TTT.view.admin.CompanyTree', {
    extend: 'Ext.tree.Panel',
    xtype: 'companytree',
    title: 'Company -> Projects -> Tasks',
    requires: ['TTT.store.CompanyTree'],
    store: 'CompanyTree',
    lines: true,
    rootVisible: false,
    hideHeaders: false,
    viewConfig: {
        preserveScrollOnRefresh: true
    },
    initComponent: function() {
        var me = this;
        Ext.applyIf(me, {
            tools: [{
                type: 'expand',
                qtip: 'Expand All'
```

```
    }, {
        type: 'collapse',
        qtip: 'Collapse All'
    }, {
        type: 'refresh',
        qtip: 'Refresh Tree'
    }],
    columns: [{
        xtype: 'treecolumn',
        text:'Node',
        dataIndex: 'text',
        flex: 1
    },
    {

        dataIndex: 'id',
        text : 'ID',
        width:60
    }]
});
me.callParent(arguments);
    }
});
```

We have also added the `text` property to each column, which is displayed in the header row, and enabled headers with `hideHeaders:false`. These minor changes will result in the following tree being displayed when fully expanded:

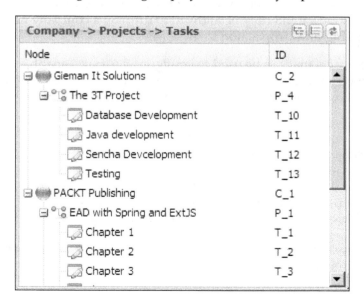

Drag-and-drop made easy

Dragging and dropping nodes within trees is easy with Ext JS 4. To allow the drag-and-drop action within a tree, we need to add the `TreeViewDragDrop` plugin as follows:

```
Ext.define('TTT.view.admin.CompanyTree', {
    extend: 'Ext.tree.Panel',
    xtype: 'companytree',
    title: 'Company -> Projects -> Tasks',
    requires: ['TTT.store.CompanyTree','Ext.tree.plugin.
TreeViewDragDrop'],
    store: 'CompanyTree',
    lines: true,
    rootVisible: false,
    hideHeaders: true,
    viewConfig: {
        preserveScrollOnRefresh: true,
        plugins: {
            ptype: 'treeviewdragdrop'
        }
    }, etc
```

This simple inclusion will enable the drag-and-drop support for your tree. You will now be able to drag-and-drop any node to a new parent. Unfortunately, this is not exactly what we need. A task node should only be allowed to drop on a project node, while a project node should only be allowed to drop on a company node. How can we restrict the drag-and-drop action to these rules?

There are two events that can be used to configure this functionality. These events are fired from the `TreeViewDragDrop` plugin and can be configured in the `doAfterActivate` function of the `AdminController` in the following way:

```
doAfterActivate:function(){
  var me = this;
  me.getCompanyStore().load();
  me.getProjectStore().load();
  me.getTaskStore().load();
  me.getCompanyTreeStore().on('append' , me.doSetTreeIcon, me);
  me.getCompanyTree().getView().on('beforedrop', me.isDropAllowed,
    me);
  me.getCompanyTree().getView().on('drop', me.doChangeParent, me);
  me.getCompanyTreeStore().load();
}
```

The `beforedrop` event can be used to test whether the `drag` and `drop` actions are valid. Returning `false` will stop the `drop` action from occurring and animate the node back to the origin of the action. The `drop` event can be used to process the `drop` action, most likely to persist the change to the underlying storage.

The `isDropAllowed` function returns `true` or `false` depending on whether the drop target is valid for the node:

```
isDropAllowed: function(node, data, overModel, dropPosition) {
    var dragNode = data.records[0];
    if (!Ext.isEmpty(dragNode) && !Ext.isEmpty(overModel)) {
        var dragIdSplit = dragNode.getId().split('_');
        var dropIdSplit = overModel.getId().split('_');
        if (dragIdSplit[0] === 'T' && dropIdSplit[0] === 'P') {
            return true;
        } else if (dragIdSplit[0] === 'P'
                    && dropIdSplit[0] === 'C') {
            return true;
        }
    }
    return false;
}
```

This function will restrict the `drag` and `drop` actions to two valid scenarios: dragging a project to a new company and dragging a task to a new project. All the other `drag` and `drop` actions are not allowed.

Dragging and dropping alone is not enough; we now need to save the new parent after a successful drop. This action is handled in the `doChangeParent` function:

```
doChangeParent: function(node, data, overModel, dropPosition, eOpts) {
    var me = this;
    var dragNode = data.records[0];
    if (!Ext.isEmpty(dragNode) && !Ext.isEmpty(overModel)) {
        var dragIdSplit = dragNode.getId().split('_');
        var dropIdSplit = overModel.getId().split('_');
        if (dragIdSplit[0] === 'T' && dropIdSplit[0] === 'P') {
            var idTask = Ext.Number.from(dragIdSplit[1]);
            var idProject = Ext.Number.from(dropIdSplit[1]);
            var rec = me.getTaskStore().getById(idTask);
            if (!Ext.isEmpty(rec)) {
                rec.set('idProject', idProject);
                rec.save();
            }
        } else if (dragIdSplit[0] === 'P'
```

```
                        && dropIdSplit[0] === 'C') {
            var idProject = Ext.Number.from(dragIdSplit[1]);
            var idCompany = Ext.Number.from(dropIdSplit[1]);
            var rec = me.getProjectStore().getById(idProject);
            if (!Ext.isEmpty(rec)) {
                rec.set('idCompany', idCompany);
                rec.save();
            }
        }
    }
}
```

Dragging a valid node to a new parent is now persisted when the record is saved. You will now be able to drag-and-drop between valid tree nodes and automatically save the changes.

The animations provided by Ext JS 4 trees will guide your `drag` and `drop` actions. Dragging the **Database Development** node will animate the action as shown in the following screenshot:

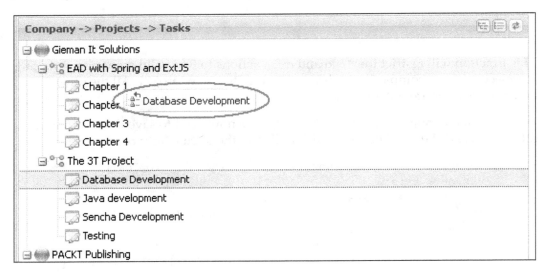

Should the drop action not be allowed, the node will animate back to the original position, providing instant visual feedback for the user.

Ext JS 4 trees are very flexible components, and there is still much to learn if you want to fully leverage trees in your application. We recommend that you explores the many tree examples on the *Sencha Docs* website for more complex examples including the `drag` and `drop` actions between trees and persisting model-based data nodes.

Summary

The **3T Admin** interface introduced the tree component for displaying hierarchical data. The company, project, and task relationship was loaded into the tree via a single JSON request and allowed the user to maintain and add new entities.

Dynamic loading of tree nodes was then explained and implemented. This strategy is best suited for very large trees with potentially complex data structures. Node-by-node dynamic loading is easily achieved with minimum changes required in the Ext JS 4 client and Java backend.

Displaying multiple tree columns and the basic drag-and-drop functionality was also explored and implemented to show the flexibility of the Ext JS 4 tree.

Our final step in the enterprise application development with Ext JS and Spring journey is building our 3T project for production deployment. Thankfully, Maven and Sencha Cmd can help make this an easy task as you will learn in our final chapter, *Chapter 13, Moving Your Application to Production*.

13
Moving Your Application to Production

The development work is over and it is time to deploy our application to the production server. If only it were so simple! Enterprise applications require formal processes to be followed, customer or business owner sign-offs, internal testing, **User Acceptance Testing (UAT)**, and many more such hurdles to be overcome before an application is ready for production deployment. This chapter will explore the following two key areas:

- Using Maven to build and compile Ext JS 4 applications for production use
- GlassFish 4 deployment and configuration concepts

We will start by examining the Sencha Cmd compiler.

Compiling with Sencha Cmd

In *Chapter 9*, *Getting Started with Ext JS 4*, we went through the process of using Sencha Cmd to generate the Ext JS 4 application skeleton and to create basic components. This section will focus on using Sencha Cmd to compile our Ext JS 4 application for deployment within a **Web Archive (WAR)** file. The goal of the compilation process is to create a single JavaScript file that contains all of the code needed for the application, including all the Ext JS 4 dependencies.

The index.html file that was created during the application skeleton generation is structured as follows:

```
<!DOCTYPE HTML>
<html>
  <head>
    <meta charset="UTF-8">
```

```
        <title>TTT</title>
        <!-- <x-compile> -->
            <!-- <x-bootstrap> -->
                <link rel="stylesheet" href="bootstrap.css">
                <script src="ext/ext-dev.js"></script>
                <script src="bootstrap.js"></script>
            <!-- </x-bootstrap> -->
            <script src="app.js"></script>
        <!-- </x-compile> -->
    </head>
<body></body>
</html>
```

The open and close tags of the x-compile directive enclose the part of the index. html file where the Sencha Cmd compiler will operate. The only declarations that should be contained in this block are the script tags. The compiler will process all of the scripts within the x-compile directive, searching for dependencies based on the Ext.define, requires, or uses directives.

An exception to this is the ext-dev.js file. This file is considered to be a "bootstrap" file for the framework and will not be processed in the same way. The compiler ignores the files in the x-bootstrap block and the declarations are removed from the final compiler-generated page.

The first step in the compilation process is to examine and parse all the JavaScript source code and analyze any dependencies. To do this the compiler needs to identify all the source folders in the application. Our application has two source folders: Ext JS 4 sources in webapp/ext/src and 3T application sources in webapp/app. These folder locations are specified using the -sdk and -classpath arguments in the compile command:

```
sencha –sdk {path-to-sdk} compile -classpath={app-sources-folder} page
-yui -in {index-page-to-compile}-out {output-file-location}
```

For our 3T application the compile command is as follows:

```
sencha –sdk ext compile -classpath=app page -yui -in index.html -out
build/index.html
```

This command performs the following actions:

- The Sencha Cmd compiler examines all the folders specified by the `-classpath` argument. The `-sdk` directory is automatically included for scanning.

- The `page` command then includes all of the script tags in `index.html` that are contained in the `x-compile` block.

- After identifying the content of the `app` directory and the `index.html` page, the compiler analyzes the JavaScript code and determines what is ultimately needed for inclusion in a single JavaScript file representing the application.

- A modified version of the original `index.html` file is written to `build/index.html`.

- All of the JavaScript files needed by the new `index.html` file are concatenated and compressed using the YUI Compressor, and written to the `build/all-classes.js` file.

The `sencha compile` command must be executed from within the `webapp` directory, which is the root of the application and is the directory containing the `index.html` file. All the arguments supplied to the `sencha compile` command can then be relative to the `webapp` directory.

Open a command prompt (or terminal window in Mac) and navigate to the `webapp` directory of the 3T project. Executing the `sencha compile` command as shown earlier in this section will result in the following output:

Opening the `webapp/build` folder in NetBeans should now show the two newly generated files: `index.html` and `all-classes.js`. The `all-classes.js` file will contain all the required Ext JS 4 classes in addition to all the 3T application classes. Attempting to open this file in NetBeans will result in the following warning: "**The file seems to be too large to open safely...**", but you can open the file in a text editor to see the following concatenated and minified content:

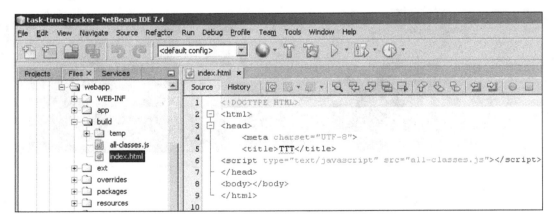

Opening the `build/index.html` page in NetBeans will display the following screenshot:

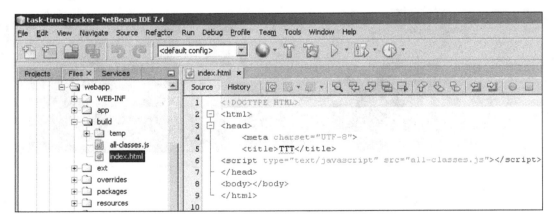

You can now open the `build/index.html` file in the browser after running the application, but the result may surprise you:

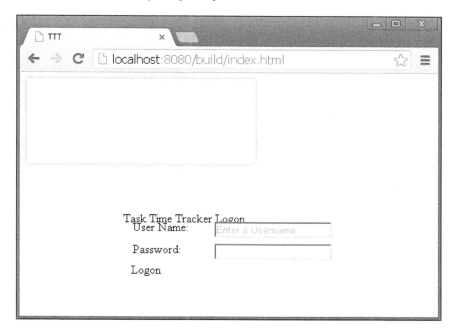

The layout that is presented will depend on the browser, but regardless, you will see that the CSS styling is missing. The CSS files required by our application need to be moved outside the `<!-- <x-compile> -->` directive. But where are the styles coming from? It is now time to briefly delve into Ext JS 4 themes and the `bootstrap.css` file.

Ext JS 4 theming

Ext JS 4 themes leverage **Syntactically Awesome StyleSheets (SASS)** and Compass (`http://compass-style.org/`) to enable the use of variables and mixins in stylesheets. Almost all of the styles for Ext JS 4 components can be customized, including colors, fonts, borders, and backgrounds, by simply changing the SASS variables. SASS is an extension of CSS that allows you to keep large stylesheets well-organized; a very good overview and reference can be found at `http://sass-lang.com/documentation/file.SASS_REFERENCE.html`.

Theming an Ext JS 4 application using Compass and SASS is beyond the scope of this book. Sencha Cmd allows easy integration with these technologies to build SASS projects; however, the SASS language and syntax is a steep learning curve in its own right. Ext JS 4 theming is very powerful and minor changes to the existing themes can quickly change the appearance of your application. You can find out more about Ext JS 4 theming at http://docs.sencha.com/extjs/4.2.2/#!/guide/theming.

The bootstrap.css file was created with the default theme definition during the generation of the application skeleton. The content of the bootstrap.css file is as follows:

```
@import 'ext/packages/ext-theme-classic/build/resources/ext-theme-classic-all.css';
```

This file imports the ext-theme-classic-all.css stylesheet, which is the default "classic" Ext JS theme. All of the available themes can be found in the ext/packages directory of the Ext JS 4 SDK:

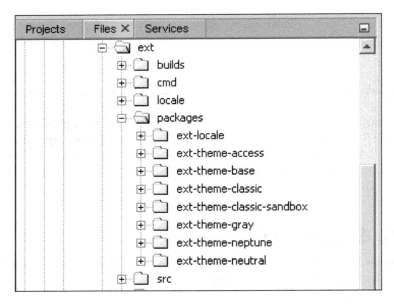

Changing to a different theme is as simple as changing the bootstrap.css import. Switching to the **neptune** theme would require the following bootstrap.css definition:

```
@import 'ext/packages/ext-theme-neptune/build/resources/ext-theme-neptune-all.css';
```

This modification will change the appearance of the application to the Ext JS "neptune" theme as shown in the following screenshot:

We will change the `bootstrap.css` file definition to use the `gray` theme:

```
@import 'ext/packages/ext-theme-gray/build/resources/ext-theme-gray-all.css';
```

This will result in the following appearance:

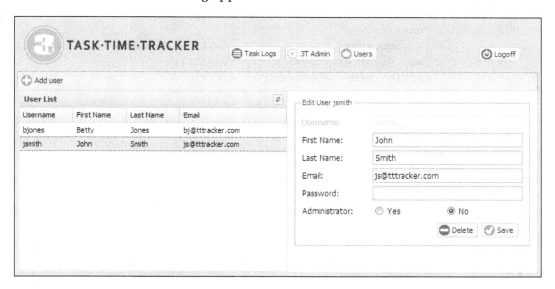

You may experiment with different themes but should note that not all of the themes may be as complete as the `classic` theme; minor changes may be required to fully utilize the styling for some components.

We will keep the `gray` theme for our `index.html` page. This will allow us to differentiate the (original) `index.html` page from the new ones that will be created in the following section using the `classic` theme.

Compiling for production use

Until now we have only worked with the Sencha Cmd-generated `index.html` file. We will now create a new `index-dev.html` file for our development environment. The development file will be a copy of the `index.html` file without the `bootstrap.css` file. We will reference the default `classic` theme in the `index-dev.html` file as follows:

```
<!DOCTYPE HTML>
<html>
  <head>
    <meta charset="UTF-8">
    <title>TTT</title>
    <link rel="stylesheet" href="ext/packages/ext-theme-classic/build/
resources/ext-theme-classic-all.css">
    <link rel="stylesheet" href="resources/styles.css">
    <!-- <x-compile> -->
      <!-- <x-bootstrap> -->
        <script src="ext/ext-dev.js"></script>
        <script src="bootstrap.js"></script>
      <!-- </x-bootstrap> -->
      <script src="app.js"></script>
    <!-- </x-compile> -->
  </head>
<body></body>
</html>
```

Note that we have moved the `stylesheet` definition out of the `<!-- <x-compile> -->` directive.

> If you are using the downloaded source code for the book, you will have the `resources/styles.css` file and the `resources` directory structure available. The stylesheet and associated images in the `resources` directory contain the 3T logos and icons. We recommend you download the full source code now for completeness.

We can now modify the Sencha Cmd `compile` command to use the `index-dev.html` file and output the generated compile file to `index-prod.html` in the `webapp` directory:

```
sencha -sdk ext compile -classpath=app page -yui -in index-dev.html -out
index-prod.html
```

This command will generate the `index-prod.html` file and the `all-classes.js` files in the `webapp` directory as shown in the following screenshot:

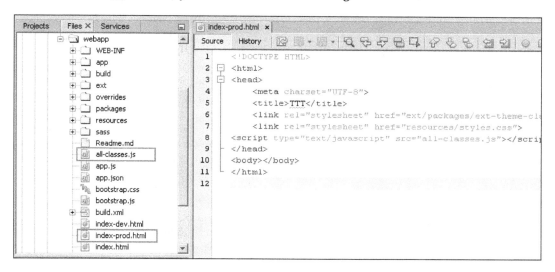

The `index-prod.html` file references the stylesheets directly and uses the single compiled and minified `all-classes.js` file. You can now run the application and browse the `index-prod.html` file as shown in the following screenshot:

You should notice a **significant** increase in the speed with which the logon window is displayed as all the JavaScript classes are loaded from the single `all-classes.js` file.

The `index-prod.html` file will be used by developers to test the compiled `all-classes.js` file.

Accessing the individual pages will now allow us to differentiate between environments:

The logon window as displayed in the browser	Page description
Task Time Tracker Logon User Name: bjones Password: ••••• Logon	The `index.html` page was generated by Sencha Cmd and has been configured to use the `gray` theme in `bootstrap.css`. This page is no longer needed for development; use `index-dev.html` instead. You can access this page at `http://localhost:8080/index.html`
Task Time Tracker Logon User Name: bjones Password: ••••• Logon	The `index-dev.html` page uses the `classic` theme stylesheet included outside the `<!-- <x-compile> -->` directive. Use this file for application development. Ext JS 4 will dynamically load source files as required. You can access this page at `http://localhost:8080/index-dev.html`
Task Time Tracker Logon User Name: bjones Password: ••••• Logon	The `index-prod.html` file is dynamically generated by the Sencha Cmd `compile` command. This page uses the `all-classes.js` all-in-one compiled JavaScript file with the `classic` theme stylesheet. You can access this page at `http://localhost:8080/index-prod.html`

Integrating Sencha Cmd compiling with Maven

Until now we have executed the Sencha Cmd `compile` command from the terminal. It would be far better to execute the command during the Maven build process. The `index-prod.html` and compiled `all-classes.js` files can then be generated automatically every time a build is performed. The following `plugin` when added to the Maven `pom.xml` file will perform the following action:

```
<plugin>
   <groupId>org.codehaus.mojo</groupId>
   <artifactId>exec-maven-plugin</artifactId>
   <version>1.2.1</version>
   <executions>
     <execution>
       <id>sencha-compile</id>
       <phase>compile</phase>
       <goals>
         <goal>exec</goal>
       </goals>
       <configuration>
         <executable>C:\Sencha\Cmd\4.0.0.203\sencha.exe</executable>
         <arguments>
           <argument>-sdk</argument>
           <argument>${basedir}/src/main/webapp/ext</argument>
           <argument>compile</argument>
           <argument>-classpath</argument>
           <argument>${basedir}/src/main/webapp/app</argument>
           <argument>page</argument>
           <argument>-yui</argument>
           <argument>-in</argument>
           <argument>${basedir}/src/main/webapp/index-
dev.html</argument>
           <argument>-out</argument>
           <argument>${basedir}/src/main/webapp/index-prod.html</
argument>
         </arguments>
       </configuration>
     </execution>
   </executions>
</plugin>
```

The following are a few points to note:

- The plugin is executed during the `compile` phase of the Maven build process.

- The Sencha Cmd executable is defined with a complete filesystem path. Only then is it possible to build different projects with different versions of Sencha if required.

- The `${basedir}` property represents the full path to the root of the Maven project. Full paths are required for each argument as we are not executing the Sencha Cmd `compile` command from within the `webapp` directory.

The `index-prod.html` and `all-classes.js` files will now be updated every time a build is performed. The output of this plugin can be seen in the following Maven build log:

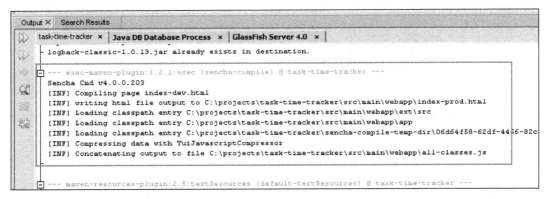

Adding the build version and timestamp

It is important to be able to identify different builds, not just the build version but also when the build was compiled. The project version is defined in the `pom.xml` file using the `version` property:

```
<groupId>com.gieman</groupId>
<artifactId>task-time-tracker</artifactId>
<version>1.0</version>
<packaging>war</packaging>
```

Performing a Maven build will result in a WAR file being generated with the filename `task-time-tracker-1.0.war`; it is a combination of the `artifactId` and `version` fields with the `.war` extension.

In enterprise environments, a new release could be anything from a minor change (for example, Release Version 1.3.2) to a major release (such as Release Version 4.0). The exact naming conventions for the `version` value in use will depend on the enterprise organization. Regardless of the naming convention, it is important to identify **when** the build was made. This is obvious when the timestamp on the WAR file is examined, but not so obvious for the testers of the application, who only have access to the frontend. We recommend adding the release version and build timestamp to the Ext JS application to allow users to identify the version they are using. The logon window is an obvious place to display this information and we will add the build version and timestamp as shown in the following screenshot:

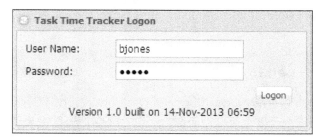

The first change that we will make is add two constants to the `Application.js` file in the `init` function:

```
init : function(application){
  TTT.URL_PREFIX = 'ttt/';
  Ext.Ajax.on('beforerequest', function(conn, options, eOpts){
    options.url = TTT.URL_PREFIX + options.url;
  });
  TTT.BUILD_DATE = '$BUILD_DATE$';
  TTT.BUILD_VERSION = '$BUILD_VERSION$';
}
```

The `TTT.BUILD_DATE` and `TTT.BUILD_VERSION` fields define tokens (or placeholders) that will dynamically be replaced in the `all-classes.js` file during the Maven build. These tokens will **not** be populated for the `index-dev.html` file and the logon window for development will look like the following screenshot:

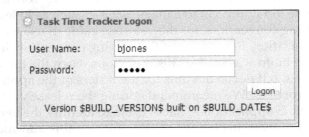

The token replacement with the correct build and timestamp is defined in the `pom. xml` file and requires several additions, the first being the `maven.build.timestamp. format` property:

```
<properties>
  <endorsed.dir>${project.build.directory}/endorsed</endorsed.dir>
  <project.build.sourceEncoding>UTF-
8</project.build.sourceEncoding>
  <maven.build.timestamp.format>dd-MMM-yyyy HH:mm</maven.build.
timestamp.format>
  <spring.version>3.2.4.RELEASE</spring.version>
  <logback.version>1.0.13</logback.version>
</properties>
```

The `maven.build.timestamp.format` property defines the format of the timestamp in the `LogonWindow.js` file. The second change is the addition of the `maven-replacer-plugin`:

```
<plugin>
  <groupId>com.google.code.maven-replacer-plugin</groupId>
  <artifactId>maven-replacer-plugin</artifactId>
  <version>1.3</version>
  <executions>
    <execution>
      <phase>prepare-package</phase>
      <goals>
        <goal>replace</goal>
      </goals>
      <configuration>
        <ignoreMissingFile>false</ignoreMissingFile>
        <file>src/main/webapp/all-classes.js</file>
        <regex>false</regex>
          <replacements>
```

```
        <replacement>
          <token>$BUILD_DATE$</token>
          <value>${maven.build.timestamp}</value>
        </replacement>
        <replacement>
          <token>$BUILD_VERSION$</token>
          <value>${project.version}</value>
        </replacement>
      </replacements>
    </configuration>
  </execution>
</executions>
</plugin>
```

This plugin examines the `src/main/webapp/all-classes.js` file and replaces the `$BUILD_DATE$` token with the build timestamp defined by the Maven property `${maven.build.timestamp}`. The `$BUILD_VERSION$` token is also replaced by the project version defined by the Maven property `${project.version}`.

The final change required is to display these properties in the logon window. We will simply add a `container` below the toolbar in the `LogonWindow.js` file's `items` array:

```
{
  xtype:'container',
  style:{
    textAlign:'center'
  },
  html:' Version ' + TTT.BUILD_VERSION + ' built on ' +
TTT.BUILD_DATE
}
```

Running the project will now display the build version and timestamp in the application logon window of the `index-prod.html` page:

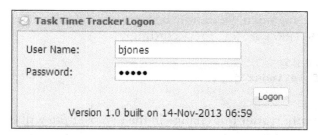

Building a slimmer WAR file

The generated WAR file, `task-time-tracker-1.0.war`, is very large in size at the moment; in fact, it is approximately 32 MB! The default behavior of the `maven-war-plugin` is to add all of the directories in the `webapp` folder to the WAR file. For production deployments we do not need a large number of these files, and it is best practice to trim down the WAR file by excluding the content that is not required. We will exclude the entire Ext JS 4 SDK and all of the Sencha Cmd-generated folders under the `webapp` directory. We will also exclude all the resources that are not applicable for production use, including the `index*.html` files used during development. The only file served by GlassFish will be the yet-to-be-created `index.jsp`:

```
<!DOCTYPE HTML>
<html>
  <head>
    <meta charset="UTF-8">
    <title>TTT</title>
    <link rel="stylesheet" href="resources/ext-theme-classic-all.css">
    <link rel="stylesheet" href="resources/styles.css">
<script type="text/javascript" src="all-classes.js"></script>
  </head>
<body></body>
</html>
```

You will note that the location of the `ext-theme-classic-all.css` file is in the `resources` directory, not in the deeply nested `ext/packages/ext-theme-classic/build/resources` location that is used in the HTML pages. The WAR file generation process will copy the appropriate content to the `resources` directory from the Ext JS 4 SDK location. This removes the need to include the SDK directory structure in the WAR file.

The production `index.jsp` file will now become our default `welcome-file` and we will adjust the `WEB-INF/web.xml` file accordingly:

```
<welcome-file-list>
  <welcome-file>index.jsp</welcome-file>
</welcome-file-list>
```

Running the application after this change in the `web.xml` file will ensure that the `index.jsp` file is served by GlassFish when a resource is *not* specified in the URL.

The changes required in the `maven-war-plugin` for building a slimmer production WAR file are highlighted in the following code snippet:

```
<plugin>
  <groupId>org.apache.maven.plugins</groupId>
  <artifactId>maven-war-plugin</artifactId>
  <version>2.3</version>
  <configuration>
    <warName>${project.build.finalName}</warName>
    <failOnMissingWebXml>false</failOnMissingWebXml>
    <webResources>
      <resource>
        <directory>src/main/webapp/ext/packages/ext-theme-classic/
build/resources</directory>
        <targetPath>resources</targetPath>
        <excludes>
          <exclude>ext-theme-classic-all-*</exclude>
        </excludes>
      </resource>
    </webResources>
    <packagingExcludes>.sencha/**,app/**,sass/**,overrides/**,buil
d/**,ext/**,app.json,bootstrap.css,bootstrap.js,build.xml, index.
html,index-dev.html,index-prod.html,app.js</packagingExcludes>
  </configuration>
</plugin>
```

The `webResources` definition will copy the content of the Ext JS 4 `classic` CSS theme to the `resources` directory. The `targetPath` property is always relative to the `webapp` directory; hence, we do not need a full path for the `resources` directory. The `directory` property is always relative to the root of the Maven project; hence, it needs a full path.

The `packagingExcludes` property lists all of the directories and files that should not be included in the WAR file. The `**` symbol denotes that all of the subdirectories should be excluded. This will ensure that all of the Sencha Cmd-generated folders that are not required by our production WAR file will be excluded.

Executing the Maven build will now generate a WAR file of approximately 6.6 MB that contains only the files required for a production application.

Deploying the WAR file to GlassFish

Until now we have always deployed the 3T application to GlassFish via NetBeans using the **Run Project** command. In production environments we deploy applications through the GlassFish admin console or from the command line using `asadmin`. We will now learn how to deploy the `task-time-tracker-1.0.war` file to GlassFish using the admin console.

Opening the GlassFish admin console

Start GlassFish either in NetBeans or in a console window using the `asadmin` command. We recommend using `asadmin` as this is normally the way GlassFish is managed in an enterprise environment.

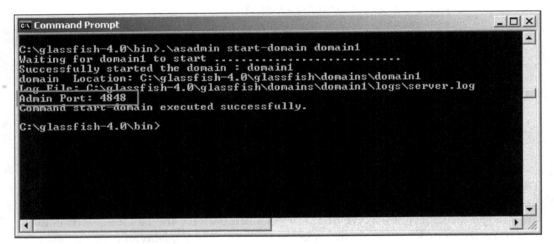

As we can see in the preceding screenshot, the default GlassFish `Admin port` value is `4848`, as shown in the preceding screenshot, but it will be different if multiple GlassFish domains are configured. Open this location in the browser to display the GlassFish admin console:

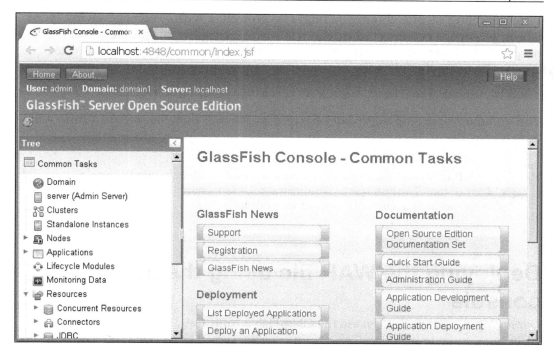

GlassFish security basics

Working on the `localhost` will normally not prompt you for a password when using the default GlassFish installation provided by NetBeans. If you are prompted, the default username is `admin` with a blank password. The previous versions of GlassFish had a default password of `adminadmin`; at the time of writing, this is no longer the case. You should be aware that this may change again in the future.

Working on remote hosts where GlassFish is running on a server other than the browser will always prompt you for a username and password when you try to access the admin console. This is the situation with enterprise environments where different servers are usually running multiple instances of GlassFish. In this environment, remote access to the admin console will be disabled by default and you will only be able to access the admin console from the `localhost`. Allowing remote access from different clients can be enabled by executing the following commands on the host running the GlassFish server:

```
asadmin --host localhost --port 4848 enable-secure-admin
asadmin restart-domain domain1
```

When enabling secure admin, you might be prompted with a message saying "**your admin password is empty**" (the default scenario). To solve this problem you will need to first change the admin password from the default (empty) password to another by using the following command:

```
asadmin --host localhost --port 4848 change-admin-password
```

You will then be prompted to enter the new password. Enabling secure admin will then be possible.

 It is beyond the scope of this book to delve too deeply into the world of the GlassFish server administration. We recommend you browse the excellent documentation and user guides at `https://glassfish.java.net/`.

Deploying the WAR file using the admin console

Deploying a web application via the GlassFish admin console is a simple process. After logging on to the GlassFish admin console, click on and open the **Applications** node as shown in the following screenshot:

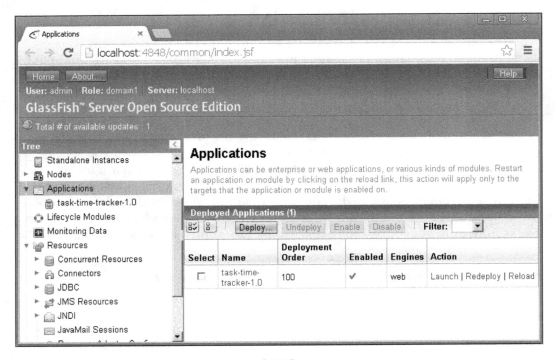

There may already be a **task-time-tracker** application deployed as a result of a previous NetBeans deployment (as shown in the preceding screenshot). If this is the case, select the checkbox next to the application name and then click on **Undeploy**.

Click on the **Deploy...** button and enter the following details:

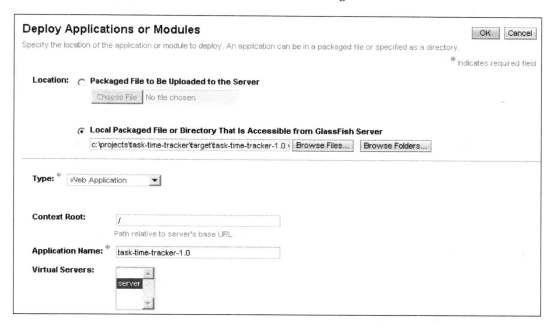

The **Local Packaged File or Directory That Is Accessible from GlassFish Server** field will define the location of the task-time-tracker-1.0.war file on the local file system. If deploying to a remote server, you will need to use the **Package File to be Uploaded to the Server** option.

The **Context Root** field defines the URL path to the deployed application. We will deploy the 3T application to the context root.

The **Application Name** field defines the name of the application within the GlassFish server and is displayed in the application listing.

The **Virtual Server** dropdown defines the virtual server(s) that will be used to host the application. A virtual server, sometimes called a virtual host, is an object that allows the same physical server to host multiple Internet domain names deployed to different listeners. It is possible to select multiple virtual servers (if configured) from this list.

Click on the **OK** button to deploy the `task-time-tracker-1.0.war` file. This action will then return you to the deployed applications listing:

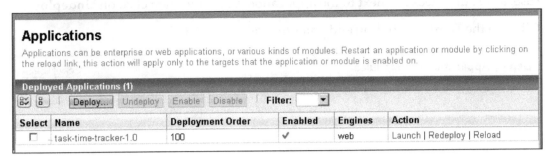

The **task-time-tracker-1.0** application is deployed to the default **Virtual Server** with the name `server` and is accessible via the following two listeners:

- `http://localhost:8080/`
- `https://localhost:8181/`

This is the default virtual server/HTTP service configuration after installing GlassFish. Note that in a production enterprise environment that allows user logons, only the HTTPS version would be enabled to ensure encrypted SSL connections with the server. You can now access these URLs to test the deployment. Opening the `https://localhost:8181/` link will result in a warning due to an invalid certificate as shown in the following screenshot:

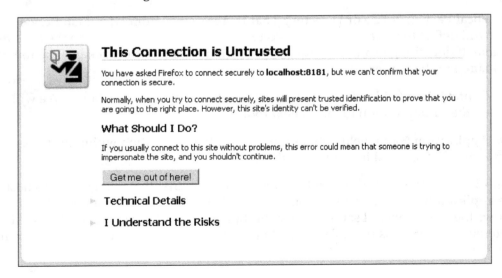

This can be ignored and you may continue to the link by clicking on **I Understand the Risks** and confirming the exception (the exact message displayed will depend on the browser). Right-clicking on the logon page and selecting **View Page Source** will confirm that you are working with the production WAR file; this can be seen in the following screenshot:

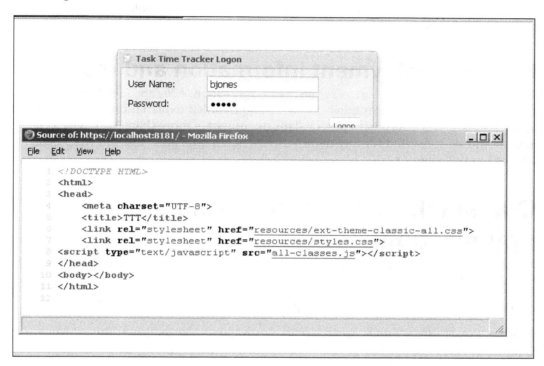

 Configuring HTTP listeners and virtual servers is once again beyond the scope of this book. We recommend you browse the appropriate documentation at `https://glassfish.java.net/documentation.html`.

Deploying the WAR file using asadmin

It is also possible to deploy the `task-time-tracker-1.0.war` file using the `asadmin` command. This is a common situation in enterprise organizations where the GlassFish admin console is not enabled for security reasons. The syntax of the `asadmin deploy` command is:

```
asadmin deploy --user $ADMINUSER --passwordfile $ADMINPWDFILE
--host localhost --port $ADMINPORT --virtualservers $VIRTUAL_SERVER
--contextroot --force --name $WEB_APPLICATION_NAME $ARCHIVE_FILE
```

This command must be executed on a single line and each uppercase variable name prefixed with $ must be replaced with the correct value. The exact syntax and parameters may depend on the environment and we will not go further into the structure of this command. If you are interested in learning more about this command, you may browse the detailed documentation at `http://docs.oracle.com/cd/E18930_01/html/821-2433/deploy-1.html`; please note that this document refers to the GlassFish 3.1 reference manual.

Further deployment information and reading

The document at `https://glassfish.java.net/docs/4.0/application-deployment-guide.pdf` contains extensive and detailed explanations for deploying applications to the GlassFish 4 server. This document is more than 200 pages long and should be consulted for any deployment-related questions that have not been covered in this chapter.

GlassFish performance tuning and optimization

The definitive guide to performance tuning and GlassFish server optimization can be found here at

`https://glassfish.java.net/docs/4.0/performance-tuning-guide.pdf`.

This guide includes sections on tuning your application as well as tuning the GlassFish server itself. Configuring aspects such as thread pools, web container settings, connection pools, garbage collection, server memory settings, and much more are covered. We recommend you consult this document to learn as much as possible about this important aspect of enterprise development and deployment.

Summary

Our final chapter has covered key production enterprise deployment concepts. We have compiled our Ext JS 4 application into a single `all-classes.js` file for production use and added the build version and timestamp to the `LogonWindow.js` file. We then reduced the size of the Maven-generated `task-time-tracker.war` file by removing all of the resources that were not required for production deployment. This production WAR file only contains the resources required by the application at runtime and excludes all the Ext JS 4 SDK resources and directories that are not required. We then examined the GlassFish deployment process and deployed the `task-time-tracker-1.0.war` file via the GlassFish admin console. There is still much more for the you to learn about the GlassFish server, but the entrée has been served!

Our Ext JS and Spring development journey now comes to an end. This book has covered an enormous amount of territory and provided a solid foundation for enterprise application development using these key technologies. We sincerely hope that your development journey will be easier and more rewarding as a result of reading this book.

Introducing Spring Data JPA

The Spring Data JPA website, `http://projects.spring.io/spring-data-jpa/`, has an opening paragraph that succinctly describes the problems of implementing a JPA-based DAO layer:

> *Implementing a data access layer of an application has been cumbersome for quite a while. Too much boilerplate code has to be written to execute simple queries as well as perform pagination, and auditing. Spring Data JPA aims to significantly improve the implementation of data access layers by reducing the effort to the amount that's actually needed. As a developer you write your repository interfaces, including custom finder methods, and Spring will provide the implementation automatically.*

In *Chapter 4, Data Access Made Easy*, we implemented the DAO design pattern to abstract database persistence into a well-defined layer. We deliberately decided *not* to introduce Spring Data JPA in this chapter, as the target audience were intermediate developers who may not have had experience with the Java Persistence API. JPA terminology, concepts, and practical examples were introduced to give you an understanding of how JPA works. The use of Java interfaces, Java generics, and named query concepts are fundamental to understanding the elegant way in which Spring Data JPA works.

Spring Data JPA does not require you to write an implementation of the repository interface. The implementations are created "on the fly" when you run the Spring Data JPA application. All that the developer needs to do is write the DAO Java interfaces that extend `org.springframework.data.repository.CrudRepository` and adhere to the Spring Data JPA naming conventions. The DAO implementation is created for you at runtime.

Internally, Spring Data JPA will implement the code that performs the same functionality that was implemented in *Chapter 4, Data Access Made Easy*. Using Spring Data we could, for example, rewrite the `CompanyDao` interface as:

```
package com.gieman.tttracker.dao;

import com.gieman.tttracker.domain.Company;
import java.util.List;
import org.springframework.data.repository.CrudRepository;

public interface CompanyDao extends CrudRepository<Company, Integer>{

}
```

The `CompanyDao` implementation will include the `findAll` method as it is defined in the `CrudRepository` interface; we do not need to define it as a separate method.

If you are comfortable with JPA and the content covered in *Chapter 4, Data Access Made Easy*, you should explore the Spring Data JPA framework. Implementing JPA-based repositories will then become significantly easier!

Index

H

handler function 314
hashCode() method
    refactoring 86-89
helper beans
    defining 130, 131

I

iconCls property 367
id attribute 149
idCompany property 209
idParam property 301
id property 366
index.html file 274
initComponent() function
    using 289
init function 314, 321, 373
Integrated Development Environment (IDE) 9
Inversion of Control (IoC) 126
IoC container
    working, URL 126
isDropAllowed function 383
isValidUser method 169
itemId property 292, 297

J

Jackson
    URL 199
Java classes, refactoring
    bidirectional mapping 72
    Company.java file 62-66
    owning entity 72
    Projects.java file 68
    Task.java file 73-76
    TaskLog.java file 80
    User.java file 76, 77
Java Enterprise Edition (Java EE) 9
Java generics
    URL 97
Java Persistence API. *See* JPA
Java Persistence Query Language. *See* JPQL
Java SE Development Kit. *See* JDK
JDBC Connection Pool
    configuring 250-253

JDBC DataSource
    creating 129
jdbc.properties file 121, 122
jdbc property 129
JDBC Resource
    configuring 253, 254
JDK
    installing 12
    URL 12
JNDI (Java Naming and Directory Interface) 237
JPA
    implementing 54
    using, reason for 54
JPA traps
    for unwary 153-156
JPQL
    about 84, 85
    and SQL, difference between 85
    named queries, defining 86
JSON 203, 204
JsonArrayBuilder object 370
JSON generation
    Company addJson method, implementing 200
    preparing for 199, 200
    Project addJson method, implementing 200
    Task addJson method, implementing 201
    TaskLog addJson method, implementing 202, 203
    User addJson method, implementing 202
JsonObject.getInt(key) method 209
JSON tree
    generating, in CompanyHandler class 368
JTA (Java Transaction API) 62
JUnit test cases
    CompanyDaoTest.java file, running 144, 145
    CompanyDaoTests.testFindAll test case, results for 147, 148
    CompanyDaoTests.testFind test case, results for 148, 149
    CompanyDaoTests.testMerge test case, results for 145-147
    CompanyDaoTests.testPersist test case, results for 150

CompanyDaoTests.testRemove test case,
results for 151-153
running, with Maven 142-144

K

Keep It Simple, Stupid (KISS) 204

L

launch function 321
LDAP 50
LDAP integration 50
Lightweight Directory Access Protocol. *See*
LDAP
log4J framework
URL 101
logback configuration
URL 124
logback.xml file
about 122-124
adding, to resources directory 246
Logoff button 323
logon action
controlling 307
logon activity audits 51
Logon button 310
logon method 214
logon window
about 287, 288
displaying 284, 285
initComponent() function, using 289
logonwindow button 310
Logout button 310
Log Out button 210

M

MainCards.js file 292, 293
MainController.init() function 310
MainController.js 308-310
mainheader button 310
MainHeader.js view 291, 292
ManageTaskLogs.js file 331, 333
ManageTasks.js file 356, 357
ManageUsers.js file 294
mappedBy property 64

Maven
about 15, 16
JUnit test cases, running with 142-144
Sencha Cmd, integrating with 397, 398
URL 15
Maven build
executing 28
Maven-build plugins
about 25-27
URL 25
maven.build.timestamp.format property
400
Maven dependency mechanism and scoping
URL 24
Maven environment
enabling, for testing 133, 137
Maven pom.xml file
configuring 239, 244
Maven properties
defining 24
maven-war-plugin options
URL 25
Maven Web Application project
creating 16-19
dependency management 20-22
dependency scope 23, 24
Maven build, executing 28
Maven-build plugins 25-27
Maven properties, defining 24
POM 20-22
merge method 94
models
AJAX proxy and REST proxy, comparing
302, 303
naming 264
Project model 341
proxy, defining 300, 301
reader, defining 304
TaskLog model 338, 340
Task model 342
validations, defining 306
writer, defining 304, 305
model skeletons
generating, Sencha Cmd Tool used 278-280
msg property 209
multiple tree columns
displaying 380, 381

test-persistence.xml file 124, 125
text property 381
timestamp
  adding 398-401
toJsonString method 209
Top-Level Domain (TLD) 17
tpl property 335
transaction manager
  configuring 132
transaction-type attribute 62
tree nodes
  loading 375-380
TreeStore function 363
TTT.console function 321
TTT.getApplication().doAfterLogon()
    function 310
TTT.getApplication().getUser() function 349
TTT.getApplication().isAdmin() function
    292

U

unitName property 102
unit testing
  about 118
  benefits 118
useNull:true property 340
useNull property 340
User Acceptance Testing (UAT) 387
User addJson method
  implementing 202
UserDaoImpl class 108-110
UserDaoImpl.findByUsernamePassword
    method 110
UserDao interface 98
UserForm.js file 295, 297
UserHandler.remove method 302
UserHandler.store method 305
User.java file 76, 77
UserList.js file 297, 298
user management components
  ManageUsers.js file 294
  UserForm.js file 295-297
  UserList.js file 297, 298
  User store 299
user object 210

users
  authenticating 215
  maintaining 323-325
Users button 323-325
User store 299
user table 47
user views
  controlling 311, 314
  doAddUser function 314, 315
  doDeleteUser function 318, 319
  doSaveUser function 317, 318
  doSelectUser function 316

V

validations 305
value property 214
view components
  defining 285-287
viewConfig property 352
viewport
  about 290, 291
  MainCards.js file 292, 293
  MainHeader.js view 291, 292
viewport action
  controlling 307
views
  building 287
  generating, Sencha Cmd Tool used 280, 281
  logon window 287, 288
  naming 264, 265
  user management components 294
  viewport 290
  Welcome panel 293

W

WAR file
  building 402, 403
  deploying, admin console used 406-409
  deploying, asadmin used 409, 410
  deploying, to GlassFish 404
  GlassFish admin console, opening 404
  GlassFish security 405, 406
Web Archive file. *See* WAR file
WebDataBinder object 232

Web MVC
  history 197, 198
web.xml file 237, 238
Welcome panel 293
writeAllFields property 305
writer 304, 305

X

xtype function 277
xtype property 289
xtypes
  naming 265

Y

Yahoo User Interface (YUI) 259
Yet another Setup Tool (YaST) 11

Thank you for buying
Enterprise Application Development with Ext JS and Spring

About Packt Publishing

Packt, pronounced 'packed', published its first book "*Mastering phpMyAdmin for Effective MySQL Management*" in April 2004 and subsequently continued to specialize in publishing highly focused books on specific technologies and solutions.

Our books and publications share the experiences of your fellow IT professionals in adapting and customizing today's systems, applications, and frameworks. Our solution based books give you the knowledge and power to customize the software and technologies you're using to get the job done. Packt books are more specific and less general than the IT books you have seen in the past. Our unique business model allows us to bring you more focused information, giving you more of what you need to know, and less of what you don't.

Packt is a modern, yet unique publishing company, which focuses on producing quality, cutting-edge books for communities of developers, administrators, and newbies alike. For more information, please visit our website: www.packtpub.com.

About Packt Open Source

In 2010, Packt launched two new brands, Packt Open Source and Packt Enterprise, in order to continue its focus on specialization. This book is part of the Packt Open Source brand, home to books published on software built around Open Source licences, and offering information to anybody from advanced developers to budding web designers. The Open Source brand also runs Packt's Open Source Royalty Scheme, by which Packt gives a royalty to each Open Source project about whose software a book is sold.

Writing for Packt

We welcome all inquiries from people who are interested in authoring. Book proposals should be sent to author@packtpub.com. If your book idea is still at an early stage and you would like to discuss it first before writing a formal book proposal, contact us; one of our commissioning editors will get in touch with you.

We're not just looking for published authors; if you have strong technical skills but no writing experience, our experienced editors can help you develop a writing career, or simply get some additional reward for your expertise.

Spring Web Services 2 Cookbook

ISBN: 978-1-84951-582-5   Paperback: 322 pages

Over 60 recipes providing comprehensive coverage of practical real-life implementations of Spring-WS

1. Create contract-first Web services

2. Explore different frameworks of Object/XML mapping

3. Secure Web Services by Authentication, Encryption/Decryption and Digital Signature

Spring Roo 1.1 Cookbook

ISBN: 978-1-84951-458-3   Paperback: 460 pages

Over 60 recipes to help you speed up the development of your Java web applications using the Spring Roo development tool

1. Learn what goes on behind the scenes when using Spring Roo and how to migrate your existing Spring applications to use Spring Roo

2. Incrementally develop a Flight Booking enterprise application from scratch as various features of Spring Roo are introduced

3. Develop custom add-ons to extend Spring Roo features

Please check **www.PacktPub.com** for information on our titles

Ext JS 4 Plugin and
Extension Development

A hands-on development of several Ext JS plugins and extensions

Abdullah Al Mohammad

PACKT open source

Ext JS 4 Plugin and Extension Development

ISBN: 978-1-78216-372-5   Paperback: 116 pages

A hands-on development of several Ext JS plugins and extensions

1. Easy-to-follow examples on Ext JS plugins and extensions

2. Step-by-step instructions on developing Ext JS plugins and extensions

3. Provides a walkthrough of several useful Ext JS libraries and communities

Sencha MVC Architecture

A practical guide for designers and developers to create scalable enterprise-class web applications in Ext.JS and Sencha Touch using the Sencha MVC architecture

Ajit Kumar

PACKT open source

Sencha MVC Architecture

ISBN: 978-1-84951-888-8   Paperback: 126 pages

A practical guide for designers and developers to create scalable enterprise-class web applications in Ext JS and Sencha Touch using the Sencha MVC architecture

1. Map general MVC architecture concept to the classes in Ext JS 4.x and Sencha Touch

2. Create a practical application in Ext JS as well as Sencha Touch using various Sencha MVC Architecture concepts and classes

3. Dive deep into the building blocks of the Sencha MVC Architecture including the class system, loader, controller, and application

Please check **www.PacktPub.com** for information on our titles

www.ingramcontent.com/pod-product-compliance
Lightning Source LLC
Chambersburg PA
CBHW060921060326
40690CB00041B/2857